D0084664

# Corporate Welfare

# Corporate Welfare

## Crony Capitalism That Enriches the Rich

# James T. Bennett

### Foreword by Ralph Nader

**Transaction Publishers**

New Brunswick (U.S.A.) and London (U.K.)

Copyright © 2015 by Transaction Publishers, New Brunswick, New Jersey.

All rights reserved under International and Pan-American Copyright Conventions. No part of this book may be reproduced or transmitted in any form or by any means, electronic or mechanical, including photocopy, recording, or any information storage and retrieval system, without prior permission in writing from the publisher. All inquiries should be addressed to Transaction Publishers, 10 Corporate Place South, Piscataway, New Jersey 08854. www.transactionpub.com

This book is printed on acid-free paper that meets the American National Standard for Permanence of Paper for Printed Library Materials.

Library of Congress Catalog Number: 2014032117
ISBN: 978-1-4128-5598-3
Printed in the United States of America

Library of Congress Cataloging-in-Publication Data

Bennett, James T.
Corporate welfare : crony capitalism that enriches the rich / James T. Bennett.
    pages cm
ISBN 978-1-4128-5598-3
1. Subsidies--United States. 2. United States--Economic policy.
3. Capitalism--United States. I. Title.
HC110.S9B46 2015
338.973'02--dc23

                                                    2014032117

# Contents

# Acknowledgments

I am grateful to many for their assistance with and support of the research and editing of this book. The research would not have been possible without the generous financial support of the Sunmark Foundation. John G. MacDhubbain provided excellent research assistance. I also owe profuse thanks to my editor, Bill Kauffman, for I am indebted to him for significant contributions to this study.

James T. Bennett
George Mason University
Fairfax, VA

# Foreword

*by Ralph Nader*

Given its magnitude, consequences, and unfairness, corporate welfare —the governmental disbursements of unearned and unpaid-for taxpayer assets to corporate claimants—has received too little notice, or analytical review. This is not surprising. When the powerful few profit at the expense of the paying many, the varieties of crony capitalism with their shielding jargon, secrecy, and complexities are in the shadows.

Professor James T. Bennett, a conservative economist at George Mason University, shines a spotlight on the early ideology foreshadowing government subsidies, handouts, giveaways, inflated contracts, and bailouts of commercial firms in the era of Alexander Hamilton's persistent advocacy. Bennett assesses some of Hamilton's policy legacies as they apply to contemporary examples of corporate welfare. These examples include: the parasitic industry of economic development giveaways, privileges, and immunities such as the immensely tragic story of the Poletown community in Detroit. This neighborhood was destroyed by a General Motors demand that city officials use eminent domain to take diversely occupied private property and give it to GM. The vast taking of over four hundred acres was sweetened with accompanying huge federal, state, and local subsidies. The unabashed guaranteed carriage of largely giant exporters by taxpayers to conduct sales overseas in the form of the Export-Import Bank and the civilian Supersonic Transport (SST), which in 1971 airplane manufacturers tried but failed to stampede Congress into underwriting, are also painful reminders that corporate welfare has few limits.

Throughout these thoroughly engrossing narrations are insights, tinctured with some well-appointed satiric humor, that demonstrate the critical difference between authentic conservatism and unbridled corporatism—critical because the strategy of these corporate welfare kings is to use conservative doctrine and rhetoric to camouflage their grasping avarice that drains their powerless victims in communities throughout the land.

Professor Bennett's plea for an anti-corporate welfare alliance already exists in the all-important realm of what Abraham Lincoln called "the public sentiment." Left-Right coalitions are the next step to give this converging revulsion the operational drive toward more critical media inquiries and more incumbents and candidates having to put discussion of these giveaways on the table. This is what happened in the 1983 defeat of the boondoggle Clinch River Breeder Reactor Project and its backers—President Reagan, the powerful Senator Howard Baker, and corporate lobbyists for companies including General Electric and Westinghouse, savoring the honey pots of this limitless over-budget, hazardous technology.

Left-Right convergence passed the 1986 False Claims Act and the 2013 Federal Whistleblower Protection Act empowering and protecting federal civil servants who blow the whistle on corporate defrauding of the taxpayers, such as Pentagon contracts or Medicare services.

This book addresses various ways to generically prevent corporate welfare or, in the alternative, subject it to factual scrutiny, which, in my view, would include specific public procedures that would place the burden of proof on proponents of each specific program to show that it is a wise use of taxpayer monies for truly public purposes, compared to its costs. The author also raises potential challenges in the future using the commerce clause or equal protection of the laws under our constitution. At present there are almost no limits, no boundaries to the federal government's extension of taxpayer largess to private companies, other than directly funding religious places of worship.

Professor Bennett alludes often to the lack of revealed or even collected data that would spark more public reporting and evaluation. There is, in fact, no compilation of the myriad corporate welfare programs in the Executive Branch and certainly no related comprehensive budgeting, other than an abstruse tax expenditure budget. In a society that touts "Big Data," such a condition is intolerable. Data on corporate welfare should be organized so that the citizenry can access this unquantified bazaar of accounts receivables with fingertip keyboard immediacy.

As Supreme Court Associate Justice Louis Brandeis once wrote: "Sunlight is the best disinfectant." Imagine the benefits of placing the full texts of government contracts online. Such revelations would impede the gigantic national outsourcing state from easily hiding corporate subsidies through endless programs where contractors are chronically over budget and over schedule with Congressional protection, greased by campaign cash, instead of regular Congressional oversight.

Decade after decade of burgeoning corporate welfare, regardless of which political party is dominant, feeds the maturation of the corporate state, the immunized institutionalization of entrenched corporate-owned "annuities." So, the Strategic Defense Initiative (star wars) continues to provide Raytheon and other companies with US Treasury checks regardless of its chronic failure to produce what taxpayers have to fund at a level of $9 to $10 billion a year. Ever more tightly interwoven, the corporate government, or crony capitalism, becomes an expected handout by companies either too big to fail, too big to cut off, or too big to survive a separation of corporation and state. All this of course turns competitive capitalism on its head in many ways and reshapes the basic contours of our political economy and the priorities for the general interest that it should be competitively serving from elections to markets, from production to consumption, from internalities to externalities.

In this and other writings, Professor Bennett has moved these phenomena to wider public attention. This volume continues his exploration of what is happening in our economy but is rarely taught in business and law schools, much less in undergraduate and high school curricula. Instead, occlusion, populated by myths, shapes the perspectives of unsuspecting young minds that are being processed for service and obedience to the status quo and the powers that be. Professor Bennett, with apologies to Shakespeare, is urging the citizenry, "get thee to reality"—the essential precursor for change.

Ralph Nader
Washington, DC
June 2014

# 1

# Introduction and Overview

The term "corporate welfare" may well have been coined by civic advocate Ralph Nader in the 1950s. Throughout his long career, Nader has shined the light of publicity on many instances of corporate welfare, both egregious and subtle. In doing so he has earned the gratitude of the American people and the scorn of the recipients of these alms from the state.

While there is often disagreement at the margins over exactly which programs might qualify as corporate welfare—controversial weapons systems? Tax rebates for filmmakers?—students of the subject generally agree on its rough outlines. Stephen Moore and Dean Stansel of the Cato Institute, the Washington, DC–based libertarian think tank, define the term succinctly as "special government subsidies or benefits that are targeted to specific industries or corporations."[1] Ralph Nader defines it somewhat more expansively as "the enormous and myriad subsidies, bailouts, giveaways, tax loopholes, debt revocations, loan guarantees, discounted insurance and other benefits conferred by government on business."[2] And while we're at it, let's throw in a journalistic definition, taken from *Time* magazine's ambitious 1998 special report on corporate welfare, which describes it as "any action by local, state, or federal government that gives a corporation or an entire industry a benefit not offered to others. It can be an outright subsidy, a grant, real estate, a low-interest loan or government service. It can also be a tax break—a credit, exemption, deferral or deduction, or a tax rate lower than the others pay."[3]

Estimates of the total annual cost of corporate welfare vary according to the definition, but even a conservative estimate pegs the bill at somewhere in the neighborhood of $100–$150 billion at the federal level and upward of $80 billion at the state and local levels.[4]

Note that a general tax reduction, or even tax abolition, is *not* corporate welfare. The term is reserved for those tax breaks that are targeted to firms singled out by the government or the economic development czars for special treatment. Those firms are given favorable treatment by the authorities that is not made available to their competitors.

Criticizing corporate welfare is not akin to criticizing business per se. This should be glaringly obvious, though shills for the welfare takers like to muddy the waters by claiming that those who condemn business subsidies are actually condemning business, or—in that most venerable smear—standing in the way of progress.

This is utter nonsense. The distinguished historian Forrest McDonald, in his foreword to Burton W. Folsom Jr.'s pathbreaking revisionist work, *The Myth of the Robber Barons*, refers to Folsom's taxonomy of "political entrepreneurs" and "market entrepreneurs." He explains:

> The former were in fact comparable to medieval robber barons, for they sought and obtained wealth through the coercive power of the state, which is to say that they were subsidized by government and were sometimes granted monopoly status by government. Invariably, their products or services were inferior to and more expensive than the goods and services provided by market entrepreneurs, who sought and obtained wealth by producing more and better for less cost to the consumer. The market entrepreneurs, however, have been repeatedly—one is tempted to say systematically—ignored by historians.[5]

The progressive historian Charles Beard, writing in 1931 about what he called "the myth of American individualism," traced the evolution of federal activity in various fields—shipping, railways, aviation—to men of business, especially big business. They often received a boost from wartime, as the demands of and on the central government multiply during hostilities, and the canny operator with an eye for the main chance has plenty of opportunities to cash in. The party of business, the Republicans, were from the outset the party of "subsidies, bounties, internal improvements, tariffs, and other aids to business," wrote Beard.[6] Being "Apro-business," in the parlance of American politics, has often meant being anti-free enterprise.

To those who viewed the Hoover Republicans as the party of parsimony and economy, Beard retorted with a vision of the

> Department of Commerce, its magnificent mansion near the Treasury Department, and its army of hustlers scouting for business at the uttermost ends of the earth. Who is responsible for loading on the Government the job of big drummer at large for business? Why shouldn't these rugged individualists do their own drumming instead of asking the taxpayers to do it for them? Business men have been

behind this enormous expansion, and Mr. Hoover, as Secretary of Commerce, outdid every predecessor in the range of his activities and the expenditure of public money. Who proposes to take the Government out of the business of hunting business for men who ought to know their own business?[7]

More than four score years later, Beard's final question still hangs in the air. Neither party seems terribly interested in cutting even the most stupendously offensive forms of corporate welfare. Why alienate your most fervent supporters—those who depend on subsidies and grants from Washington, DC? The constituency for slashing corporate welfare is vast, but the benefits of reducing this pork are spread very thinly, while the benefits themselves are concentrated. Thus those who profit from corporate welfare take an intense interest in its continuance: they employ lobbyists, they plant favorable stories on the Internet, they cajole and threaten, they donate large sums to those politicians who do their bidding.

Their welfare is big business.

Americans were outraged by corporate welfare before there was even a name for it. The nineteenth-century Democrats used to run under the banner "Equal rights for all, special privileges for none," which cut to the quick like few other political slogans. Favorable treatment for influential corporations has never had any real popular constituency in the United States, which is not to say that it hasn't had a constituency among the powerful beneficiaries of such aid. Boeing and Lockheed in the "pro" category outweigh five hundred Jane Does and Joe Smiths in the anti-corporate welfare column.

One's attitude toward corporate welfare has never really split along left-right or liberal-conservative lines. Ralph Nader, for instance, is often placed on the left end of the American political spectrum (though he is really more a populist than a leftist), while one of today's elected scourges of corporate welfare, Senator Tom Coburn (R-OK), is a stalwart conservative. North of the border, corporate welfare was made an issue in 1972 by David Lewis, national leader of the New Democratic Party, Canada's leading left-wing party. Lewis published a book, *Louder Voices: The Corporate Welfare Bums*, that castigated corporate recipients of Canadian tax monies.

Winona LaDuke, a Native American activist and former vice presidential candidate of the Green Party, points out that corporate welfare "is not the mysterious hand of Adam Smith" at work.[8] It has nothing whatsoever to do with free enterprise or entrepreneurship. It is the granting of favors by the government for influential corporations, (im)pure and simple.

Economically, the effects of subsidies are perverse. Granting such favors to powerful companies fortifies their dominant position and disadvantages their competitors. Subsidizing weak companies, on the other hand, "may allow the corporation to stay in business despite the fact that demand is not high enough to justify keepings its doors open," as Steven R. Little explains.[9] In either case, a subsidy disrupts the workings of the market, singles out certain companies for preferential treatment and effectively punishes the unsubsidized competitors of those companies, and saddles taxpayers with higher bills. It is a sweet deal for the few and a rip-off for the many.

Although corporate welfare can raise the hackles of the ordinary taxpayer, it is of curiously little interest to most lawmakers. The first-ever congressional hearing on the subject wasn't held until June 1999 by the House Budget Committee. Though it would seem ripe with promise for politicians seeking to make populist waves, the subject seldom intrudes into the national political conversation. Perhaps it just makes too many powerful interests (and politicians beholden to these interests) uncomfortable. Calling the CEO of Boeing or General Electric a "welfare bum" is a trifle too audacious for your average member of Congress. It can also be hazardous to his political health.

In his classic essay "The Theory of Economic Regulation," Nobel Prize–winning economist George J. Stigler explained that government economic regulation is typically "designed and operated" by the industries themselves, for their own benefit. The state, with its monopoly on legal coercion, can "prohibit or compel . . . take or give money," and "selectively help or hurt a vast number of industries."[10]

Stigler instances the airline industry in his essay, pointing to its longtime airmail subsidy. (That industry was also bred and prospered in wartime to a great extent.) The major players in an industry will usually not try to simply squeeze direct grants of money from the government, says Stigler, for in doing so they would invite numerous other potential beneficiaries into the field. Rather, they often seek to limit entry into the field or employ such legislative expedients as the protective tariff, price-fixing, or the subsidy or suppression of complementary or substitute industries.

There is a real sense in which the tariff, to take one of Stigler's examples, is a tool of corporate welfare, as are large sections of US agriculture policy (the sugar and peanut programs are particular viola-tors of even elemental standards of fairness), but this book focuses on the blunt and direct forms that such welfare takes: direct subsidies to favored companies.[11] (Despite the ballyhooed "Freedom to Farm" act of 1996, which was supposed to phase out agricultural subsidies, farm-ers have in some ways become even more dependent on government checks. And the monies have even kept flowing to prosperous persons whose farming is pretty much limited to government subsidies.[12] The farm program remains riddled with bizarre subsidies to inexplicable recipients. But then perhaps the federal government is sending agri-cultural corporate welfare checks to denizens of Manhattan high-rises because the federal bureaucracy regards Manhattan as a rural outpost. As a *Washington Post* investigation amusingly revealed, the federal government "has at least 15 official definitions of the word 'rural.'" As this book went to press, the Senate was trying to reduce the number of definitions to nine, while the House seemed satisfied with fifteen. The wheels of reform turn slowly on Capitol Hill. Mighty slowly.[13])

In recent years, the most mind-blowing cases of corporate welfare have made fine fodder for publicity-seeking members of Congress. Senator William Proxmire (D-WI) grabbed regular headlines in the 1970s and '80s with his "Golden Fleece" awards, which he bestowed on particularly galling giveaways. (One of Proxmire's finest hours—his successful assault on the SST—is reviewed in some detail in Chapter 3.) In today's Congress, the champion exposer of flagrant corporate charity is the aforementioned Senator Tom Coburn, an Oklahoma Republican.

Senator Coburn's bête noire is the "welfare millionaire." In his atten-tion-getting report *Subsidies of the Rich and Famous* (2011), Coburn cast a wide net, pillorying millionaires who cash Social Security checks (in 2009, the year of Coburn's survey, 38,217 millionaires received $1.142 billion in Social Security payments), receive unemployment benefits (2,362 of them accepted more than $20.799 million in 2009), partake of farm program payments (in 2009, 3,432 received $45.724 million in such aid), take out taxpayer-subsidized college loans for their children (in 2010, 270 such loans totaling $5.327 million were disbursed), and accept disaster assistance from the federal government (in 2010, claims from millionaires amounted to $2.37 million).[14] These figures cast an interesting light on the whole question of means testing for entitlements.

But at least, in keeping with current fashions, many of these welfare millionaires are green. Or pretend to be. Coburn discusses the US

Department of Agriculture's Wetlands Reserve Program (WRP), which pays landowners to *not* use wetlands. The WRP forbids payments to anyone with an adjusted gross income of over $1 million, unless that person receives a waiver. In 2009 and 2010, Coburn discovered, USDA shelled out more than $84 million to individuals whose AGI exceeded that million-dollar mark. Among the chief beneficiaries was a family-owned company that received $22 million for not growing anything on wetlands on its Florida ranch. (That's some waiver!) Lest you get the impression that this family company has a passion for wetlands restoration, it also owns "multi-tenant office buildings, parking lots, a for-profit educational institution, restaurants, and retail property."[15] Real greenies, it would seem. (There are also plenty of federal subsidies that menace the environment or artificially distort land use patterns in the West, from irrigation subsidies to water projects. As Edward A. Chadd documented for *Common Cause*, "The biggest beneficiaries of federal water projects are not small farmers but huge agribusinesses," among them the company of J. G. Boswell II, who until his death in 2009 was "believed to have more land—as much as 192,000 acres—under cultivation than anyone else in America."[16])

Following up on Senator Coburn's report, Walter Williams, a professor of economics at George Mason University, and Stephen Moore proposed in the *Wall Street Journal* "The Millionaire Subsidy Elimination Act," which would "prohibit anyone with an annual income of over $1 million from receiving any government benefits."[17] The proposal is ingenious in its simplicity and justice, which is, perhaps, why it has zero chance of enactment.

Corporate welfare programs exist in almost every nook and cranny of the federal behemoth. From NASA to the Small Business Administration, from the Department of Defense to the Federal Maritime Administration, from energy conservation programs within the Department of Energy to great swathes of the Departments of Commerce and Homeland Security, the national bureaucracy is pockmarked and mottled with spending initiatives that transfer taxpayer dollars into the coffers of US (and even foreign) business interests. The Cato Institute has identified 46 corporate welfare programs in the federal budget whose aggregate annual outlay approaches $100 billion.[18]

Some of the biggest feeders at the trough really do have no shame. During the 1990s, Martin Marietta, the defense contractor whose very existence was in good part due to the largesse extended by the American taxpayer, actually billed the government for such expenditures as a Smokey Robinson concert for its employees ($263,000), a recreational park for its Oak Ridge, Tennessee, employees ($417,629), and even volleyball referees ($4,032) for an Oak Ridge league.[19] The word *chutzpah* doesn't do justice to Martin Marietta's effrontery. But these ridiculous examples demonstrate the extent to which some large corporations take it as a matter of course that the federal government has as a primary purpose the support, the nurture, the coddling of those same corporations. And of course if the likes of Martin Marietta, which later merged with Lockheed, were asked to summarize their mission, they would offer guff on the order of Defending the American Way of Life—a way of life that now seems to have as a more or less permanent condition the transfusion of billions of dollars from the Treasury to favored and prepotent business interests.

Corporate welfare takes many forms. Although the locus is often Washington, DC, sometimes it is as blatant as a payoff from a state or local government to a big company that is threatening (or teasing) to relocate. This phenomenon is explored in detail in Chapter 4, but two examples are given here as a foretaste. In 1999, the state of Maryland lavished tax credits, job training grants, and infrastructure improvements totaling approximately $80 million to keep Marriott International, the hotel chain, which had been based in Montgomery County since 1955, from moving its corporate headquarters to neighboring Virginia. At stake were 3,500 Marriott jobs plus another 700 the corporation pledged to add over the next five years. Central to the package was an outright gift of $9 million for the "extraordinary economic development opportunity" it was affording the Old Line State just for taking its money and staying put.[20]

The usual left-right anti-corporate welfare coalition lined up to criticize the deal. "It's disgraceful for them to come looking for government subsidies of that magnitude when they are a profitable company—and not just profitable but making profits of hundreds of millions of dollars," thundered Maryland State Senator Brian E. Frosh, a Democrat. "It's a harmful precedent, and not the way the free market economy is supposed to work."[21]

Maryland "won" the bidding war. Eight years later, Jay Hancock of the *Baltimore Sun* assessed the "dubious benefits" of the deal. Yes, Marriott stayed in Maryland. But those 700 jobs never materialized. Instead, the hotel giant added a grand total of 117 jobs. A spokesman for the Maryland Department of Business and Economic Development blamed the shortfall on . . . get this . . . "the reasonably long-term effects that 9/11 had."[22]

Yes, you heard it right: *It was 9/11's fault* that Marriott didn't keep its word (though it did keep that $9 million cash gift). Truly, the terrorists had won.

A second example: In 2003, at the height of the semi-prohibitionist anti-smoking campaign, Richmond, Virginia, convinced Philip Morris to move its Manhattan headquarters to the former capital of the Confederacy with a menu of subsidies that New York City could not and did not want to match. The tobacco titan received a grant of $3 million from the Virginia Governor's Opportunity Fund, $2 million in incentives from the City of Richmond, another $1 million from Henrico County, and $25 million in regular payments from the Virginia Investment Partnership Grant.

Philip Morris had been incorporated in New York in 1902. A century later, the city enacted draconian regulations on indoor smoking as part of Mayor Michael Bloomberg's seemingly comprehensive efforts to regulate the eating, drinking, and sumptuary habits of his subjects. Moreover, as S. Mohsin Reza notes in the *University of Richmond Law Review*, in 2003, when Philip Morris made its move, New York state taxed cigarettes at $1.50 per pack compared to Virginia's per-pack tax of 2.5 cents.[23] Now *that* is a differential. Company spokesmen denied that Bloomberg's anti-smoking law had anything to do with the move, and perhaps it didn't, though "tobacco-friendly" Richmond made its pitch at the right time and with enough inducements to lure Philip Morris southward,[24] inducements obtained at the expense of Virginia taxpayers.

One last example, this from the Obama administration, before we get to the lineaments of our story. In 2011, an investigation by the *Washington Post* found that in 2009 the administration had pressured reviewers for the federal Office of Management and Budget to hasten their decision on whether or not to approve a $535 million loan guarantee to Solyndra, a California-based manufacturer of solar panels.

It seems that Vice President Biden was due to appear at a ground-breaking ceremony for the company's new plant, and it was thought that his announcement of a more than half a billion dollar federal loan would supply the necessary buzz.

As the *Post* reported, OMB officials balked at the pressure, telling the vice president's domestic policy advisor that "We would prefer to have sufficient time to do our due diligence reviews."[25] Nevertheless, the loan, which was from the US Department of Energy, went through. The following year, the president himself appeared at the Solyndra factory, enthusing that "It's here that companies like Solyndra are leading the way toward a brighter and more prosperous future."[26]

The future was somewhat dimmer than the president envisioned: another year later, on August 31, 2011, Solyndra filed for bankruptcy. Eleven hundred workers lost their jobs.

The backstory, as unearthed by reporters in the wake of the company's failure, was a classic case of political favoritism and corporate welfare. Obama's DOE had not picked Solyndra's name out of a hat, or selected it after a rigorous comparison with the 143 other solar-panel manufacturers that had at one time or another been part of the loan application process. But it seems that Solyndra's major investor (with over one-third ownership) was a foundation backed by Obama fundraiser and billionaire George B. Kaiser. Moreover, the company "spent nearly $1.8 million on Washington lobbyists, employing six firms with ties to members of Congress and officials of the Obama White House," according to the *New York Times*.[27]

Such cronyism was rife within the Obama administration, especially with regard to its vaunted "green energy" initiatives. (Call something *green* and the money cascades.) The *Washington Post* reported that "$3.9 billion in federal grants and financing flowed to 21 companies backed by firms with connections to five Obama administration staffers and advisers."[28] The only thing green about these showy initiatives was the color of the money funneled into the Obama campaign.

Pressed to give a postmortem, President Obama said, "Now there are going to be some failures" when government picks corporations to back. "Hindsight is always 20/20."[29] But spending other people's money means never having to say you're sorry. Or broke.

\* \* \*

*Corporate Welfare* is not a general survey of corporate welfare; some books already address various aspects of that topic.[30] Nor is it a potpourri of outrageous instances of government giveaways to business, though these are encountered in the pages to follow. Rather, *Corporate Welfare* begins by tracing the evolution of corporate welfare from Alexander Hamilton's "Report on Manufactures" up through its practical application during the Great Depression, as towns and cities sought to lure footloose companies to their precincts by lavishing on them an array of benefits, from providing them with taxpayer-financed factories to exempting them from local taxes to giving them outright gifts of money.

From this historical foundation, modern manifestations of corporate welfare in four broad areas are examined in depth.

The first case, nestled within what President Dwight D. Eisenhower termed the military-industrial complex, is the aviation industry—more specifically, the epochal debate of the 1960s and 1970s over government subsidy of a supersonic transport aircraft, or SST. The fight over the SST was one of the first and greatest instances of corporate welfare assuming center stage in the national political arena. The political battle illuminated the fault lines in the corporate welfare fight, helped to introduce the "strange bedfellows" who seem to come together with impressive frequency to represent taxpayers in these contests, and gave us a rare case in which corporate welfare suffered a high-profile defeat in Congress.

The second case has its origins in the Southern factory relocation programs of the 1930s. Going under anodyne monikers like economic or industrial development, the practice of state and local governments granting companies taxpayer-financed incentives (subsidies, tax exemptions or deferrals or abatements not enjoyed by competitor firms, infrastructure improvements, subsidies for worker training) has become so ubiquitous as to seem just a part of the economic air we breathe. Yet economists are by and large dubious that these subsidies are, on balance, salutary, and they constitute today the most widespread and visible example of corporate welfare.

The third case under examination also has its roots in early American corporate welfare. This is the taking of private property for the enrichment of business interests. Under the legal cloak of eminent domain, governments have stolen, even destroyed, not just individual businesses or homes but entire neighborhoods at the request of such corporate behemoths as General Motors. Ralph Nader himself was at the center of one of the most legendary corporate welfare/eminent domain fights, that which goes by the shorthand of Poletown. In Poletown, the city of Detroit and "the soulless juggernauts of mercantilism," in Nader's piquant phrase, spent $200 million in taxpayer subsidies to condemn, acquire, and demolish, on behalf of General Motors, about 1,300 homes (housing 4,200 people), 143 businesses, 16 churches, a hospital, and 1,176 buildings.[31] As will be seen with Poletown and similar travesties, this is corporate welfare at its ugliest.

The fourth case of corporate welfare (Chapter 6) has its genesis in the New Deal but really has come into its own only in recent decades: the Export-Import Bank. Dubbed a "reverse Robin Hood" by its critics, the Ex-Im Bank subsidizes the international business exchanges of some of America's largest corporate entities.[32] As is always the case, supporters supply a fig leaf of justification: that these subsidies, in time, create jobs, but the number of jobs that might have been created by alternative uses of this money is never calculated, or even mentioned. Ex-Im survived a brief moment of vulnerability in the early 1980s, when some of the Reagan administration's more dedicated free-marketeers had it in their sights; under President Obama, it is enjoying its age of wine and roses, and those who challenge the idea of funding exports by Fortune 500 companies are belittled as libertarian extremists or anti-business leftists. Ex-Im is corporate welfare as unapologetic big-business boosterism.

Chapter 7, the book's conclusion, examines the prospects for a successful anti-corporate welfare coalition of libertarians, free-market conservatives, Greens, and populists. The coalition is out there. Whether a canny politician can ever put it together and keep it together long enough to mount a taxpayer counterattack on corporate welfare is an intriguing question.[33]

## Notes

1. Stephen Moore and Dean Stansel, "How Corporate Welfare Won: Clinton and Congress Retreat from Cutting Business Subsidies," *Cato Policy Analysis* No. 254, May 15, 1996, p. 3.
2. Ralph Nader, *Cutting Corporate Welfare* (New York: Seven Stories Press, 2000), p. 13.
3. Donald L. Bartlett and James B. Steele, "Corporate Welfare," *Time*, November 9, 1998.
4. Scott Lincicome, "Calculating the Real Cost of Corporate Welfare," *The Federalist*, September 30, 2013, http://thefederalist.com/2013/09/30/calculating-the-real-cost-of-corporate-welfare/.
5. Forrest McDonald, Foreword, *The Myth of the Robber Barons: A New Look at the Rise of Big Business in America*, by Burton W. Folsom, Jr. (Herndon, VA: Young America's Foundation, 2010/1987), pp. ix–x.
6. Charles A. Beard, "The Myth of Rugged Individualism," *Harper's Monthly*, December 1931, p. 19.
7. Ibid., p. 16.
8. Winona LaDuke, Foreword, *Cutting Corporate Welfare*, p. 8.
9. Steven R. Little, "Corporate Welfare Wars: The Insufficiency of Current Constitutional Constraints on State Action and the Desirability of a Federal Response," *Hamline Law Review* (Vol. 22, No. 3, 1998–1999): 860.
10. George J. Stigler, "The Theory of Economic Regulation," *Bell Journal of Economics and Management Science* (Vol. 2, No. 1, Spring 1971): 3.

11. "Regular peanut subsidy checks go out to upscale 'urban farmers' in places such as McLean, Va., and Grosse Point, Mich. At the same time, mothers in inner-city Washington, DC, and Detroit have to pay an extra 36 cents in subsidies every time they buy an 18-ounce jar of peanut butter." See "Mr. Peanut and Sugar Daddy," *Wall Street Journal*, September 29, 1995.

12. For high-profile and often indefensible examples of welfare for the rich, see Dan Morgan, Gilbert M. Gaul, and Sarah Cohen, "Farm Program Pays $1.3 Billion to People Who Don't Farm," *Washington Post*, July 2, 2006; and Thomas A. Fogarty, "Freedom to farm? Not likely," *USA Today*, January 2, 2002.

13. David A. Fahrenthold, "What does rural mean? Feds Have 15 answers," *Washington Post*, June 9, 2013; David A. Fahrenthold, "Fighting waste, and often losing," *Washington Post*, December 28, 2013.

14. Senator Tom A. Coburn, "Subsidies of the Rich and Famous," November 2011, pp. 6, 11, 15, 21, and 26.

15. Ibid., p. 16.

16. Edward A. Chadd, "Manifest Subsidy," *Common Cause Magazine*, Fall 1995.

17. Stephen Moore and Walter E. Williams, "The Millionaire Subsidy Elimination Act," *Wall Street Journal*, December 9, 2011.

18. Tad DeHaven, "Corporate Welfare in the Federal Budget," *Cato Institute Policy Analysis* No. 703, July 25, 2012, pp. 3–5.

19. "Taxpayers get stuck with tab for 'morale' of contractors," Associated Press, *Washington Times*, October 18, 1994.

20. Jay Hancock, "The 1999 Deal to Keep Marriott's Bethesda, Maryland Corporate Headquarters from Moving to Virginia Draws Criticism," *Baltimore Sun*, January 28, 2007.

21. Scott Wilson, "Marriott Takes Deal To Stay in Maryland," *Washington Post*, March 12, 1999.

22. Hancock, "The 1999 Deal to Keep Marriott's Bethesda, Maryland Corporate Headquarters from Moving to Virginia Draws Criticism," *Baltimore Sun*.

23. S. Moshin Reza, "*DaimlerChrysler v. Cuno*: An Escape from the Dormant Commerce Clause Quagmire?" *University of Richmond Law Review* (Vol. 40, 2005–2006): 1232.

24. Terry Pristin, "Philip Morris USA Starts Its Move to a Historic Building," *New York Times*, November 26, 2003.

25. Joe Stephens and Carol D. Leonnig, "Solyndra loan: White House pressed on review of solar company now under investigation," *Washington Post*, September 13, 2011.

26. Eric Lipton and John M. Broder, "In Rush to Assist a Solar Company, U.S. Missed Signs," *New York Times*, September 22, 2011.

27. Ibid. See also Joe Stephens and Carol D. Leonnig, "Solyndra: Politics infused Obama energy programs," *Washington Post*, December 25, 2011.

28. Carol D. Leonnig and Joe Stephens, "Federal funds flow to clean-energy firms with Obama administration ties," *Washington Post*, February 14, 2012. For more on the close connections between Obama and the titans of "green energy," see Timothy P. Carney, "Obama Cabinet picks show his coziness with industry," *Washington Examiner*, March 7, 2013, p. 14.

29. Carol D. Leonnig and Joe Stephens, "Obama was advised against visiting Solyndra after financial warnings," *Washington Post*, October 3, 2011.

See also Tim Cavanaugh, "I, Panel: Solyndra's story, with apologies to Leonard E. Read," *Reason Reader* (Fall 2012): 9–10.

30. For a penetrating examination of the myriad ways that Washington funds the largest and most lobby-savvy corporations, see Timothy P. Carney, *The Big Ripoff: How Big Business and Big Government Steal Your Money* (Hoboken, NJ, Wiley, 2006). For a look at how government subsidies distort the food market and enrich "the biggest and most profitable businesses in the world," see Thomas M. Kostigen, *The Big Handout: How Government Subsidies and Corporate Welfare Corrupt the World We Live in and Wreak Havoc on Our Food Bills* (New York: Rodale, 2011), p. ix.

31. Ralph Nader, Foreword, *Poletown: Community Betrayed*, by Jeanie Wylie (Urbana: University of Illinois Press, 1989), p. xii.

32. Leslie Wayne, "A Guardian of Jobs or a 'Reverse Robin Hood'?" *New York Times*, September 1, 2002.

33. There are clearly gray areas. When is corporate welfare not really corporate welfare but instead a sincere effort to facilitate commerce or the extraction of raw materials from the earth?

Consider the 1872 Mining Act, which is often held up as among the most egregious examples of a corporate giveaway. Typically, the act is denounced as an outrageous gift on a silver platter, a blatant example of corporate welfare that sickens all right-thinking people. It is "anachronistic, corporate welfare, a relic of pioneer days, and a source of major environmental problems" (Andrew P. Morriss, Roger E. Meiners, and Andrew Dorchak, "Homesteading Rock: A Defense of Free Access Under the General Mining Law of 1872," *Environmental Law*, Vol. 34, 2004: 745). In the words of a *Seattle Post-Intelligencer* investigation of 2001, the act gives away "Gold, silver, platinum and other precious metals for free. Land for $5 an acre or less." It encourages destructive mining practices that have left parts of the West "pockmarked by huge craters" and imposes costly cleanups, borne by taxpayers (Robert McClure and Andrew Schneider, "The General Mining Act of 1872 has left a legacy of riches and ruin," *Seattle Post-Intelligencer*, June 10, 2001). Under the act, the public lands have been sold to private interests at ridiculously low prices.

The estimable Ralph Nader, who has done so much to publicize the concept of corporate welfare, calls the 1872 Mining Act a "corporate mineral giveaway" (Nader, Introduction to Carl J. Mayer and George A. Riley, *Public Domain, Private Dominion: A History of Public Mineral Policy in America*, San Francisco: Sierra Club Books, 1985, p. ix).

The 1872 Mining Act, charges Sam Kalen in the *University of Colorado Law Review*, "stands alone in the field of public land laws as the last vestige of a nineteenth century congressional public land policy designed to settle and promote development in a now-populous West" (Sam Kalen, "An 1872 Mining Law for the New Millennium," *University of Colorado Law Review*, Vol. 71, 2000: 343). Prior to 1872, the appropriation of minerals from public lands had been lightly regulated. Localities tended to enact statutes governing claims that reflected local custom. In practice, this meant that they "usually made the right to hold a claim dependent, first, upon discovery followed by appropriation, and second, upon continuing to work upon or develop the ground." In effect, the publicly owned lands of the United States were open fields for those who wished to mine them. Interference with these jealously guarded rights was frowned on. One district in California provided "for the whipping and banishment . . . of practising [sic] lawyers," according to Bancroft G. Davis in his seminal 1937 *Harvard Law Review* article "Fifty Years of Mining Law" (Bancroft G. Davis, "Fifty Years of Mining Law," *Harvard Law Review*, Vol. 50, No. 6, 1937: 898, 900).

A Federal Mining Act of 1866 sought to accommodate "the local customs or rules of the miners in the several mining districts," but it was judged inadequate, so six years later an act was passed that still, admitting many amendments and modifications, sets the rules by which minerals are taken from publicly owned lands (Davis: 898–99). (Among the biggest changes since 1872 is the removal of oil, gas, oil shale, sodium, stone, gravel, cinders, and pumice from coverage under the Mining Act. Hardrock mining, however, remains governed under a still-recognizable modification of the 1872 law.)

The 1872 Act arrived almost a quarter century after the Gold Rush in then pre-statehood California set off a mineral mania in the West. It provided a means whereby miners could locate and lay claim to both "rock in place" and "loose rock on or near the earth's surface" (Kalen: 348–49). Claims for the former were set at $5 per acre; the latter could be claimed at $2.50 an acre. To attain legitimacy, claims must pass what has become known as the "prudent person" test; that is, the site claimed must be such that "a person of ordinary prudence would be justified in the further expenditure of his labor and means, with a reasonable prospect of success, in developing a valuable mine" (http://idahomining.com/page3.html). This requirement ruled out fishing expeditions in which a miner or mining company might stake claims in the dark in the hope that somewhere under all that rock exists a gold mine.

In recent years, claimants have been required to pay annual fees of $100. They needn't pay royalties on any minerals they find or extract; nor do they ever have to find minerals. (Profits from mining on federal lands are, of course, taxable.) If it is determined that the claimants are working on "an economically viable mineral deposit," they are entitled to apply for a patent which grants them "fee simple title" to mineral and surface rights. Then the claim fees of $2.50 and $5 per acre kick in; claims do not exceed 20 acres (Morriss et al.: 756–57).

The purpose of the Act was stated in 1872 by Rep. Aaron A. Sargent (R-CA), who said: "We are inducing miners to purchase their claims, so that large amounts of money are thereby brought into the Treasury of the United States, causing the miners to settle themselves permanently, to improve and establish homes; to go down deeper in the earth, to dig further into the hills, and in every way to improve their own condition, and to build up the communities and the States where they reside" (Kalen: 343).

This sounds good, say contemporary critics of the law, and they are as numerous as sands in the desert, but in fact "large sums" are precisely what are *not* paid into the Treasury. Instead, they charge, the 1872 law, in its current form, virtually gives away the public lands and the hard-rock minerals underneath to greedy mineral companies. When Bruce Babbitt was secretary of the interior under President Clinton, he denounced the law in theatrical set pieces; in one, he made a show of giving $10 billion in mineral riches for just $10,000 in mining fees (Kalen: 345).

Yet there are those who argue that the 1872 Mining Act is an admirable, if not exemplary, law. It "provides a rational basis for allocating resources in a principled manner that solves critical information and incentive problems inherent in public ownership of resources," argue Andrew P. Morriss, Roger E. Meiners, and Andrew Dorchak in the scholarly journal *Environmental Law*. The trio of authors defends the Mining Act on virtually every one of its supposed weak points. For one thing, they say, it is not a giveaway. Mining is a risky, capital-intensive venture. Once the considerable costs of exploration and production are factored in, they say, the "net value of mineral rights privatized under the Mining Law is relatively small" (Morriss et al.: 751, 745).

True, the claim fees of $2.50 and $5 per acre seem absurdly small. This is what generally provokes the cry of *Giveaway!* And so reformers often suggest that a system of royalties be instituted. After all, isn't it only fair that those who profit from mining the public lands be required to pay some percentage of their profits back to the owners of that land, the federal government?

But before a claim is staked, the mineral deposits must be discovered. This is not cheap; nor are such explorations sure things. Most, in fact, fail to bear out the hopes of the discoverers. As Morriss, Meiners, and Dorchak write, "the giveaway charge is based on ex post information on land values, not on ex ante estimates" (Morriss et al.: 759). Yes, some claims turn out to be the hard-rock equivalent of gushers, but far more are duds.

Most mineral deposits are on federal lands in the West. Unless these are to be locked up or entirely privatized, some method of opening them to exploration is necessary. The Mining Act, its defenders argue, is a rational way to permit persons and companies to assert claims to extract minerals from government-owned grounds. They also note that the law does not require those with legitimate claims to actually mine those claims. Production is not mandated. Preservation and environmental groups are free to stake claims and then preserve the land. Moreover, the total of federal lands patented under the Mineral Act is 3.3 million acres, or barely 1.5 percent of all federal lands that have been patented for any reason. Those 3.3 million acres pale, assert the scholarly Mining Act defenders, next to the 213 million acres of federal land claimed by settlers under the various homestead acts (Morriss et al.: 760).

The quintet of Nevada, Montana, California, Arizona, and Wyoming accounts for 80 percent of all current hard-rock mining claims. The total workforce is around thirty thousand, so this is not a politically powerful workforce or industry. In political terms, ten US senators are, at least theoretically, protecting the interests of the mining industry, while ninety are looking out for either the taxpayer or the federal treasury, depending on your point of view. Indeed, the history of mining politics is a history of "easterners seeking federal revenue and westerners seeking free access" (Morriss et al.: 753). There are far more of the former than the latter, and yet the Mining Act of 1872 endures.

The manager of a project in Arizona told the *Post-Intelligencer*, "If massive royalties are put on federal land, you're going to see a lot less mining."

Critics continue to take aim at the Mining Act of 1872 as a flagrant example of corporate welfare. Its most vigorous defenders, Morriss, Meiners, and Dorchak, insist that it is "an institutional response to the incentive problems of public ownership of resources and an effective, evolved mechanism for solving the problem of determining how to use those resources" (Morriss et al.: 763).

While most instances of corporate welfare are obvious in the Justice Potter Stewart sense of knowing it when you see it, the Mining Act of 1872 is that relatively rare case marked by ambiguity.

# 2

# Alexander Hamilton, Canals, and Railroads

Surveying the myriad subsidies and interventions involved in President Clinton's proposals for a new "industrial policy" in 1993, Roger Pilon, a senior fellow at the Cato Institute and constitutional scholar, asked, "Where, in America, is the constitutional authority for such a policy?"[1]

Skeptics of corporate welfare have been asking that same question for two and a quarter centuries now. Defenders of the policy have not been able to provide a pithy, let alone lucid, answer, though the lack thereof has done nothing to stem the flow of federal dollars to business beneficiaries.

The historic fountainhead of federal aid to business is Secretary of the Treasury Alexander Hamilton, whose "Report on the Subject of Manufactures" was a foundational document in American economic history.

Hamilton's report, which he sent to Congress December 5, 1791, in response to a question of January 15, 1790, from the US House of Representatives on how the US government might encourage manufacturing, was "the first government-sponsored plan for selective industrial planning in America," as Hamilton's recent biographer Ron Chernow has written.[2] The report also "contains the first attempt ever made to survey the industrial resources and activities of the United States."[3]

The United States that Hamilton sought to turn toward manufacturing was an agricultural nation, though its eastern ports conducted a brisk trade in certain goods. The Revolutionary War had spurred the development of firearms and munitions manufactories, but the pace of industrialization was far too laggard for Hamilton's taste. It needed a spur, a goad. And so the request from Congress for a report on the state of American manufacturing came as a godsend to Hamilton, who would use the opportunity to "breath[e] new vigor into the moribund system of restriction and government interference," in the words of Arthur Harrison Cole, editor of *The Industrial and Commercial Correspondence of Alexander Hamilton Anticipating His Report on Manufactures.* Hamilton's Report, writes Cole, "marks the first revolt from the free-trade doctrines of Adam Smith" that had gained in currency since the publication of *Wealth of Nations* in the epochal year of 1776.[4]

Along with Alexander Hamilton's "Report on the Public Credit" (January 9, 1790) and his "Report on a National Bank" (December 14, 1790), the "Report on the Subject of Manufactures" laid the groundwork for the Federalist economic system—much to the displeasure of Thomas Jefferson, James Madison, and the rather more laissez-faire faction of the early republic.

On receiving the request for a report from the Congress, Hamilton did what any author facing a mammoth task would do: he asked for help. He sent out a query to the various local societies for the promotion of manufactures that were then dappling the new nation. Among the recipients was Tench Coxe, a prominent Philadelphia trader and secretary of the Philadelphia Manufacturing Society, who was "without a doubt the most important pro-manufacturing merchant in the United States" and a prolific essayist withal.[5]

Coxe responded the way that enthusiasts respond to questions about their special passions: at length, and with gusto. He provided the treasury secretary, who was strong on theory but a little weak on particulars, with detailed information on the condition of manufactures, in Pennsylvania and in the United States as a whole. This was drawn from his "encyclopedic knowledge of the American economy." Hamilton, impressed, appointed Coxe assistant secretary of the treasury, in which capacity he undertook "the task of collecting additional data on American manufacturers and preparing a report on their current state and the means whereby they might be encouraged."[6] (Coxe later defected to the Jeffersonian side of American politics. He was something of an Anglophobe, while Hamilton was something of an Anglophile.)

Contrary to the assertions of some Hamilton biographers, Coxe played an "instrumental" role in the composition of Hamilton's report, argued Jacob E. Cooke in the *William and Mary Quarterly.* He compiled much of the information and drew up a first draft. Coxe contributed the "utilitarian arguments in support of manufactures," claims Cooke, while Hamilton provided the "theoretical justification." In one important respect the secretary and his assistant differed: while Coxe shied from a "strenuous recommendation" of explicit subsidies to manufacturing concerns, Hamilton would make it a centerpiece of his report.[7] (Not that Coxe had any philosophical objections to such aid; indeed, he would urge it in his later writings.)

In requesting this report, Congress had merely asked Hamilton for his thoughts on "the promotion of such manufactures as will tend to render the United States independent of other nations for essential, particularly for military, supplies." But given the opportunity to expound on the necessity for an activist federal government and his pet economic theories, Alexander Hamilton was not about to limit himself within the boundaries of the request. He needed an expanse over which to roam—and he created one, albeit a "prolix and repetitious" document that serves as a superior sleep-aid.[8]

Hamilton's report was a lengthy explication of his view that the United States needed to develop a manufacturing base, and that this could best be accomplished by significant increases in government spending and direction of the economy. He tied this recommendation to national security, citing the "extreme embarrassments of the United States during the late war, from an incapacity of supplying themselves." To take its place among the nations, the United States must become self-sufficient in its "means of subsistence, habitation, clothing, and defence."[9] This would not be the last time that subsidization of industry would be defended on national defense grounds. Indeed, few rationales are as enduring as the claim that giving public monies to favored industries or firms is essential to the security of the nation. "National defense" is right up there with "for the sake of the children" as an all-purpose rationale for government spending.

The "Report on the Subject of Manufactures" merits a close reading, both for its rhetoric and its substance. Hamilton begins, ingeniously and perhaps a bit disingenuously, by stating, "The expediency of encouraging manufactures in the United States, which was not long since deemed very questionable, appears at this time to be pretty generally admitted."[10]

So Hamilton starts his report by asserting as a truism what is in fact a controversial statement. "Encouraging manufactures" was *not* "pretty generally admitted" to be a desirable thing in 1791, at least if one assumes that the federal government, issuer of the report, is the means of encouragement.

Certainly the partisans of strict construction of the Constitution did not favor any such encouragement. Thomas Jefferson, secretary of state and Hamilton's rival within the Washington cabinet, would have objected strongly to Hamilton's opener, as James Madison did.

In the interests of fairness, or the appearance of fairness, Hamilton essays to summarize the views of his opponents. (Those opponents might say he caricatures them.) These benighted discouragers of manufactures, he says, believe that "agriculture is the most beneficial and productive object of human industry." To interfere with this state of affairs, in their view, is to defy nature. He encapsulates, not unfairly, the Jeffersonian view thus:

> To endeavor, by the extraordinary patronage of government, to accelerate the growth of manufactures is, in fact, to endeavor, by force and art, to transfer the natural current of industry from a more to a less beneficial channel. Whatever has such a tendency, must necessarily be unwise; indeed, it can hardly ever be wise in a government to attempt to give a direction to the industry of its citizens. . . . To leave industry to itself, therefore, is, in almost every case, the soundest as well as the simplest policy.[11]

Subsidy, in this Jeffersonian line of thinking, enriches the well connected: "If, contrary to the natural course of things, an unseasonable and premature spring can be given to certain fabrics, by heavy duties, prohibitions, bounties, or by the other forced expedients, this will only be to sacrifice the interests of the community to those of particular classes."[12]

This is not an inaccurate précis of the agriculturally inflected laissez-faire predilections of many followers of Jefferson, though it should be noted that this tendency also had adherents among many mechanics and working men in the new nation's cities. (Contrariwise, as Lawrence A. Peskin notes in the *Journal of the Early Republic*, "many urban republicans sympathized with manufacturing."[13]) If the Jeffersonian philosophy was not quite "anarchy plus the police constable," it did look askance at an activist federal government. But it was, Hamilton suggested, outmoded. Old-fashioned. Yesterday's philosophy. To be au courant, one must support state encouragement of industry. And that has been a consistent theme of corporate welfare boosters over the years: the past may have been laissez-faire, but the future belongs to government direction of the economy.

Governmental "encouragement of manufactures," stated Hamilton, was "recommended by the most cogent and persuasive motives of national policy."[14] He adduced seven reasons why industry ought to be nurtured; these ranged from its role in ensuring a proper division of labor to its promotion of immigration ("it is the interest of the United

States to open every possible avenue to emigration from abroad") to its expansion of options for enterprising and talented men (so that "each individual can find his proper element") to the use made by factories of women and children. This last has been cause for throat clearing by Hamilton partisans over the years. In praising industry for "the employment of persons who would otherwise be idle," Hamilton went on to say that "women and children are rendered more useful, and the latter more early useful, by manufacturing establishments, than they would otherwise be."[15]

A century later, progressives—Hamilton's descendants, economically —would reverse field on the desirability of sending children into the factories.

Foreshadowing later arguments for state intervention, Hamilton conceded that in a perfect world, subsidy might not be needed, but given the imperfections of the world, and the practice of protection and subsidy by other nations, the United States had no real choice but to imitate those nations.

The idea that "industry, if left to itself, will naturally find its way to the most useful and profitable employment . . . without the aid of government" struck Hamilton as naïve. Among those who might wish to enter manufacturing, the fear of failure was so strong that absent state subvention they would stay on the sidelines. "It is of importance," Hamilton lectures, "that the confidence of cautious, sagacious capitalists, both citizens and foreigners, should be excited. And . . . they should be made to see that in any project which is new . . . the prospect of such a degree of countenance and support from government, as may be capable of overcoming the obstacles inseparable from first experiments." Only government assistance could overcome the general wariness of "want of success in untried enterprises."[16]

Launching a business is difficult. An agricultural people may need inducements to forsake the farm for the factory. If left to their own devices, Hamilton fretted, potential entrepreneurs might be crippled by worries about their own inadequacy or the lack of demand for their product in the marketplace. To assuage those worries was the purpose of "the incitement and patronage of government."

If foreign nations enabled their factory owners with "bounties, premiums, and other artificial encouragements," then it was up to the federal government to match those prizes. It was simply impossible for domestic manufacturers to compete on an equal footing with long-established foreign businesses. To even the playing field, to use a trope drawn from the late twentieth century, was not doable absent "the extraordinary aid and protection of government." This "extraordinary" aid could assume various forms, from outright grants and remunerations to protection against imports, but one thing was clear: "to contend with success, it is evident that the interference and aid of their own governments are indispensable."[17]

Might such assistance fortify monopoly? Might it enrich a single domestic manufacturer at the expense of the people of the States, who would be better off purchasing lower-cost items from foreign sources? This is not an "unreasonable supposition," concedes Hamilton, who then assures his readers (members of Congress) that once this single domestic manufacturer has "attained to perfection," competitors will rapidly take the field, and prices will fall accordingly.[18] (He does not bother to provide any examples.)

Hamilton also denies that subsidy will favor any particular section. With an eye to the South, whose statesmen generally viewed with disfavor schemes for protection, he declares that "every thing tending to establish substantial and permanent order in the affairs of a country, to increase the total mass of industry and opulence, is ultimately beneficial to every part of it."[19] Yes, the Middle Atlantic and New England states would be likelier venues for manufacturing than the agrarian South, but as the source of raw materials for these factories the South would profit, too. It was a good try—but the South wasn't buying it.

Hamilton admits that American manufacturing and production is flourishing, or at least emerging, in various fields. These included iron, spirits and liquors, flax and hemp, refined sugars, bricks, paper, copper, tinware, carriages, gunpowder . . . seventeen areas in all, not to mention those articles produced within the household: shirts, coats, linens, coverlets, and numerous items made of cotton and wool, so that up to four-fifths of the clothing in America is made within the home.[20]

Getting down to the nitty-gritty, Hamilton describes the forms that government assistance may take. These include protective duties; prohibitions on the import of domestically manufactured articles; prohibitions on the export of materials used by rival foreign manufacturers; exemptions of materials from duties; "exclusive privileges" for inventions, or what we would call patents; government inspection of manufactured commodities; making bank paper negotiable across state lines; and the improvements of roads and canals and waterways, or what was called "internal improvements."

But for our purposes, "pecuniary bounties" are the cynosure. For here is the Hamiltonian case for what would later be called corporate welfare. In Hamilton's view, "pecuniary bounties" were superior to the protective tariff. Direct, and not indirect, subsidy was the desideratum. ("Pecuniary bounties" is also the longest of the eleven means of assistance that this report examines.)

Pecuniary bounties, avers Hamilton, are "one of the most efficacious means of encouraging manufactures." These bounties—which are, in effect, grants from the government to chosen manufacturers—are "positive and direct."[21] They do not artificially inflate prices, as is the case with protective duties, nor do they lead to scarcity. They are a "stimulus and a support" to new industries, and besides, other countries are in the habit of granting them.[22]

Admittedly, says Hamilton, these bounties should not become permanent. Businesses ought not to depend on them as lifelines of infinite length. They must be temporary, and any expense "is more than compensated by an increase of industry and wealth; by an augmentation of resource and independence; and by the circumstances of eventual cheapness" once the industry has attained maturity.

In this formulation, pecuniary bounties are the very model of public-spiritedness; objections thereto are mean, even selfish. Incredibly, says Hamilton, "there is a degree of prejudice against bounties, from an appearance of giving away the public money . . . and from a supposition that they serve to enrich particular classes, at the expense of the community."

Well, yes. And what does Hamilton say to that? What is his response to critics of corporate welfare? That such dislike does not "bear a serious examination" because "There is no purpose to which public money can be more beneficially applied, than to the acquisition of a new and useful branch of industry."[23]

That settles *that*.

Historian Lawrence A. Peskin argues that Hamilton's report betrayed those working men who made up the forgotten segment of the Federalist Party. For although "all mechanics, rich and poor, would benefit more or less equally from tariffs affecting their respective trades, only a few influential manufacturers stood to benefit from Hamilton's program" of pecuniary bounties.[24]

As for those constitutionalist pettifoggers who whine that direct grants of public monies to favored industries are a violation of the nation's new charter, Hamilton huffs that "there is certainly no good foundation for such a question."[25]

Skeptics of the constitutionality of his schemes are beneath notice, it seems. The Constitution, notes Hamilton, authorizes the federal government to provide for the "general welfare," and this term was "doubtless intended to signify more than was expressed" in the actual words preceding this authorization ("to lay and collect taxes, duties, imposts, and excises, to pay the debts"). True, these powers did not include gifts to private industries, but the phrase *general welfare* "is as comprehensive as any that could have been used." The omission of this power should be interpreted as its inclusion. To question this is to question reality: "there seems to be no room for a doubt, that whatever concerns the general interests of learning, of agriculture, of manufactures, and of commerce, are within the sphere of the national councils, as far as regards an application of money."[26]

In fact, there were plenty of doubters, as Hamilton would discover after his report was issued. Foremost among them were Thomas Jefferson and James Madison, authors, respectively, of the Declaration of Independence and the Constitution (to which Hamilton, who was a marginal figure at the Philadelphia Convention of 1787, contributed almost nothing of note).

Hamilton appended to "pecuniary bounties" the narrower idea of "premiums"; that is, monetary rewards for "some particular excellence or superiority" with an eye toward stimulating others to emulate those so awarded. Characteristically, he noted that while in other nations these premiums tended to be awarded by "voluntary associations" for the promotion of commerce and manufactures, in the United States these premiums should be "supplied and supported by the Government of the Union."[27]

This would seem an inversion of the roles played by the New World and the Old: the former, Americans contended, was to be free of the shackles and confinement of government direction and patronage, while the latter was absolutely permeated by statism. But Hamilton felt so strongly about the necessity for federal government subsidies to business that he closed his famous report with this plea:

"In countries where there is great private wealth, much may be effected by the voluntary contributions of patriotic individuals; but in a community situated like that of the United States, the public purse must supply the deficiency of private resources. In what can it be so useful, as in prompting and improving the efforts of industry?"[28]

The report was tabled. And so, unlike Hamilton's reports on credit and a national bank, the report on manufactures stalled before becoming national policy. But it provoked horror and detestation from Hamilton's rivals. A frank plea for wide-scale economic intervention was not about to pass unopposed. There was a segment of the political and popular world that supported the attitude expressed by the Jeffersonian philosopher-economist Thomas Cooper, who wrote that "every treatise on political economy ought to have its first page occupied with . . . LET US ALONE."[29] A country in which that sentiment had considerable popular support was unlikely to adopt wholesale the recommendations of Mr. Hamilton.

Thomas Jefferson saw within Hamilton's Report the seeds of a total government. He charged that "under color of giving *bounties* for the encouragement of particular manufactures," Hamilton's expansive reading of the Constitution "permitted Congress to take everything under their management which *they* should deem for the public *welfare*."[30]

James Madison objected most vigorously to Hamilton's interpretation of the document whose first draft he had written in 1787. Madison scholar Colleen A. Sheehan writes that in Madison's view, the Report indicated that "Hamilton meant, by administrative fiat, to undermine the Constitution as ratified and adopted by the American people, and to alter the substance, and perhaps the form, of American republicanism." Indeed, "The pages of the 'Report on Manufactures' revealed to Madison that Hamilton intended nothing less than the transformation of the economic and political life of America."[31] This was, in a real sense, a revolution—or counter-revolution.

In a letter of January 1, 1792, to Henry Lee, Madison wrote, "I enclose the report of the Secy. of the Treasury on Manufactures. What think you of the commentary . . . on the terms 'general welfare'? The federal Govt. has been hitherto limited to the Specified powers. . . . If not only the *means*, but the *objects* are unlimited, the parchment had better be thrown into the fire at once."[32] The primary author of the Constitution was saying that if Hamilton's interpretation of the document held, then it might as well be burned to ashes.

This was in response to Hamilton's claim in the Report that the general welfare clause permitted the federal government to offer "pecuniary bounties" as "the most efficacious means of encouraging manufactures." Writing to Henry Lee later that same month, Madison speaks of the "usurpation of power recommended in the report on manufactures," which if enacted "I shall consider the fundamental & characteristic principle of the Govt. as subverted."[33]

Strong words—but to Madison, enabling the federal government to directly subsidize businesses was an act of subversion. Writing to Edmund Pendleton on January 21, 1792, he again sounds the tocsin, telling Pendleton that the Report on Manufactures "broaches a new constitutional doctrine of vast consequence. . . . I consider it myself as subverting the fundamental and characteristic principle of the Government, as contrary to the true & fair, as well as the received construction, and as bidding defiance to the sense in which the Constitution is known to have been proposed, advocated and adopted." The philosophy embodied in the Report, says Madison, holds that "the Government is no longer a limited one possessing enumerated powers, but an indefinite one subject to particular exceptions."[34]

He took to the floor of Congress to expand on these points. In Madison's "longest recorded speech of the first session of Congress,"[35] he made the distinction between "a mere commutation and modification of a drawback," e.g., a tariff reduction, and "an allowance in the nature of a real and positive bounty," e.g., a subsidy. The very term "bounty" he found offensive and misleading; the commutation of drawbacks was certainly within the power of Congress to grant, but the granting of bounties was subversive of "a limited government tied down to the specified powers" of the Constitution.

He told the House, "Arguments have been advanced, to shew, that because, in the regulation of trade, indirect and eventually encouragement is given to manufactures, therefore congress have power to give money in direct bounties, or to grant it in any other way that would answer the same purpose."[36] Nonsense, replied Madison, who after all was the chief architect of the Constitution under dispute. The power to lay duties was explicitly granted the Congress, whereas no power was granted, or even contemplated, permitting the direct subsidy of industry. (The word "bounty" was stricken from the bill under debate, which then passed.)

Hamilton later wrote (in 1801) that "In matters of industry, human enterprise ought doubtless to be left free in the main, not fettered by too much regulation, but practical politicians know that it may be beneficially stimulated by prudent aids and encouragements on the part of the government."[37] He makes it sound like an anodyne, blandly uncontroversial position. But just how stimulating these "prudent aids and encouragements" should be is the stuff of fierce, cleaving, philosophical debates. Or at least it was: today the Hamiltonian position is seldom contested.

The ultimate influence of the "Report on the Subject of Manufactures" is "indeterminable,"[38] says historian Jacob E. Cooke, although economic historian Carter Goodrich writes that "The Report on Manufactures has perhaps been quoted more often than any other document in American economic history."[39] Certainly it lacks literary polish and has the flavor of special pleading, and it sent James Madison into a state of high dudgeon, but it is undeniable that eventually, though not totally, Hamilton's more interventionist philosophy prevailed over the laissez-faire Jeffersonian view.[40]

\* \* \*

New York was one of the few states that took a cue from Hamilton, as "between 1790 and 1820 special acts were passed lending a total of $273,000 to forty-eight new or prospective manufacturing enterprises," writes economic historian Carter Goodrich in *The Government and the Economy, 1783–1861*.[41] But the primary means by which government entered the economy on the side of favored businesses was in getting people and goods from one place to another. Antebellum "governmental measures to promote the construction of the means of transport—roads, river improvements, canals, and railroads"—were "extensive."

For instance, about 70 percent of total investment in canals in the 1815–1860 period came from governmental sources.[42] Protectionism, of course, was an example of governmental promotion of favored domestic industries, though it was of an indirect sort as opposed to the direct subsidy of manufacturers of the kind proposed by Alexander Hamilton.

Still, the political heirs to Jefferson and Madison refused to yield to the Hamiltonian persuasion. They contended that "internal improvements" was code for "eternal taxation."[43] The high-water mark of the early opposition to such subsidy came in President Andrew Jackson's veto of legislation authorizing "a subscription of stock in the Maysville, Washington, Paris and Lexington Turnpike Road Company."

In his veto message of May 27, 1830, President Jackson explained his rejection of the bill. He was "Sincerely friendly to the improvement of our country by means of roads and canals," Jackson asserted, yet the Maysville Road was of "purely local character" and would set off "a scramble for appropriations" which would "shift upon the Government the losses of unsuccessful private speculation," thereby tending to "sap the foundations of public virtue and taint the administration of Government with a demoralizing influence."[44]

Forrest McDonald points out that while the nineteenth-century Whigs and Republicans, heirs to the Hamiltonian tradition, spoke a language of business and development, "the policies they advocated, such as subsidies, grants of special privileges, protective tariffs, and the like, actually worked to retard development and to stifle innovation." The nineteenth-century Democrats of a Jacksonian kind, on the other hand, may have *sounded* anti-business in their condemnation of special privileges, but "the results of their policies were to remove or reduce governmental interferences into private economic activity, and thus to free market entrepreneurs to go about their creative work. The entire nation grew wealthy as a consequence."[45]

In condemning the government underwriting of "private speculation," Jackson was preaching the old Jeffersonian gospel. But that gospel was fast being superseded by Hamiltonian doctrines. For the railroads were coming—and quickly.

Railroad track mileage in the United States increased from three thousand in 1840 to thirty thousand in 1860, making it "the largest railroad network in the world."[46] Political discussion soon ran along a parallel track.

Consider the debate in the US Senate over the first railroad land grant. In 1850, Senators Stephen Douglas (D-IL) and William R. King (D-AL) teamed up to propose the grant of 3.75 million acres for the construction of a North-South railroad running from Illinois to Mobile—not coincidentally, from Douglas's state to King's state. Senator Douglas, who would come down to us as the man who debated Abraham Lincoln in 1858 and lost the presidency to him in 1860, was joined in the debate by Senator William Seward (Whig-NY), who would serve as Lincoln's secretary of state, a man whose vision of permissible government projects knew no bounds. "I have no trouble myself, Mr. President," Seward told the Senate, "about the constitutional power of the Government of the United States to make works of national improvement."[47]

In opposition, Senator Andrew P. Butler (D-SC) proclaimed that "I am opposed to the whole principle of using the public lands for building private roads." Butler added, "It is absolutely using public property for private purposes."[48] Senator Butler was voicing the old Jeffersonian skepticism of an activist federal government; that is, he was delivering the classic argument against corporate welfare. He lost.

The Constitution, though it might surprise Mr. Madison to hear this, apparently looked kindly on internal improvements.

The railroads are often held up as an example of corporate welfare that worked. The federal and state governments showered grants of land and lavish subsidies on these iron horses. Eventually, some states even delegated the power of eminent domain to railroads, permitting them to appropriate land for rights-of-way.

Assisting in the crisscrossing of America by tracks was the governmental power of eminent domain, whose often brutal modern application will be examined in Chapter 5. This was one of the earliest tools in the corporate welfare arsenal. The construction of roads—including toll roads—has long been held so fundamental a societal undertaking that it excused the expropriation of property from its rightful owners and its transfer to the road builders, even when those road builders were private and not governmental concerns.

This kind of taking of private property for public use has it defenders. Historians often justify it as necessary for the construction of canals, roads, and railways. In the formulation of Harry N. Scheiber of the University of California-San Diego, writing in *Law & Society*, nineteenth-century judges who broadly constructed the power of eminent domain "mobilized boldly creative expediting doctrines to reduce entrepreneurial costs of mill-dam builders, canal and railroad promoters, miners, lumbering companies, and other types of private firms."[49] *Boldly creative expediting doctrines*: a fancy way of euphemizing what seemed to the victims clear-cut cases of theft. (This joins a long list of euphemisms covering corporate welfare; one of the more recent is "statutory competitive advantage.")

But the path of Hamilton and of *boldly creative expediting doctrines* was not the only road to prosperity. In Burton W. Folsom Jr.'s usefully revisionist work *The Myth of the Robber Barons*, the author analyzes the early history of the steamship industry through the aforementioned lens of "political entrepreneurs" versus "market entrepreneurs." The former, which folklore has dubbed "robber barons," would include Robert Fulton, who was granted by the New York State Legislature a thirty-year monopoly on steamship traffic in New York waters. The latter include the man who busted that monopoly, Cornelius Vanderbilt, whose steamboats undercut the Fulton monopoly and drastically reduced the cost of passenger traffic on such ships.

As Folsom notes, steamships remained a corporate welfare vessel until the Civil War. Congress lavished subsidies on such political entrepreneurs as Edward K. Collins, who was granted $3 million down and an annual payment of $385,000 (later boosted to $858,000) for building five ships to carry the mail as well as passengers. (He only built four, says Folsom, and these were equipped with nonessential—for purposes of mail-carrying, at least—features such as "elegant saloons, ladies' drawing rooms, and wedding berths." Two of the ships would ultimately sink, costing five hundred lives.) Others, sensing that profits could be made from exploiting the government's postal monopoly, followed. Cornelius Vanderbilt offered to carry mail for less than half of the subsidy Collins was receiving; when a heavily lobbied Congress turned him down, Vanderbilt took on Collins anyway, saying, "The share of prosperity which has fallen to my lot is the direct result of unfettered trade, and unrestrained competition. It is my wish that those who are to come after me shall have that same field open before them."[50]

Vanderbilt charged less than Collins did for carrying both the mail and persons. He also added a cheap third-class passenger fare. Though he found competition with the federally subsidized Collins onerous—"It is utterly impossible for a private individual to stand in competition with a line drawing nearly one million dollars per annum from the national treasury, without serious sacrifice"—Vanderbilt persevered.[51] By 1858, lawmakers had climbed out of Collins's back pocket. They repealed the steamship subsidy. Collins went under; Vanderbilt prospered.

Or consider another of Folsom's heroes: James J. Hill, the Canadian immigrant and railroad man known as the "Empire Builder." We are not used to thinking of railroad barons as independent men who forswear government subsidies. Rather, we imagine them as moustache-twirling villains buying off venal politicians and stealing land from widows and orphans on which to lay their trackage.

Hill had the moustache, but there the resemblance to the cartoon ends. As Burton W. Folsom Jr. writes, the Union Pacific and Central Pacific railroads had had their path to Promontory Point smoothed by forty-four million acres of federal land grants and more than $61 million in federal loans. The corruption seeded by these transcontinental railroads and their smaller brethren was legendary; examples ranged from petty graft—"In Congress and in state legislatures, free railroad passes were distributed like confetti"—to the Credit Mobilier stock scandal, often considered the ethical lowlight of the Gilded Age.[52]

On a parallel track, the Northern Pacific, which ran from Minnesota to Washington State, from the Great Lakes to the Pacific Ocean, had a bumpier ride. Chartered by Congress in 1864, it received land grants twice as generous as those received by the Union Pacific. Its golden spike was not driven until 1883, and that only after years of exorbitant construction costs and bankruptcy.

But the troubled Northern Pacific was not the only railroad cutting its way through the wild Northwest. James J. Hill did the same with the Great Northern, and "he did it with no federal aid." Instead, Hill plotted a careful, deliberate course across the Northwest, even importing settlers, crops, and cattle to populate the new towns along his rail line. He avoided, when possible, the daunting topographical challenges that had bedeviled the Northern Pacific. Said Hill, "What we want is the best possible line, shortest distance, lowest grades and least curvature that we can build. We do not care enough for Rocky Mountain scenery to spend a large sum of money developing it."[53]

Federal aid to those railroads suckling on it was gauged to mileage; the more track you laid, the more alms you received. This encouraged unwise choices by the subsidized railroads. Hill's Great Northern, with no federal cash cow to milk, built fewer miles of track than the Northern Pacific. As Folsom points out, subsidized railroads also had to carry US mail at cut rates, and they were required to use American-made steel rather than possibly superior steel from elsewhere. As is so often the case, he who takes the king's shilling becomes the king's man.

In the Gilded Age, as in ours, access to power was a source of prestige for some pathetic souls. To have a pipeline to corporate welfare was a mark of being in the In Crowd. But James J. Hill was proud of his independence. He proclaimed that the Great Northern "was built without any government aid, even the right of way, through hundreds of miles of public lands, being paid for in cash."[54]

The lesson? Following Hamilton's doctrines was not the only way to run—or build—a railroad.

The latter third of the nineteenth century saw legal doctrines evolving to treat the practice of corporate welfare. If the first half of the nineteenth century was a boom time—relatively speaking—for state and local subsidy of business, the latter years of the century were quite a different story. The Civil War, like all wars, had greatly increased the role of the federal government in the economy. This, in turn, had spurred concerns about widespread corruption. Whenever money is appropriated, bribery and fraud flourish. The most powerful and unscrupulous forces were able to steer government assistance their way; this violated not only the basic sense of fair play shared by most Americans but also the regnant economic philosophy of laissez-faire. As a result, challenges

31

to corporate welfare popped up in state legislatures and state courts, leading to significant US Supreme Court rulings.

In *Olcott v. Supervisors* (1872), the US Supreme Court took up the matter of state rail subsidies. In 1867, the Wisconsin state legislature had authorized Fond du Lac County to hold a referendum on the question of the county aiding the Sheboygan and Fond du Lac Railroad in the construction of a line linking the Wisconsin cities of Fond du Lac and Ripon. The voters approved the measure; the county prepared "orders" payable to the Sheboygan and Fond du Lac Railroad Company. In stepped the Wisconsin State Supreme Court, which in 1870 voided the act authorizing the referendum on the grounds that the legislature lacked the power "to raise money or to authorize it to be raised by taxation, for the purpose of donating it to a private corporation." Yes, admitted the state court, railroads were sometimes delegated by the state to exercise eminent domain, but in all other respects—"rolling stock, buildings, fixtures, and other property pertaining" to them— railroads were private property, and thus ineligible, under the Wisconsin Constitution, for subsidy from tax revenues.[55] Public taxes cannot be levied for private purposes, argued the attorneys defending the right of the state to nullify the Fond du Lac action. Moreover, the US Supreme Court was in the practice of respecting state court interpretations of state constitutions (remember—this was long, long ago and far, far away; no such deference exists today); therefore, the High Court must let stand the decision of the Wisconsin Supreme Court.

US Supreme Court Associate Justice William Strong delivered the Court's opinion. Yes, he conceded, "It is undoubtedly true in general, that this court does follow the decisions of the highest courts of the States respecting local questions peculiar to themselves, or respecting the construction of their own constitutions and laws."[56] But—there had to be a *but*—denying subsidies to railroads was carrying this respect too far! Railroads, huffed Justice Strong, "though constructed by private corporations and owned by them, are public highways." The fact that states condemn private land and transfer that property to private railroads surely signifies that the building of a rail line is a public use. "Though the ownership is private, the use is public."[57]

Justice Strong noted that "The argument most earnestly used against the constitutionality of the act is that it attempted to authorize Fond du Lac County to assist the railroad company by a donation. It is stoutly contended that the legislature could not authorize the county to impose taxes to enable it to make a donation in the aid of the construction of the railroad, even if its ultimate uses are public." To which the learned jurist replies: "But why not?"[58]

Well, that certainly settles the matter!

A direct subsidy—a donation—is every bit as valid a way of assisting this "public use" railroad as would be the gift of land via eminent domain. Municipal corporations may subscribe to stock issued by a railroad; so, reasoned Justice Strong, may counties impose taxes to assist such a venture. So much for the Wisconsin state constitution.

Beyond railroads, however, the legal territory was murkier. In *Citizens Savings and Loan Association v. Topeka* (1874), the US Supreme Court was called on to decide a case in which the state of Kansas had authorized the city of Topeka to issue municipal bonds (one hundred at $1,000 each) in order to assist the King Wrought-Iron Bridge Manufacturing and Iron-Works Company "in establishing and operating bridge shops" in Topeka.[59]

The High Court, acting on a suit filed by the Citizens' Savings and Loan Association of Cleveland, which was seeking to collect interest on its bonds, ruled the Kansas statute which permitted such a subsidy unconstitutional. The act, wrote Justice Samuel Freeman Miller for the majority, "authorizes the towns and other municipalities . . . by issuing bonds or loaning their credit, to take the property of the citizen under the guise of taxation to pay these bonds, and use it in aid of the enterprises of others which are not of a public character, thus perverting the right of taxation, which can only be exercised for a public use, to the aid of individual interests and personal purposes of profit and gain."[60]

Justice Miller conceded that the "aid voted to railroads by counties and towns" had generally been upheld by the courts, at least in cases where the aid was "for a public purpose" and not merely the gain of the railroad corporation. (Just how one distinguishes between the two is a matter perhaps best left to expert casuists and champion hair splitters.) For carefully defined "public purposes," which generally involve transportation—railroads, canals, highways—municipal aid is within the realm of the permissible. To go beyond this, however, is "an unauthorized invasion of private right."[61]

To the layman, bridges, the principal product of the King Wrought-Iron Bridge Manufacturing and Iron-Works Company, might seem to fall at or even within the margins of public purpose, but Justice Miller drew a sharp line. When "towns are authorized to contribute aid by way of taxation to any class of manufacturers," he announced, "there is no difficulty in holding that this is not such a public purpose as we have been considering." His next point is one that might profitably be engraved today on the wall of every taxpayer organization seeking to stop the Industrial Development Authorities (IDAs) and Economic Development Agencies (EDAs) and every other economic development agency that subsidizes favor-seeking businesses:

> If it be said that a benefit results to the local public of a town by establishing manufactures, the same may be said of any other business or pursuit which employs capital or labor. The merchant, the mechanic, the innkeeper, the banker, the builder, the steamboat owner are equally promoters of the public good, and equally deserving the aid of the citizens by forced contributions. No line can be drawn in favor of the manufacturer which would not open the coffers of the public treasury to the importunities of two-thirds of the businessmen of the city or town.[62]

That line, no longer drawn with any precision, has been blurred almost out of existence by importunate subsidy seekers. Yet Justice Miller's ringing declaration speaks to us even today: "To lay with one hand the power of the government on the property of citizen, and with the other to bestow it on favored individuals to aid private enterprises and build up private fortunes, is nonetheless a robbery because it is done under the forms of law and called taxation."[63] This principle, if followed, would effectively nullify almost all of what we call corporate welfare. But this principle has long been discarded in US jurisprudence.

Nevertheless, this "public purpose" doctrine held sway, making "the period from 1875 through the early portion of the twentieth century, a low-water mark for government assistance and government regulation of private enterprise," writes Martin Gold in *The Urban Lawyer*.[64]

The nadir for corporate welfare—a century before it would be taken on by Nader—lasted into the twentieth century. As Gold notes, "Through the end of the nineteenth century and the first half of the twentieth century, state courts, citing *Loan Association v. Topeka*, repeatedly struck down programs providing governmental assistance for economic development projects."[65] Then came the Great Depression and Franklin D. Roosevelt and the New Deal and a US Supreme Court both cowed by Roosevelt and adapting to changing circumstances.

For example, the State of New York Constitution, adopted in 1846 and since amended but still in effect, prohibited government loans to private firms. In 1874, this prohibition was extended to include gifts of money to private firms. This ban was never repealed; an effort to amend the constitution in 1967 to permit "gifts and loans to private corporations whose purpose was economic or community development" was beaten back. Yet the ban is toothless today. As Martin Gold observes, at present "There are virtually no restraints under the public purpose doctrine in New York State." A 1923 ruling by the state court of appeals (*Schieffelin v. Hylan*) defined public purpose as an activity that "contribut[es] to the comfort and happiness of citizens," a loophole through which one could ram the Empire State Building and still have room for the Statue of Liberty.[66] As a result, explains Buffalo attorney James Ostrowski, who filed a much-discussed but ultimately unsuccessful anti-corporate welfare lawsuit in New York, "state officials have acted as though the 1967 amendment had become the law."[67]

Today in New York, a virtual cornucopia of gifts and loans are lavished on favored corporations. But that story must wait until Chapter 4.

## Notes

1. Roger Pilon, "On the Folly and Illegitimacy of Industrial Policy," *Stanford Law & Policy Review* (Vol. 5, Fall 1993): 103.
2. Ron Chernow *Alexander Hamilton* (New York: Penguin, 2004), p. 374.
3. Arthur Harrison Cole, editor, *The Industrial and Commercial Correspondence of Alexander Hamilton Anticipating His Report on Manufactures* (Chicago: A.W. Shaw Co., 1928), p. xvi.
4. Ibid.
5. Lawrence A. Peskin, "How the Republicans Learned to Love Manufacturing: The First Parties and the 'New Economy,'" *Journal of the Early Republic* (Vol. 22, No. 2, Summer 2002): 242.
6. Jacob E. Cooke, "Tench Coxe, Alexander Hamilton, and the Encouragement of American Manufactures," *William and Mary Quarterly* (Vol. 32, No. 3, July 1975): 380, 370.
7. Ibid.: 369, 374, 377.
8. Ibid.: 372, 374.
9. Alexander Hamilton, "Report on the Subject of Manufactures," *The Industrial and Commercial Correspondence of Alexander Hamilton Anticipating His Report on Manufactures*, p. 284.
10. Ibid., p. 247.
11. Ibid., pp. 247–48.
12. Ibid., p. 248.
13. Peskin, "How the Republicans Learned to Love Manufacturing: The First Parties and the 'New Economy,'" *Journal of the Early Republic*: 237.
14. Hamilton, "Report on the Subject of Manufactures," *The Industrial and Commercial Correspondence of Alexander Hamilton Anticipating His Report on Manufactures*, p. 249.
15. Ibid., pp. 256–61, *passim*.
16. Ibid., pp. 266–67.
17. Ibid.

18. Ibid., p. 281.
19. Ibid., p. 287.
20. Ibid., pp. 280–81.
21. Ibid., p. 290.
22. Ibid., p. 292.
23. Ibid.
24. Peskin, "How the Republicans Learned to Love Manufacturing: The First Parties and the 'New Economy,'" *Journal of the Early Republic*: 239.
25. Hamilton, "Report on the Subject of Manufactures," *The Industrial and Commercial Correspondence of Alexander Hamilton Anticipating His Report on Manufactures*, p. 292.
26. Ibid., p. 293.
27. Ibid., p. 294.
28. Ibid., p. 320.
29. Peskin, "How the Republicans Learned to Love Manufacturing: The First Parties and the 'New Economy,'" *Journal of the Early Republic*: 259.
30. Thomas Jefferson, *The Complete Anas of Thomas Jefferson* (New York: Round Table Press, 1903), p. 55.
31. Colleen A. Sheehan, "Madison Versus Hamilton: The Battle over Republicanism and the Role of Public Opinion," *The Many Faces of Alexander Hamilton*, edited by Douglas Ambrose and Robert W.T. Martin (New York: NYU Press, 2006), p. 169.
32. "To Henry Lee," January 1, 1792, *The Papers of James Madison*, Vol. 14, edited by Rutland, Mason, Brugger, Sisson, and Teute (Charlottesville: University Press of Virginia, 1983), p. 180.
33. "To Henry Lee, January 21, 1791," *The Papers of James Madison*, Vol. 14, p. 193.
34. "To Edmund Pendleton, January 21, 1792," *The Papers of James Madison*, Vol. 14, p. 195.
35. *The Papers of James Madison*, Vol. 14, p. 112.
36. "Bounty Payments for Cod Fisheries," February 6, 1792, printed in *Federal Gazette*, *The Papers of James Madison*, Vol. 14, pp. 220–23.
37. Chernow, *Alexander Hamilton*, p. 377.
38. Cooke, "Tench Coxe, Alexander Hamilton, and the Encouragement of American Manufactures," *William and Mary Quarterly*: 374.
39. Carter Goodrich, editor, *The Government and the Economy, 1783–1861* (Indianapolis: Bobbs-Merrill, 1967), p. 188.
40. The Society for Establishing Useful Manufactures was one progeny of the Hamilton report. This "most ambitious industrial experiment in early American history" was set up in 1791 and chartered by the state of New Jersey. Its purpose was to harness the power of the Great Falls of the Passaic River; its means was the founding of a mill town, named after New Jersey Governor William Paterson. The enterprise was to enjoy a ten-year exemption from property taxes. The Society failed, expiring in 1796, but Paterson, which became known as the Silk City, would eventually flourish. Cooke, "Tench Coxe, Alexander Hamilton, and the Encouragement of American Manufactures," *William and Mary Quarterly*: 380.
41. Goodrich, editor, *The Government and the Economy, 1783–1861*, p. 196.
42. Ibid., p. xvi.

43. Ibid., p. xxxii.
44. Andrew Jackson, "The Maysville Road Veto," May 27, 1830, in *The Government and the Economy, 1783–1861*, pp. 44–51.
45. McDonald, Foreword, *The Myth of the Robber Barons: A New Look at the Rise of Big Business in America*, p. x.
46. Timothy Sandefur, "A Gleeful Obituary for *Poletown Neighborhood Council v. Detroit*," *Harvard Journal of Law & Public Policy* (Vol. 28, No. 2, 2004–2005): 655.
47. "The Debate over the First Railroad Land Grant," *The Government and the Economy, 1783–1861*, p. 114.
48. Ibid., p. 118.
49. Harry N. Scheiber, "Federalism and the American Economic Order, 1789–1910," *Law & Society Review* (Vol. 10, Fall 1975): 64.
50. Folsom, *The Myth of the Robber Barons: A New Look at the Rise of Big Business in America*, pp. 6–7.
51. Ibid., p. 9.
52. Ibid., p. 21.
53. Ibid., pp. 25, 27.
54. Ibid., p. 29.
55. *Olcott v. Supervisors* (1872), 83 U.S. 680.
56. Ibid.: 689.
57. Ibid.: 694–95.
58. Ibid.: 697.
59. *Loan Association v. Topeka* (1874), 87 U.S. 656.
60. Ibid.: 659.
61. Ibid.: 660–62.
62. Ibid.: 665.
63. Ibid.: 664.
64. Martin E. Gold, "Economic Development Projects: A Perspective," *The Urban Lawyer* (Vol. 19, No. 2, Spring 1987): 205.
65. Ibid.: 207.
66. Ibid.: 214, 213.
67. Howard Owens, "Buffalo attorney's lawsuit aims to halt government funds used in economic development," www.thebatavian.com, April 7, 2009.

# 3

## Corporate Welfare Takes Flight: How the SST Was Launched (and Shot Down)

In post–World War II America, the role of the federal government in subsidizing research and development had become almost an article of faith. (See my book *The Doomsday Lobby: Hype and Panic from Sputniks, Martians, and Marauding Meteors* for an account of the debate over federal support of R&D, from the time of John Quincy Adams till the present day.[1]) But it remained part of the pro-R&D strategy to tie such aid to defense-related concerns, whether real or putative. Whenever the federal government undertook a large-scale research and development project, it was advertised as essential to national security.[2]

The defense card seemed unbeatable. But if it was not played, or played poorly, the corporate welfare known as R&D became assailable—even beatable. Enter, stage right, the SST.

The debate over the supersonic transport (SST) airplane, which in its early stages was centered on questions of technology, soon encompassed many more issues, from the environmental to the defense related, but for our purposes what was most remarkable about the SST fight was the way it thrust corporate welfare into the spotlight and installed as the sharpest critics of such welfare not the caricatured penny-pinching miserly conservatives of liberal imagination but, instead, those very liberals. For this flying species of corporate welfare was a project of what President Dwight D. Eisenhower had, in his famous and prescient Farewell Address, disparagingly termed the "military-industrial complex," and that complex often found its most committed supporters among conservatives. Whatever qualms they might have had about the federal government taking a lead role in the

39

development and promotion of a commercial supersonic transport plane was overcome, in most cases, by their fealty to the defense industry, which had supported the SST. And there was also the sense that the anti-SST crowd consisted of sandal-wearing hippies and anti-Vietnam War leftists. This was a caricature, every bit as exaggerated as the image of conservatives as hard-hearted misers who didn't care about the poor. But in politics, partisans are often motivated by such caricatures of their enemies, and so the SST debate broke down along curious lines: conservative Republican supporters of corporate welfare, or at least this example thereof, versus liberal Democrat foes of this instance of corporate welfare. (There were, of course, exceptions: the biggest SST boosters were liberal Democrats—hawkish liberal Democrats—from Washington State, Senators Warren Magnuson and Henry "Scoop" Jackson, while free-market economists such as Milton Friedman were within the anti-SST ranks.)

But if there were new players and new alliances in this game, the usual suspects were not absent, either. Foremost among them was Boeing, which weaves in and out of these pages like an arrogant mendicant, begging billions from the federal treasury as if those tax dollars are part of the aviation giant's birthright.

The Boeing Company was, in a sense, bred and spoon-fed on government contracts. From the start, it has been a creature of corporate subsidy. Boeing was founded by a wealthy young Yale dropout named William E. Boeing, who left his native Midwest in the early twentieth century to seek his fortune in the Pacific Northwest. Though his family fortune came from lumber, young Boeing was fascinated by the emerging science of flight. He purchased a bankrupt shipyard and began making vehicles for the air rather than the sea. His Pacific Aero Products was born in 1916, just a year before the United States entered the First World War. What perfect timing that was; Boeing built a seaplane and, as T. M. Sell relates in *Wings of Power: Boeing and the Politics of Growth in the Northwest* (2001), he proceeded to "bomb Seattle with red cardboard shells, extolling the virtues and importance of aircraft: 'For our national defense, encourage aviation . . . for our country needs more airplanes.'"

Thus the Boeing Airplane Company, as the firm was known by 1918, solicited government contracts from almost the very moment of its birth. In fact, the very next year, 1919, Boeing "had an office in Washington, DC, seeking airplane contracts with the Navy."[3]

Its main office remained in Seattle, however, and Boeing thrived, its early growth based primarily on military contracts. It made a good product, though, and achieved any number of distinctions in aviation with its pioneering manufacture of fighter planes, mail planes, and bombers. Uncle Sam was a very good patron. Boeing survived the Depression years on government contracts, for its commercial aviation wing flew not nearly so well.

And then came another world war. As T. M. Sell writes, "World War II kept Boeing afloat just as World War I had." The company secured $1 billion in military contracts in 1943, which as Sell notes was almost double the total of Washington State's entire manufacturing production of just four years earlier. The feds even assisted Boeing in the construction of plants in Seattle and nearby Renton through aid from the Defense Plant Corporation, a child of the Reconstruction Finance Corporation. The DPC was the federal government's means by which wartime factories were built; its assistance, as well as federal R&D monies, "boosted the company into the big time . . . and permanently altered the landscape."[4]

Peace was bad news for Boeing. The company lost money in 1946, setting off alarm bells in Seattle. What if peace endured? What if spending on armaments decreased? What if the world were to know a period in which it was not at war? The possibilities were terrifying.

But never fear: lobbyists were hard at work! The company put on a full-court press, assisted by prominent members of the Air Force and beholden politicians. Air power, it was said, was the key to keeping the peace, and the keystone of American air power was Seattle. As Sell writes, "The Cold War and Korea bailed the company out in the late 1940s and 1950s, before commercial jet airplanes made Boeing a household word."[5]

War was good for Boeing, if not for the rest of the country.

Seattle was now an industry town: a Boeing town, a town dependent on federal contracts for defense and aviation. Its politicians became subservient to Boeing, virtual errand boys. How things had changed. Once upon a time, being a senator from Washington was not synonymous with being a senator from Boeing. Consider that in February and March 1934, Senator Homer Bone, a Washington state Democrat, had denounced Boeing on the Senate floor, asserting that it had "made 90 percent profit out of the government."[6] Senator Bone charged that Boeing was paying $25,000 annually to a vice president whose job was pursuing federal government contracts. (This is the kind of thing that shocked our ancestors; today we would wonder about the soundness of a company that *didn't* hire a vice president in charge of chasing down corporate welfare.)

In 1934, when Senator Bone lit into Boeing, the company was influential in the Seattle area but not yet dominant. It employed about one thousand persons, giving it the largest workforce in the state, but Washington was by no means a one-industry state. Timber and agriculture were more important. No one had to bow and scrape before the aviation god. As Richard S. Kirkendall, professor of American History at the University of Washington, notes, by 1958, almost a quarter-century after Homer Bone's salvos, the Seattle-area Boeing workforce was about sixty thousand. The new senators were no Homer Bones; they were the very hawkish Democrats Warren Magnuson and Henry Jackson, the latter nicknamed "Scoop."

Senator Jackson, often credited as the political father of today's neoconservatives, was perhaps the most indiscriminate supporter of defense spending in American political history. He spent the 1950s railing against the Eisenhower administration as insufficiently committed to national defense. For instance, in October 1957, after the Russians launched into orbit a 184-pound artificial satellite called *Sputnik*, which President Eisenhower dismissed as "one small ball in the air," Senator Jackson breathlessly declared it a "National Week of Shame and Danger."[7] Senator Jackson was no stranger to hyperbole, or panic, for that matter.

As Richard S. Kirkendall writes in *Columbia Magazine*, "Often Jackson's demands for more defense spending focused on Boeing products," such as the B-52 bomber, the KC-135 jet tanker, and the ground-to-air missile Bomarc. By the late 1950s he had earned the moniker "the Senator from Boeing," a tag that would hang on him for the rest of his career and that originated in his home state and his own party, "among Democrats in western Washington who regarded him as a militaristic warmonger."[8]

While the SST had no obvious link to the Vietnam War for which Senators Jackson and Magnuson expressed vigorous support, the debate was inevitably caught up in broader controversies. Many of the SST opponents were sharp critics of the war and what they viewed as excessive military spending by the United States.

Boeing profited from the Saturn and Apollo space programs as well as the Vietnam War; when these began to wind down, the company was thrown into a mini-tailspin. A popular billboard at the time read

"Will the last person leaving Seattle turn out the lights?" Layoffs hit the company, with 41,000 workers let go in 1970 alone. The unemployment rate in the region hit 17 percent in 1971.[9] The SST may have been a corporate welfare boondoggle to observers in most of the nation, but in Seattle it meant desperately needed jobs.

But Boeing was only the most prominent and importunate corporation in an industry that had long been a government dependent. . . .

\* \* \*

In *Clipped Wings: The American SST Conflict* (1982), Mel Horwitch divides the SST story into four stages:

1—the prelude of the 1950s and early 1960s, when the prospects of a commercial SST came to be discussed and analyzed;
2—the Kennedy administration's vigorous push for an SST, led by FAA administrator Najeeb E. Halaby;
3—the "fragmentation" period lasting from the end of 1963 until 1968, as the project's Kennedy-era momentum was slowed by "bureaucratic jealousies, economic doubt, lack of managerial confidence, changing loci of policy-making power, technical uncertainty, ambiguous presidential support, a growing number of participants, the beginnings of criticism in the media, and the emergence of organized public opposition"; and
4—the "explosion" of 1968 till 1971, as the SST became a hot political issue and its opponents came in for the kill.[10]

The prelude begins with the National Advisory Committee for Aeronautics, or NACA, which was a hotbed of early SST enthusiasts, as would be its more glamorous successor, NASA, and the Federal Aviation Administration. In fact, as a pair of economists has written, "the SST program seems to have been more the result of pushing from within the government than pressure from the outside."[11] The airlines themselves, as opposed to aircraft manufacturers crafty enough to land on the public dole, were decidedly unenthusiastic about the SST.

The NACA was the federal government's first major step into the new field of aviation. Born in 1915 and enjoying its salad days during the 1920s and '30s, NACA undertook research and development in such areas as "aircraft streamlining, design of engine parts, properties of fuels, and structural aspects of aircraft design," but it stopped short of direct subsidy of private or commercial aviation.[12] NACA's work had both military and civilian applications; like the aviation industry, it boomed as a result of the world wars. It was most famous for its wind tunnels. (In 1958 NACA traded a C for an S and became the National Aeronautics and Space Administration, or NASA.)

The aircraft industry was in something approaching the doldrums circa 1960. The Korean War was in the rearview mirror and Vietnam was just ahead, but for an industry dependent on ramped-up military spending, peace—even the precarious peace of the Cold War—was not good for business. Missiles were all the rage; manned aircraft were taking a back seat in military-related spending. The military side of the aviation industry was struggling with the recent diminution of the Air Force's B-70 bomber. David S. Lawrence, writing in the *American Journal of Economics and Sociology*, referred to the aviation industry's "historical" and "symbiotic" relationship with government; that is, as we saw in the Boeing case, it was nurtured in its infancy by government in the hailstorm of World War I, matured with mail contracts in the interwar years, and grew to adulthood in World War II. But it was panicked by "the pre-Viet Nam lull in military expenditures." Peace might be breaking out! If that were so, commercial air transport was in trouble, for as Lawrence wrote in 1971, "virtually all commercial air transport technology is derived from military applications."[13]

Lawrence explained, "In January 1960, industry representatives began to plump for government sponsorship of a commercial supersonic transport."[14] Private industry, its captains feared, was not up to the task of rejuvenating itself without public sector support. The House Committee on Science and Astronautics recommended just such a plan in June 1960. Representative Overton Brooks (D-LA), chairman of the committee's Special Investigating Subcommittee, trumpeted as the primary reasons for federal support of the SST "global tension and instability, the apparent progress of communism, the far-flung nature of American military and commercial operations, and the threat of foreign SST competition," as Mel Horwitch writes.[15]

President Eisenhower, who kept a more watchful eye on what he termed the military-industrial complex than any post–World War II president before or since, was not terribly enthusiastic about federal development of a commercial SST, though at the end of his second term a fairly meager $5 million was directed toward SST feasibility work. But the supersonic transport didn't really take off as a federal project until Eisenhower's successor, President John F. Kennedy, who was at once more hawkish and more spendthrift than Eisenhower, took office. The "optimism" of Kennedy's New Frontier, under which no project was too grandiose or expensive to pursue as long as it reflected glory on its initiators, was capacious enough to include federal funding for a supersonic transport.

The prefix "super" probably didn't hurt; it had the ring of that early 1960s sense that all things were possible. The sky was the limit—or maybe even the sky was *not* the limit—when the US government set its sights on technological advancement. In this case, the job of building a political constituency for an SST was entrusted to the Federal Aviation Agency. (The agency had something of an identity crisis. In previous incarnations it had been the Civil Aeronautics Authority and the Civil Aeronautics Administration. In 1958, the CAA was transmogrified into the Federal Aviation Agency, or FAA. In 1967 it would become the Federal Aviation Administration, lodged in the new US Department of Transportation.)

FAA administrator Najeeb E. Halaby was the Kennedy administration's point man for the SST. The Texas-born Halaby was a Syrian-Lebanese Christian whose roots in the Lone Star State stretched back to the late nineteenth century. His extraction made him one of the first prominent Arab-Americans in public life. Halaby had spent his adult life in aviation, so much that he virtually sprouted wings. He'd been flying since he was a teenager. He later tested aircraft and served as an air corps flight instructor. "I had a really fascinating war," Halaby later said of the Second World War. "Instead of slugging it out at Guadalcanal with the Marines, I was at Patuxtent, Md., slugging it out with the elements, with aerodynamics and thermodynamics."

Halaby had served in the Truman administration as a deputy assistant secretary of defense and had also worked with Laurence Rockefeller as a venture capitalist before joining the New Frontier. In later years he would ascend the corporate ladder of Pan American World Airways (Pan Am), making president in 1968, chief executive officer in 1969, and chairman in 1970 (when his visage appeared on the cover of *Time*—admittedly, in the lower right-hand corner—for a story about "superjets") before the board forced him out in 1972. To the end, he insisted that the SST was the plane of the future. "We know that worldwide supersonic flight will become as commonplace in the decades ahead as jet travel is today," he said confidently, and very wrongly, in 1971.[16] He is perhaps best remembered today as the father of Queen Noor of Jordan, who once bore the cognomen of Lisa Halaby.

But in 1961, Najeeb Halaby was the point man in what he and President Kennedy saw as the next great advance in commercial aviation.

A forceful and effective political operator, Halaby quickly succeeded in securing an $11 million congressional appropriation for the project, followed by a $20 million appropriation for fiscal year 1963.

On March 3, 1961, Halaby was charged with developing for Kennedy "a statement of national aviation goals" in enough comprehensive detail to "provide sufficient definiteness to facilitate long-range practical planning."[17]

A task force, bearing the Buck Rogers-ish title of Project Horizon, was formed, chaired by Fred M. Glass, vice president of Hertz (the rental car company that would profit handsomely from the expansion of commercial aviation). A former director of aviation for the Port Authority of New York, vice president of traffic for Capital Airlines, counsel for American Airlines, attorney for the Civil Aeronautics Board, and colonel with the Air Transport Command, Mr. Glass was the consummate airline industry insider.

In fact, the Project Horizon task force consisted almost entirely of such insiders; it was an extension of the government and commercial airline industries. Other members were:

— Vice chairman Stanley Gerwitz, former vice president of Western Air Lines, Air Transport Association of America, and National Airlines, and onetime bureaucrat with the Civil Aeronautics Board and officer with the Air Transport Command;
— Selig Altschul, aviation consultant and founder of the Aviation Advisory Service;
— Leslie A. Bryan, director of the Institute of Aviation, former Air Force consultant, and former vice president of the National Aeronautic Association and president of the American Association of Airport Executives;
— Gerald A. Bush, corporate director of marketing planning for Lockheed Aircraft Corp.;
— Francis T. Fox, general manager of the Los Angeles Department of Airports;
— John F. Loosbrock, editor of *Air Force Magazine and Space Digest*, the official journal of the Air Force Administration; and
— Paul Reiber, veteran attorney for Air Transport Association.

Doubtless these men possessed the necessary knowledge and experience to serve on the Project Horizon task force, but their personal ties to the aviation industry made them, in effect, boosters of that industry. What is missing from the task force is any hint of an independent voice, a skeptical outlook, an advocate for the taxpayer. The deck was stacked heavily in favor of an active role for government in the promotion of aviation, and that is exactly what Mr. Glass's task force served up on September 1, 1961, when it transmitted to Mr. Halaby its recommendations for aviation policy in the decade 1961–1970. (Skeptical voices were not entirely absent. Noted aeronautical engineer William Littlewood, chairman of the technical review committee of Project Horizon, expressed doubt about the advisability of anything "like the Manhattan Project which produced the atom bomb without regard to cost."[18])

On September 5, 1961, FAA administrator Halaby forwarded the Project Horizon report to President Kennedy.

Its introduction is a congestion of clichés, from its opening line— "If there is a word to characterize the times in which we live, it is change"—to its portentous declaration that "aviation today hesitates at the crossroads." (And we all know what happens to him—or even a pilot—who hesitates.) Project Horizon flies the flag, and under cover of the flag it sneaks in special favors for aviation. It echoes JFK's inaugural address in asking "what aviation can do for the Nation and for the free world," and proposes a bargain: If "the Nation [read: the taxpayers] must do some things for aviation, then this would seem to be a fair sharing of responsibilities."[19]

Consistent with the tradition of subsidy seekers, the Project Horizon authors raise the specter of war. They refer darkly to "the other side of the Iron Curtain," and posit that "Progress [that is, transferring tax monies to the aviation industry] becomes, then, not merely a prelude to national prestige and prosperity but fundamental to national survival."

Subsidize or die!

Grandiosely, Project Horizon envisioned subsidies to aviation addressing the following "problems":

— National economic growth.
— National security.
— National culture and a more closely knitted social fabric.
— International understanding through increased person-to-person contact.
— International trade and commerce, with emphasis on contributions to the economic stability of emerging economies.
— The role of the United States as the leader of freedom-loving people everywhere.

To those who might question the neediness of a $7 billion civilian industry with six hundred thousand employees, Project Horizon's authors assure us that the federal government must finance "necessary developments that may be beyond the capability or willingness of private industry." (Note how that second word—*willingness*—broadly expands the possible role of government.) As for those nitpickers who might raise constitutional objections, well, the "Federal Government's interest in aviation finds root in its responsibility for the general welfare and well-being of the American people."[20] The general welfare clause—infinitely elastic—stretches yet again!

Central to the general welfare and well-being of the American people, or so Project Horizon argued, was the development of a supersonic commercial aircraft. Racing through the skies at speeds of more than two thousand miles per hour, three times or more the speed of sound, these SSTs would facilitate the rapid movement of travelers "to a degree never before approached in commercial transportation." And these wouldn't be just any travelers. No, they would be "important segments of the population." Not Uncle Jim visiting his family in Nebraska, or a family of six flying down to see Mickey Mouse, but *truly important* people: politicians, captains of industry, and maybe even journalists.

The construction of such a plane is certainly feasible, asserted the authors, for "competent persons" have said so. In the age of technocracy, this was enough. The implications of a US-built SST were far reaching: "the first nation to build such an aircraft will be the first to sell it, and the limited potential market makes it almost mandatory that the United States attempt to capture it." This is a quaint notion: that the first company—or in the phrasing of Project Horizon, the first country—to manufacture a product will dominate the market. This would be news to, for instance, the Duryea Motor Wagon Company, the first American manufacturer of automobiles, and to such latecomers as Henry Ford.

But the economic windfall is hardly the only justification put forth for an SST. There is also "international prestige," as if the reputation of the world's most prosperous and culturally influential nation hung on a mere aircraft. And—drumroll, please—the SST would represent "a significant military asset."[21] The promise that it would "rush troops and material to remote areas of the world" was "obviously desirable."[22] (Desirable to whom, one wonders. American draftees? The people of Vietnam?)

The Soviet Union, it was darkly hinted, was cooking up an SST in its labs at that very moment. That plane, the Tupolev Tu-144, the Soviet SST (joking called the "Concordski," after the later and more successful British-French SST), was a pet project of Soviet Premier Leonid Brezhnev. As the aviation site *Historic Wings* relates, "For Brezhnev, the Tu-144 was to serve as the crowning example of the achievement of Soviet technical superiority over the West."[23]

It didn't quite work out that way. The Tu-144 took flight on July 15, 1969, far earlier than it was ready to fly. Based in part on stolen aeronautical plans from the French and English, the Tu-144 had more design flaws than a kindergartener's soapbox derby racer. The plane would prove notoriously unreliable (even down to details like seatback trays and window shades that didn't work), ridiculously expensive, and after a very public crash at the Paris Air Show of 1973 the plane became a symbol of Soviet ineptitude. But it was a useful goad to prod American politicians to support the US SST as a means of keeping up with the Russians. President Kennedy had run his 1960 campaign against Vice President Richard M. Nixon in part on what turned out to be a phony "missile gap" separating the two superpowers. With his "pay any price, bear any burden" rhetoric, Kennedy was very much in the hawkish tradition of Cold War Democrats. If advisors told him that the SST was an important feature of US national security, then he would naturally support it to the hilt.

This national security trump card is always played, and often acts as the key that opens the treasury. During the Cold War, nothing quite spurred legislators into a spending frenzy as the thought that we might be falling behind the Soviet Union in some area. (Curiously, Defense Secretary McNamara, symbol to some of the Cold War, put little stock in the aviation industry as a pillar of American prestige. He denied the SST in any way strengthened American defense, and McNamara even said, "If the Russians could build 707s cheaper I would buy them from Russia."[24])

The treasury was the target of the SST lobby. Project Horizon urged the US government to "begin immediately an intensive applied research program to establish the preferred design parameters for a Mach 3 supersonic transport." Together with air carriers and designers of airframes, the government was urged to draw up the operating requirements for an SST design competition. The winner of said competition—the "prime contractor"—would put its government bounty to work by 1964.[25]

Were there reservations expressed? Not really. Project Horizon did acknowledge the potential complication, or nuisance, of "the so-called sonic boom."[26] Data on the effects of this boom—the explosion-like noise caused by the shock waves created when an aircraft exceeds Mach 1, or the speed of sound—were meager, and further research was warranted. But we would cross that bridge in the sky when we came to it. After all, officials of the US Air Force had scoffed that the so-called sonic boom was no louder than "a good stiff windstorm" and was even less impactful than "a healthy boy jumping on the floor."[27] What kind of namby-pamby could object? Why, it sounded almost like mild entertainment!

As for any objections to the federal government underwriting this massive subsidy to the commercial air industry, "The supersonic transport will require such large research, development, test, and production costs as to make impractical any course other than direct Government financial assistance." True, the development costs of airframes for commercial transport had traditionally fallen on private aviation companies, but this was, well, a new horizon, a new frontier, whose cost might well approach $1 billion. (Which was real money in 1961.)

Research, development, and the initial production of SSTs would be expenditures "in the national interest," and who but a mossback conservative or sandal-wearing pacifist could possibly object?[28] The authors did throw fiscal conservatives a bone, saying that the recipients of SST corporate welfare could be required to pay into a "royalty system" so that the taxpayers might recoup some of their involuntary investment, but this comes off as an afterthought, an "oh-by-the-way" addendum.[29]

In any event, Project Horizon, imbued with that Kennedyesque confidence that technology can be made to follow a timeline, announced that a Mach 3 SST could be carrying commercial passengers by the early 1970s. All that was needed was a commitment by Washington to a "coordinated, Government-directed research effort . . . implemented with energy and purpose," those latter two words, apparently, being euphemisms for plenteous tax dollars.[30] (As two economists later noted, "early advocacy" of the SST "came largely from within government, not from outside."[31] There was considerable ambivalence, if not outright skepticism, in the industry, at least with respect to investing their own money in SST development. But if the feds were going to pay the bill, well, then. . . .)

In 1962, the administration devised a 75 percent federal government/25 percent industry formula for sharing the costs of developing the SST. The anticipated total cost was a billion dollars or so. Within a couple of years, the cost sharing moved to an even more lopsided 90–10 split. The wonder plane of the future was so wonderful that 90 percent of its development had to be funded out of the involuntary contributions of taxpayers rather than the rational calculations of the industry that it would supposedly revolutionize. Feasibility studies and roseate projections were a thing of the past; the SST was barreling along, and it was, almost entirely, a creature of the federal bureaucracy.

Najeeb Halaby's predecessor at Pan Am, Juan Trippe, announced in June 1963 the company's plan to buy six of the SSTs known as Concordes from the Anglo-French partnership of the British Aircraft Corporation and Aerospatiale. He called this a "protective order" in case an American-made SST was not available.[32]

With this act, Pan Am helped to goad Kennedy into one of his by-the-end-of-this-decade pledges—not, in this case, involving putting a man on the moon, but rather putting an SST into the air before 1970. The prestige of the United States was so fragile, apparently, so brittle, that it could not survive if another country happened to be the first to market a commercial supersonic airplane. (Throwing down the gauntlet, French President Charles De Gaulle had railed against "America's colonization of the skies."[33] Kennedy was not about to take *that*!)

In response to the Pan Am announcement, the president took to the stage and told the graduating class of 1963 at the Air Force Academy that "it is my judgment that this Government should immediately commence a new program in partnership with private industry to develop at the earliest practical date the prototype of a commercially successful supersonic transport superior to that being built in any other country of the world. . . . If we can build the best operational plane of this type—and I believe we can—then the Congress and the country should be prepared to invest the funds and effort necessary to maintain this Nation's lead in long-range aircraft, a lead we have held since the end of the Second World War, a lead we should make every responsible effort to maintain."[34]

Notice the way, in Kennedy's phraseology, that "Congress" and "country" are both separate entities but also of a single mind; they are also used as euphemisms for *the taxpayers of the United States*, who were not to be consulted in the matter.

Kennedy desired the manufacturers to pony up at least a quarter of the development costs. He secured $100 million dedicated to the SST in the FY 1964 budget; Pan Am and TWA pledged "$2.1 million towards the purchase of 21 SSTs."[35] The prospective builders of those planes, however, were not as bullish. They balked at Kennedy's request that they contribute 25 percent of the costs, or an envisioned $250 million. A 75 percent handout was not enough for them; they would eventually bump it up to 90 percent, or about as close to an arrant corporate handout as one can find. As Boeing Chairman of the Board William

Allen said: "If the program is considered to be in the best interest of the country. . . . Government must be prepared to render greater financial assistance than presently proposed."[36] Somehow, in Mr. Allen's mind, the "best interest of the country" became conflated with, perhaps even identical to, the best interest of Boeing.

The Concorde with which Kennedy wished to compete—unlike Kennedy's SST—actually took flight in 1969. But it ascended the skies at a moment when more than 80 percent of the commercial aircraft in service had been manufactured in the United States. This was hardly a sign of an industry in decline, or a nation slouching toward a Third World economy. Despite the historical connection between the aviation industry and the US military, American dominance of this field was not wholly or even primarily a function of federal intervention. Rather, as economists George Eads and Richard R. Nelson wrote in 1971, it was due to "the good record of the American manufacturers in deciding when to embody technological advances in commercial products. This record undoubtedly has been aided by the fact that in each case, the decision to produce a commercial design has been made by a private company risking its own funds."[37]

This is exactly what the SST was not, and perhaps this is why JFK's supersonic plane never left the ground. The conceit of Presidents Kennedy, Johnson, and Nixon—that by snapping their metaphorical fingers and showering federal dollars on R&D, an SST would appear virtually overnight—demonstrated a profound misunderstanding of the interplay between technology and private enterprise. In a market system, technological advances tend to "proceed sequentially and in small bites," with the occasional breakthrough. While they have often been "spectacular," as Eads and Nelson write, they have also "been paced over time, with the major product development efforts waiting until components were available, until research findings had clarified many of the dark places, and until the final expensive surge looked relatively certain and the returns high."[38]

Government, unlike private actors in a market, can proceed recklessly, in a helter-skelter manner, and with exceeding impatience, all because it is unchecked by any market discipline. It taxes and it spends, and if it wishes to spend more it simply taxes or borrows more. It can put a man on the moon, at extraordinary cost, but that is due to a rare confluence of factors, among them the utterly unique nature of the Apollo project, its public popularity (at least until Neil Armstrong's famous step; support later plummeted, and we haven't been back to the moon for four decades), and the incredible expenditure of tax dollars and manpower. The SST had none of these going for it. And as flat-out corporate welfare, it could never fire the patriotic enthusiasm that Apollo did, or did among some people.

The death of President Kennedy had consequences for the SST. Less than a month after his assassination, on December 19, 1963, the Black-Osborne Report was submitted to President Lyndon B. Johnson. This report had been commissioned several months earlier by President Kennedy. He had asked Eugene Black, a former president of the World Bank, to study the financial side of the SST. Black's deputy was Stanley de Jongh Osborne, president and chairman of Olin Mathieson Chemical and a former vice president of Eastern Airlines.

The Black-Osborne Report concurred with the airline industry that the feds should foot 90 percent of the cost of SST development. So this was hardly a shot across the corporate welfare bow. But it did express doubts that the FAA was up to the job, and it cautioned against any kind of Manhattan Project–type crash course.

Najeeb Halaby went into orbit. Congress had just approved $60 million for his pet SST project. And while LBJ was as indiscriminate a booster of the aviation and aeronautics industry as JFK was, the boorish new president lacked style, panache, and was, in his personal habits, Halaby later said, "kind of disgusting to me."[39]

President Johnson asked Secretary of Defense Robert Strange McNamara to review the Black-Osborne Report. McNamara, who favored a 75–25 percent cost-sharing formula, urged the President to create an independent authority to oversee the SST. While the FAA succeeded in defeating this effort at turf poaching and remained the controlling agency, it now had looking over its bureaucratic shoulder a Presidential Advisory Committee (PAC) headed by none other than Robert Strange McNamara. The Department of Defense had snuck into the FAA's backyard.

Meanwhile, the prototype SST design competition overseen by the FAA went into high gear. Perhaps predictably, the prototype contracts were awarded in 1966–67 not to daring startups or innovative under-dogs but to Boeing (with its variable sweep-wing airframe, which it later abandoned) and General Electric (for its after-burning turbojet engine)—no strangers in the corporate welfare line. Not that they beat out scrappy young go-getters: the other designs were submitted by Lockheed and North American Aviation (airframe) and Pratt & Whitney and Curtiss-Wright (engine).

Development of the SST staggered along. President Lyndon B. Johnson, no budget cutter, was uncritical of the project, as were his SST point men, FAA administrator William McKee and his handpicked director of SST development, Jewell C. Maxwell. McKee bore the unfortunate nickname of "Bozo."

Both men were Air Force generals and therefore perhaps not the best judges of the proper balance between public and private enterprise. By FY 1966, the SST was consuming $140 million of taxpayers' money. In fact, as Joshua Rosenbloom notes, in the 1966 hearings before the House and Senate Appropriations Committees, every witness was impeccably pro-SST. Technologically, the witnesses asserted, the plane was feasible. Financially, there was no doubt that private financing would eventually supplant federal subvention. As for the sonic boom, it was but an "annoyance," claimed Generals Maxwell and McKee. Not until 1967 would an SST hearing finally host an "unfriendly" witness: Representative Henry Reuss (D-WI), who criticized the requested appropriation ($198 million for FY 1968) on economic grounds as an inefficient allocation of resources.[40]

Johnson's FAA issued a report in 1967 painting a rosy picture of the future of supersonic commercial travel in the United States. (Johnson's secretary of defense, Robert McNamara, remained something of an SST skeptic, however.) Its backers brushed aside questions about the SST's commercial potential by assuming that potential travelers placed an extremely high value on the time savings the jet promised. Even that, it turned out, was a faulty assumption.

* * *

Here we should pause and hearken to the sonic boom that punctuates this debate.

The sonic boom became an important ancillary issue. Early hopes that sonic booms were more like sonic busts—annoying blips—were dashed. The boom really was a boom.

Sonic booms had been around since the 1940s. The phrase was coined by "ground crews and radar operators to denote the vibrations and loud noises accompanying supersonic flights of military aircraft."[41] When a craft exceeds Mach 1, the speed of sound, the accumulated sound waves meeting the ground causes a loud booming noise.

Bo Lundberg, director of the Aeronautical Research Institute of Sweden, told a seminar of the Flight Safety Foundation in 1961 that "We just cannot—or at least should not—bombard larger and larger portions of the earth's surface with ever-increasing sonic boom thunder without giving, in advance, full consideration to all implications."[42] Lundberg outlined the legal, economic, and environmental issues caused by the boom; did it really make sense to subsidize the development of SSTs before working out at least tentative answers to some very knotty problems? Lundberg's scientific bona fides would prove valuable to a movement that pitted citizens, taxpayers, and environmentalists against the scientific-industrial complex.

The design specs submitted to Congress in 1963 envisioned the sonic boom overpressure during the SST's acceleration to be under 2 psf (pounds per square foot) and less than 1.5 psf once it had reached cruising altitude. Writing in the *Bulletin of Atomic Scientists*, Joel Primack of the Harvard University Department of Physics and Frank Von Hippel of the Argonne National Laboratory note that the Kennedy administration anticipated that 1 psf would be "acceptable" to the general public, 1.5 psf could cause "some scattered public reaction," and 2 psf would set off "probable public reaction," particularly at night. At 2.5 psf, when the sonic boom would sound like "close range thunder or explosion," a "significant public reaction" was likely. As for engine noise, the hope was that the SST's would be similar to "current international subsonic jet transports."[43]

Although Air Force jets produced sonic booms, these were generally accepted as the price of national defense. Commercial sonic booms— which, if the SST took off in popularity as envisioned, would be much more common—were viewed far more warily. Representative Roman C. Pucinski, an Illinois Democrat, introduced legislation as early as 1963 to limit sonic booms over populated areas.

The primary study of how people respond to sonic booms came in 1964, during the charmingly titled "Operation Bongo." The shock waves known as sonic booms are rather louder than bongo drums, if just as annoying. In Operation Bongo, which was under the supervision of the Federal Aviation Agency, the three hundred thousand residents of Oklahoma City "were subjected to booms averaging 1.3 psf overpressure eight times daily for five months."[44] Now, 1.3 psf was well below the anticipated level of an SST, and far below what the final Boeing design included.

The University of Chicago's National Opinion Research Center polled the locals to assess their feeling about the booms. About three-quarters of Oklahoma City's captive sample population (73 percent) found 1.3 psf booms acceptable; the other quarter did not. There were, however, over 15,000 complaints filed about the noise, as well as nearly "5,000 filed damage claims which resulted in compensatory payments of $218,000."[45] Even at 1.3 psf, the sonic boom was more than an annoyance to many people. (As Sweden's Bo Lundberg asked, "Why should any nonmilitary boom disturbance be accepted at all?"[46])

The first week of Operation Bongo, the Oklahoma Citians heard four sonic booms a day; over the next almost half a year, OKC was serenaded by eight sonic booms a day.

As a NASA history admitted, Operation Bongo was designed to win a favorable report from Oklahoma Citians. For one thing, the city, which hosted an FAA center and an Air Force base, understood that its bread was buttered by the boom makers. For another, the booms were carefully timed throughout the day (never at night); indeed, some residents even used them as the functional equivalents of alarm clocks. The NASA house history notes that

> A secretary used the recurring booms as an alarm clock. She got out of bed at the window-rattling crack of the 7 AM boom, then took a shower. She shut off the water when she heard the next boom, for this meant it was 7:20, time to start her day. Other people also treated the eight daily booms as if they were blasts from a factory whistle. One group of construction workers used the 11 AM boom as their signal for a coffee break. Animals as well went undisturbed. In El Reno, a nearby town, a farmer saw a tom turkey chasing a hen. Though a boom rattled the barn, the tom never broke stride.[47]

In this rendering, the booms were about as offensive as cell phone rings or school bells. It's almost enough to make one wish for a day punctuated by regular and reliable sonic booms.

FAA head General Jewell C. Maxwell thought that those with sensitive ears should just shut up and get with the federal program. He later told an interviewer about sonic booms:

> "I'll bet you'll find that babies are sleeping through them. If you only hear them occasionally, if you only get 'em twice a week, you're right [that they are startling]. . . . If you get 'em with regularity, several times a day, you get to the point where you don't respond to it. So there is accommodation."[48]

The solution to the problem, evidently, was *more* sonic booms. Make daily life so loud, so constantly scored by the booms, that citizens' ears simply become inured to the sound, like workers in a slaughterhouse.

Maxwell's cavalier attitude did not play well in Peoria, however; early in the Nixon administration, Secretary of Transportation John Volpe announced that until some way could be found to mitigate the effects of the sonic boom, the SST—whether American, British, or Soviet built—would be banned from flying over populated areas.

Boeing's final design (the "swing-wing") was not accepted by the FAA until 1969. This design, as Primack and Von Hippel write, was, at 750,000 pounds, twice the weight that had been contemplated in the original design specs. The larger plane meant a larger boom. Recall that Kennedy's FAA had expected strong public reaction at anything higher than 2 pounds per square foot (psf) overpressure. The Boeing design of 1969 included a sonic boom overpressure of 3.5 during acceleration and 2.1 during cruise. This was not an accident; in the words of an anonymous administration official in 1966, "We are all out for economics now and to hell with the sonic boom." To hell with the public, he might have said. But then as FAA administrator McKee had said in 1968, "We believe that people will come to accept the sonic boom as they have the rather unpleasant side-effects of other advances in transportation."[49] On the other hand, perhaps public objection to the boom would be so clamant that overland flights would be banned—a potentially fatal blow to the SST. (The SST engine noise, which the Kennedy FAA had expected to be no worse that of the typical international subsonic jet, was also greatly increased.)

Among the critics of the sonic boom was none other than Charles Lindbergh, he of the *Spirit of St. Louis* and at one time the great American hero. Lindbergh, who sat on the board of Pan Am, told PAC, the advisory committee on the SST, that the supersonic transport was "another step upward on the exponential curve of tempo, mechanization, and distraction," and that "an over-emphasis on science will destroy us."[50] In February 1971 he would come out publicly against the SST. If the greatest hero of aviation scorned the plane, surely the opposition must consist of more than just stingy old right-wingers and environmentalist kooks.

In March 1967, two Harvard scientists, physicist William A. Shurcliff with the Cambridge Electron Accelerator and biologist John T. Edsall, founded the Citizens League Against the Sonic Boom (CLASB), an unpronounceable acronym that rapidly grew to the point where CLASB was advertising its case in the *New York Times*. Though CLASB was operated out of Shurcliff's home, with the physicist's sister and son as principal staffers, it served as an invaluable clearinghouse for information for the anti-SST forces. The CLASB quickly gained thousands of members, peaking at perhaps five thousand. It published on its own an *SST and Sonic Boom Handbook*, which Ballantine later brought out in 1970 and which sold an impressive one hundred thousand copies in paperback. From modest contributions by its enthusiastic grass-roots membership, it was able to sponsor anti-SST ads in such pricey venues as the *New York Times*, the *Washington Post*, and the *Wall Street Journal*.

William A. Shurcliff, write Primack and Von Hippel, "deserves the credit for making it politically impossible to fly SST's over populated areas."[51] Dr. Shurcliff had served as a technical aide on the Manhattan Project and later ran an optics laboratory for the Polaroid Corporation. Among his inventions was a military camouflage paint. "We all believe in progress," he explained, in response to those who charged that the anti-SST forces were standing in the way of a glorious future, "but some things just aren't progress."[52]

There were alarmists among the SST opponents, Chicken Littles who went far beyond reasonable concerns over the effects of the boom and painted horrific pictures of a boom breaking a window on an SST, "as a result of which passengers' blood would be caused to boil resulting in instantaneous death."[53] (*That* would certainly deter potential passengers.) A more likely scenario, as Robert Lang speculated in an article about the legal and insurance ramifications of the sonic boom, is that "relatively few claims" would be filed for massive structural damage—houses were unlikely to be dislodged from their foundations even by frequent sonic booms—but there would be plenty of claims for harm to "glass, plaster, and light bric-a-brac."[54]

(Scientists—many of them reputable—speculated about the effect of the boom on, say, the eggs of cliff-dwelling birds or creatures who dwelt in the upper reaches of the ocean. There were concerns raised over ozone depletion and predictions of an epidemic of skin cancer. Claims were made that the SST would be as loud as "50 jumbo jets taking off simultaneously," an assertion that must have brought a smile to the faces of ear-plug sellers. It also sounds a lot more impressive than "twice as loud as a Boeing 707," which is another way of putting it.[55])

One notable hearing specialist said of Operation Bongo: "I was witness to the fact that men were executing their brethren during six long months ... with their thunder, the sonic boom, they were punishing all living creatures on earth."[56] This was, to say the least, hyperbolic. If the SST's most determined supporters were given to gross exaggeration of its potential benefits, so were some of its harshest critics prone to a leap overboard.

The window-rattling, dish-breaking, hands-over-ears sonic boom proved more than a nuisance or footnote to the SST. (It turns out that people don't want ear-shattering noises punctuating their day. Imagine that!) But the rushed nature of the project—an SST in the sky by 1970!—precluded the kind of careful, extensive, meticulous study that might have provided answers to the sonic boom question. Despite the common complaints about gridlock and inaction, government is not good at deliberation. Delay, yes; deliberation, no.

Today, innovations in aeronautical design are lessening the effects of the sonic boom, so that eventually the many places in the world that ban SST flyovers may repeal or modify those prohibitions. It only took fifty-plus years from the release of Project Horizon.

In a fascinating account in the science journal *Minerva* of the ways in which "expert" advice was used and misused during the SST controversy, Ian D. Clark noted that on both sides of the controversy, "those who had expert advisors used their advice less to improve their own knowledge of the subjects with which they had to deal than to persuade others of the correctness of the views which they already held."[57] It was all about winning the fight, not clarifying the stakes. For instance, once it became known that the Rand Corporation, which had contracted with the Federal Aviation Administration to study the SST, was likely to conclude in 1963 that the SST would be prohibitively costly, "the FAA cancelled its contract with the Corporation and never again sought its advice on this matter." The FAA did the same thing when unfavorable reports were submitted or were in the works by the Stanford Research Institute in 1963 (which found "no economic justification for an SST program") and the consulting firm Booz Allen Hamilton in 1966.[58] If it didn't shoot the messenger, it at least defunded it. And it altered its method of analysis. Rather than rely on a single consultant, the FAA solicited calculations from various consultants and sources. It cherry-picked the most favorable analyses. Was this honest? Not particularly. But when large sums of tax dollars are on the table, what's honesty got to do with anything?

You've got to choose the right experts, Clark recommended, tongue partially in cheek. If Rand, Stanford, or Booz Allen don't play the tune you've requested, dismiss them, and promptly. Better, says Clark, to "select a person who is either an enthusiastic aircraft visionary—like

Mr. Najeeb Halaby . . . or one who makes a large part of his income from consulting for the aerospace industry . . . alternatively choose a person who had invested much of his professional career in trying to make the SST a reality."[59]

\* \* \*

Like its predecessor, the Nixon administration supported the SST, though design problems (with the airframe) and the uncertainties surrounding the sonic boom delayed consummation of the dream of supersonic travel. But if President Nixon was, like Kennedy and Johnson before him, an enthusiast for Big Science projects with military ties, budget-conscious members of his administration were not.

A Nixon White House ad hoc SST Review Committee, appointed in February 1969 and consisting of four panels representing twelve different agencies and departments (including the Departments of Transportation; State; Labor; Health, Education and Welfare; Commerce; and Interior), reached skeptical conclusions on various fronts. For instance, the economics division found "a large element of doubt" about the potential of the SST to compete successfully with subsonic jets. The environmental division of the ad hoc committee was even less supportive of the president's position. It stated that "all available information indicates that the effects of the sonic boom are such as to be considered intolerable by a very high percentage of people affected." The committee also reached a negative conclusion about the engine noise generated by the SST: "over large areas surrounding SST airports . . . a very high percentage of the exposed population will find the noise intolerable and the apparent cause of a wider variety of adverse effects."[60]

These negative conclusions came despite the fact that most of the witnesses who appeared before the Ad Hoc Committee were favorably disposed to the SST. Among the critics, interestingly, was the Eisenhower administration's FAA administrator, Elwood Quesada. Even in retirement, the Eisenhower Republicans exerted a parsimonious pull on the party. (Eisenhower's White House science advisor, George Kistiakowsky, was also an SST critic.)[61]

The president was unswayed. "The question," he said in September 1969, "is whether in the years ahead the people of the world will be flying in American supersonic transports or in the transports of other nations."[62] To which one response might be: Who cares? And who would even bother to ask such a question? It was too much of a stretch even for Nixon to claim that the SST was vital to national security;

what, therefore, did it matter if a British or French (or Anglo-French) concern was the first to manufacture a commercial plane traveling at supersonic speeds? (Talk about misreading the future: *Aviation Week and Space Technology*, a reliable booster of federal funding of anything related to aviation, space, or aeronautics, gushed that "Historically, we would not be surprised if Mr. Nixon's firm decision committing this nation to build a supersonic transport eventually ranks with the late President Kennedy's decision to send Americans to the moon."[63] Well, not quite. But that's the thing about prognosticating: no one calls you on the prophecies that don't come true.)

Nixon was echoed by James Beggs, undersecretary of transportation, who told the House Committee on Appropriations in 1969 that "The SST is more than a commercial venture. . . . It relates directly to our Nation's technical and economic leadership."[64] That a Republican policy-maker would state that our "economic leadership" would be bolstered by federal subsidies rather than within private markets should surprise only those unfamiliar with the long history of Republican support for Hamiltonian economics. Beggs would later cash in on his government service as managing director of operations for General Dynamics, a prime recipient of corporate welfare in the military-industrial complex. He would serve as NASA director under President Reagan.

A second committee generated by the Nixon administration, this one consisting of outside experts and chaired by Dr. Richard Garwin, a renowned physicist with IBM, reported to the president in April 1969 that the SST was a dud, or at least commercially doomed, and that government subsidization thereof be ended. The report was ostensibly confidential, but Garwin was not exactly a self-effacing, retiring sort. In later years, he would gain a reputation as a sharp-tongued political debater. But he was no mere political scientist; Nobel Prize–winning physicist Enrico Fermi is said to have called Garwin "the only true genius" he had ever met.[65]

The garrulous Garwin testified in congressional hearings against the supersonic jet and even lobbied individual members. He did so in his capacity as a private citizen, though the fact that he had served as a putatively confidential advisor was of course known. As Garwin told a Joint Economic Hearing of May 1970, technology that might render the SST "economically and environmentally acceptable . . . did not yet exist."[66] (Garwin is the gent who gets the perhaps dubious credit for saying that a single SST at takeoff would sound like "the simultaneous takeoff of 50 jumbo jets.")

Challenged for breaking the code of silence that, in theory at least, governs confidential advisors, Garwin explained himself: "I'm not a full-time member of the Administration and I feel like a lawyer who has many clients. The fact the lawyer deals with one doesn't prevent him from dealing with another so long as he doesn't use the information he obtains from the first in dealing with the second. Since there are so few people familiar with these programs, it is important for me to give to Congress, as well as the Administration, the benefit of my experience."[67]

Garwin seems not to have possessed a superabundance of modesty. But then geniuses typically do not. His testimony helped to give the imprimatur of science to the anti-SST case.

Consistent with its general mode of operation, the administration sought to squelch the public release of both reports. The ad hoc SST Review Committee report was made public due to the doggedness of Representative Henry Reuss (D-WI). The Garwin Committee's report, subject of a long legal battle pitting the ACLU, the CLASB, and others against Nixon's science advisor, was not officially released until August 1971, or after the SST was a rusting hulk in the corporate welfare cemetery.

For his part, Nixon ignored the recommendations of economists and scientists and pursued Kennedy's dream. But this one didn't turn out quite as well as the late president's pledge that the government would put a man on the moon. And yet to a degree not true of the previous administrations, the Nixon crew was not of one mind on the SST. Nixon's position on the transport had been somewhat ambiguous during the 1968 campaign. He was not unacquainted with free-market economists who decried it as rank corporate welfare. And as president, he often aligned himself with the environmentalists, however uncomfortable that made them. Physicist Lee DuBridge, science advisor to the president, notified the Ad Hoc Review Committee: "Granted that this is an exciting technological development, it still seems best to me to avoid the serious environmental and nuisance problems and the Government should not be subsidizing a device which has neither commercial attractiveness nor public acceptance."

DuBridge is an interesting example of the neutering effect that public service can have on a man. Despite his SST skepticism, he remained one of the president's men. He told Senator William Proxmire (D-WI) in 1970:

> Needless to say, the President has a broader view of the whole problem after he has studied all the facts and opinions which have been

brought to his attention. Thus, while each of the several of us may have, from our own restricted points of view, recommended against further federal involvement in the SST project, I, for one, believe that the President, in taking a more comprehensive view than any of us could have, came to a sound decision. . . . The President recognizes, as we pointed out, that there are still technological and environmental problems to be solved. But he has the faith, which I now share, that the ingenuity of the American industrial system can eventually solve these problems satisfactorily.

That is either a craven and cringe-inducing example of self-abasement or an admirable instance of a man sacrificing himself for the good of the team, the team in this case being the Nixon administration. DuBridge's loyalty to Nixon went beyond this statement; he fought against release of the Garwin Report. DuBridge's refusal to bolt is understandable when one considers that Nixon was the third president he had served as science advisor; the previous two were Harry Truman and Dwight Eisenhower. He was also a longtime academic administrator at the Massachusetts Institute of Technology and at the California Institute of Technology. Academic administrators, however capable, tend not to rock the boat.

As DuBridge explained to SST foe Representative Sidney Yates (D-IL), "I am a soldier. The President has made up his mind, and I am going to support the President's decision."[68] Shortly thereafter, the soldier resigned. He was replaced by an out-and-out supporter of the SST, Edward David Jr., an electrical engineer whose service had been primarily with the Bell Telephone Laboratories.

But as Primack and Von Hippel detail, the intra-Nixon administration disagreements continued. Russell Train, chairman of the executive branch Council on Environmental Quality, was a patrician blueblood and government attorney who would later serve as administrator of the Environmental Protection Agency under Nixon and Gerald Ford. Testifying in May 1970 before Senator Proxmire's Joint Economic Committee, Train raised the possibility that the harm to the ozone layer from frequent SST flights could increase the penetration of "potentially highly dangerous ultraviolet radiation."[69]

Proxmire's hearing was loaded with anti-SST witnesses—a startling reversal of form, as SST-related congressional hearings over the previous decade had been virtual lovefests for the supersonic transport. Something, it seems, was in the air—and it wasn't the SST.

* * *

The first, foremost, and certainly most active of the high-profile political critics of the SST was William Proxmire, the populist Democratic senator from Wisconsin, best known for his ceaseless ridicule of absurd-sounding federal expenditures. Proxmire, whose "Golden Fleece" awards were often bestowed on recipients of corporate or academic welfare, insisted that the SST should be developed and financed by private interests, not the federal government and its taxpayers. "The government should stay out of the free competitive market," insisted Proxmire.[70] He later wrote that the SST battle shows that corporate welfare can be defeated, even on the floor of Congress. "The right sort of pressure from those who are sufficiently concerned, even outraged, can win a victory against great odds," he said.[71]

The odds were indeed formidable. "Here was a spending program," wrote Proxmire in *The Fleecing of America*, "that seemed to have everything and everyone behind it": Presidents Kennedy, Johnson, and Nixon; the Departments of Defense and Treasury, and NASA; Boeing and its powerful senatorial tandem of Jackson and Magnuson; the AFL-CIO; and, least of all, "the country's airlines' somewhat reluctant support."[72] (Domestic airlines were the least likely to support federal funding of the SST. Those airlines with transoceanic flights, which would be SST routes, were the most likely supporters of Uncle Sam's aid, especially after the hubbub over the sonic boom made overland SST flights problematic.)

The early Senate opposition was scattered and weak. Proxmire was joined, in the ranks of precocious foes of the SST, by the Southern intellectual William Fulbright (D-AR), the liberal Democratic senators George McGovern (SD) and Ernest Gruening (AK), the Kentucky Republican Senator John Sherman Cooper, and, until his assassination in 1968, Robert Kennedy of New York. Senator Karl Mundt, a South Dakota Republican, was among the earliest GOP skeptics. Primary defenders of the SST included Senators Charles Percy (R-IL) and William Brock (R-TN), though Percy later reversed field. The redoubtable independent Virginia Democrat Harry Byrd Jr. was also a sharp critic of the subsidy.

But the ranks of the opposition began to swell. Some economists spoke of the SST as a misallocation of resources. Newspapers began to editorialize against it. Taxpayer watchdogs called it a prime example of waste in government. The Naderites criticized it as corporate welfare. And then, critically, environmentalists raised objections. The worm turned.

Some conservatives began to make known their reservations about the SST. The *Wall Street Journal* editorialized that the real question was not whether supersonic planes were feasible or even desirable, but "whether the need for such planes is so urgent that the Federal Government must finance a project that private investors find unattractive."[73] The *Journal* consistently raised questions about the SST, in particular its method of financing. As early as 1966 it was editorializing that the SST program "is all too typical of a Government that seems to think that it can fight a war, go to the moon and do practically everything else all at once."[74]

In a statement submitted to the Joint Economic Committee, economist Milton Friedman of the University of Chicago announced:

> With respect to the SST, private market incentives seem ample. If the SST cannot be justified by a sufficient demand from airlines to pay the costs of developing and building them, I do not myself see any external benefits to the community at large that justify subsidizing development or construction. On my understanding, this would seem a clear case for applying guideline 2: when in doubt, stay out. If the judgment of the public or of Congress is different from mine, then guideline 3 would be relevant: provide finance but do not administer. One way to do so would be to offer a substantial prize of a specified sum for each of the first *n* successful super-sonic transport planes constructed by US companies. This method would avoid the present detailed supervision by governmental agencies of the plans for the SST, the costly process of governmental decision on a single plan, the vested interests that get established between particular suppliers and particular governmental agencies. It would also permit and foster competition among companies rather than, as now, fostering concentration of production in a single company.[75]

In sum, said Friedman, "If the SST is worth building, the market will make it in Boeing's interest to build it."[76]

Professor Friedman was one of several prominent economists, representing various schools of thought, to speak out against the SST. Joining him were, among others, Kenneth Arrow and Wassily Leontief of Harvard, Walter Heller of the University of Minnesota, and Paul Samuelson of the Massachusetts Institute of Technology. (As chairman of the Council of Economic Advisers, Heller had raised questions about the SST within the Kennedy administration.)

Not to be outdone, the Nixon administration rounded up thirty-four economists who supported the SST. (Several had professional ties to the aerospace industry.) The FAA asserted that "reliable economists"[77]—unlike, one supposes, Friedman, Arrow, Samuelson, and Leontief: Nobel laureates all—expected an eventual SST fleet of five hundred planes, though the agency offered little evidence for this claim. Foes were not about to let such woolgathering pass by unremarked. For the dollars and cents angle—taxpayer-supplied dollars and cents—was to prove the most troublesome, in the end, for SST backers. If in fact a robust market existed for the supersonic transport, then federal subsidy would be unnecessary. And if no such market existed, as many SST critics suspected, then why on earth should the government underwrite a dud investment? If the planes existed primarily to facilitate the travels of "rich people in a hurry," then why stick harried middle-class workers and earners with the tab?[78]

Perhaps the most cogent case against the SST was made by an economist, Professor George Eads of Princeton, who specialized in the economics of the airline industry. In widely reported testimony before the Transportation Subcommittee of the Senate Appropriations Committee, Professor Eads laid aside questions of sonic booms and air pollution and the like. He began his statement to the Senators:

> As important as the environmental doubts surrounding the SST are, the economic arguments alone dictate that the Federal government should not appropriate $290 million to finance construction of the particular SST prototype you are considering.
> Neither Boeing nor G.E. has adequately explained why, for the first time in the history of US commercial aviation, the Federal government should pay the overwhelming majority of the costs associated with the construction of a civilian transport aircraft prototype.

Professor Eads gave the senators a tutorial in aviation economics. We had been down this road once before, he lectured, and the Congress had made the right choice. In 1948, Eads explained, "there was considerable support within the aircraft industry for proposals that the Federal government put up between $100 and $250 million to finance the construction of a jet transport prototype." The British were said to be spending even more than that designing their own prototype, and as seekers of corporate welfare are wont to cry, if someone somewhere in the world is spending public monies on a project, the US government also ought to do so.

*American Aviation* magazine announced: "It has been obvious for a long time that this country will see no further development of civil transport and cargo airplanes unless some agency of government foots the very heavy developmental costs. . . . It is very clear that private industry alone cannot finance such projects."

Along the same lines, the rival *Aviation Week* averred that "private industry, in its present financial condition, could never hope to undertake the construction of a prototype aircraft." The only hope resided in federal benefaction. Otherwise the British would beat us to the punch and rule the air.

It didn't happen that way. Congress said no to the request, and as Eads slyly noted, "the skies were not filled thereupon with British aircraft." Those prototypes financed by the British treasury "never got off the ground economically," and although de Haviland's privately financed Comet I and Comet II did fly, no American aviation companies placed orders for those British craft. Instead, as Eads writes, "In 1952 the Boeing company decided to invest $16 million of its own funds . . . to construct a jet transport prototype." The resultant planes "set standards for the world in speed, comfort, and, most important, economy of operation."

Technological advances had made it possible for Boeing to come up with a superior jet transport prototype for $16 million in 1952—a far cry from the quarter of a billion dollars aviation panjandrums were begging for in 1948. Eads drew the obvious parallel with the SST. A federal bureaucracy was about to shower large US corporations with public monies in order to develop a prototype craft employing technologies that seemed insufficient to meet certain challenges, among them the sonic boom. "The quickest way to make the US commercial aircraft industry as uncompetitive as the British is to push uneconomic prototypes," he argued to the senators. "American transports sell because they are the best and they are the best because *all* to date have been forced to meet the test of the free market."[79]

The free market, and not the unholy alliance of Big Government and Big Aviation, would best determine when and in what form a supersonic transport would come into existence. Writing with Richard R. Nelson in *Public Policy*, Eads emphasized the revolutionary nature of the SST program. Coupled with the proposed breeder reactor, it represented "an almost unprecedented extent and kind of governmental subsidy for the development of products for production and sale by private companies through the market to the general public." Moreover, there was no "pressing 'need' for these new departures." There was neither public clamor nor military necessity driving the projects. Eads and

Nelson noted that the usual defense of the SST by its federal benefactors was that private industry was incapable of so grand a program, and thus government subsidy was required, but "very little in the way of detailed persuasive analysis was, or is, being presented as to why the conservative attitudes of private industry were counter to the public interest."[80] The soundness of public expenditure was taken for granted; the wisdom of private reluctance to undertake this venture was never credited, never assumed to be based on rational calculation.

\* \* \*

For once, corporate welfarists were feeling the heat. The primary elements of the hardcore save the SST alliance consisted of the FAA, Boeing, and Senators Jackson and Magnuson, as Primack and Von Hippel note. Boeing created a public relations strategy utilizing "press coverage, advertising, brochures, and giveaways, speeches, technical papers, and motion pictures," including a film titled *You and Me—and the SST*. (Don't you regret missing *that*?) For its part, the FAA, seeing stars, sought unsuccessfully to enlist in the pro-SST propaganda effort the aviator-actor Jimmy Stewart and the CBS TV comedy *My Three Sons*, in which Fred MacMurray played an engineer who just might, suggested the agency public relations masterminds, get working on a certain supersonic transport.[81]

Lobbyists descended on Congress like a biblical plague. As the *Wall Street Journal* reported in September 1970, "SST contractors and subcontractors are reminding wavering legislators of the jobs and income that the project will generate in their states. Pro-SST lawmakers are pressuring colleagues to go along with promises of reciprocal support for the others' pet programs."[82]

The logs were rolling; the backs were being scratched. Chits were being called in; threats, perhaps veiled and perhaps not, were issuing from the office of Washington State's Senator Magnuson, chairman of the Senate Commerce Committee and a consummate wheeler dealer.

But the anti-corporate welfare forces refused to be logrolled. When President Nixon's Department of Transportation "sent a map to each Congressman's office showing the amounts that his state could expect to receive in SST sub-contracts," write Joel Primack and Frank Von Hippel, George Eads "prepared a map for distribution by the Coalition Against the SST which showed that all but a few states would contribute more in taxes than they would receive in subcontracts."[83]

The Coalition was in part organized by Lawrence Moss, an engineer who had served in the Nixon administration as a White House Fellow in the Department of Transportation. In that capacity he came to view the SST harshly. Moss gathered a collection of more than a dozen mostly liberal environmentalist groups, including the Sierra Club, the Friends of the Earth, the National Wildlife Federation, and the Federation of American Scientists, under the umbrella of the Coalition Against the SST. On Earth Day 1970, the Coalition issued a statement damning the supersonic jet as a monstrous entity which would "bombard millions with ear-splitting shock waves, cause unprecedented airport noise, cause heavy discharge of pollutants, and could cause possible climate changes."[84]

This emphasis on environmental factors rather than economic perhaps limited its effectiveness, but Moss and the Coalition would learn to expand their appeal. The Coalition, in the person of its coordinator Joyce Teitz, enlisted "15 prominent economists, ranging in philosophy from Milton Friedman of the University of Chicago to John Kenneth Galbraith of Harvard, to publish statements explaining their opposition on economic grounds to the SST." All but one (Henry Wallich) consented.[85]

Prominently absent from the list of Democrat-leaning SST foes was American labor. The AFL-CIO, under President George Meany, supported federal funding of the supersonic jet. The promise of government-financed jobs was the lure. Employment in the aerospace industry had fallen from 1.4 million in 1967 to 900,000 in 1971.[86] Vietnam and Apollo had been good for this government-dependent industry, but the glamour of space was wearing thin, and the end of the Vietnam War was now closer than its beginning. Not for the first or the last time, American labor unions lined up solidly behind corporate welfare.

As the hour of decision neared, Boeing's lobbying became frenzied. Workers, suppliers, and anyone whose lives were the least bit affected by the fortunes of the Seattle company were hectored to write letters and call their congressmen. Other members of the aviation-industrial complex—Northrup, the International Association of Machinists and Aerospace Workers, General Electric—contributed to the lobbying push. Institutional support for the SST came also from the US Chamber of Commerce (usually found wherever corporate welfare is dispensed), the Airline Pilots Association, and NASA. The last-named, capitalizing on Apollo fever, even wheeled in Neil Armstrong to testify on behalf of the plane in 1971. But by 1971 moon madness had waned; citizens were wondering just when astronomical budgets could be brought back to Earth.

Senators Jackson and Magnuson hit far above their weight, due to their influence in the Senate. Some environmentalist lobbies were so cowed by Jackson, chairman of the Senate Interior Committee, that they swallowed their objections to the SST in order not to anger the powerful chairman. These profiles in cowardice didn't join the anti-SST bloc at first; Friends of the Earth, which threw in with the CLASB in 1969, was an exception.

The anti-SST senators found that emphasizing populist pro-taxpayer themes resonated with the public. Indeed, they were the difference between a losing environmentalist cause and a winning anti-corporate welfare cause. Why should Joe and Josephine Sixpack shell out their hard-earned tax dollars so that millionaires could shave a few hours off their New York to Paris flights? Senator Proxmire marveled during a 1970 debate that "We are being asked to spend $290 million this year for transportation for one half of one percent of the people—the jet setters—to fly overseas, and we are spending $204 million this year for urban mass transportation for millions of people to get to work. Does that make any sense?"[87] Putting aside the question of the efficiency of those urban mass transit systems, Proxmire struck a nerve. If the jet setters desired a swifter plane and less travel time, let them pay for it. Why stick the taxpayer with the bill?

As Mel Horwitch notes in his thorough *Clipped Wings: The American SST Conflict*, as the long battle moved to its climax the "most forceful" anti-SST arguments were economic. Nobelist Paul Samuelson warned that the plane would become, like the Concorde, the "biggest lemon" in the sky. Economist Karl Ruppenthal, a former TWA pilot who earned a PhD at Stanford and taught in its business school, told a Senate hearing in 1971 that the SST was "a clear and present danger to the private enterprise system."[88]

In July 1970, Matthias Lukens, president of the Airport Operators Council, which represented the major American airports, said that the "key question of noise" was still outstanding, and unless and until it was resolved SST funding should be stopped.[89] Mayor John Lindsay of New York City, ever alert to which way the wind was blowing, vowed to stop SSTs from using Gotham's airports.

The Nixon administration, sensing that the tide was turning, deployed the classic defense of corporate welfare: that it created jobs where the free market could not. By 1970, William Magruder, a onetime test pilot who had worked for Douglas Aircraft and Lockheed, was in charge of SST development in the Department of Transportation. He told the Senate Appropriations Committee that subsidizing the SST would strengthen the aviation industry and, by some pass-it-forward magic, also lead to "better education, better housing, better law enforcement, better transportation" and even "improve our environment."[90]

There was nothing, it seems, that the judicious transfer of taxpayer monies to Fortune 500 companies could not accomplish. Borrowing a trite and tired old trick, the administration, as the writing on the wall became more and more decipherable, called its foes enemies of progress, Luddites whose fear of the future would cripple American industry. Senator Jackson sneered that those who opposed taxpayer subsidy of SST development were "know-nothings," while his partner in Washington state pork, Senator Magnuson, warned that the United States would become a "technological Appalachia" unless Congress approved the plane.[91]

If SST opponents were a mixture of dovish environmentalists and fiscal conservatives, perhaps their embodiment was Senator J. William Fulbright, the Arkansas Democrat who himself combined those qualities. Fulbright told the Senate in September 1970 that critics of the federally subsidized SST were speaking for "the taxpayers, the common, ordinary citizens of this country, who have to pay the taxes for these outrageous programs that waste the public's money."[92]

This described a broad swath of the American public, yet the politicians were slow to follow. Even as its design lagged and the sonic boom controversy swelled, the SST seemed unassailable in Congress. It had easily survived challenges in 1966 and 1967. In the latter year, when Senator Proxmire's vote to defund captured just nineteen votes, Senator Magnuson sneered, "What'd Proxmire get? Nineteen votes? I could have had half of those if I'd needed them."[93]

Hubris is always headed for a fall, though, or so one would like to think. There was no SST appropriation in FY 1969 (which would have been voted on in 1968) due to design problems on the part of Boeing, but the tin cup was out again the next year. A 1969 Proxmire amendment to end funding for the SST ($80 million in the Senate's FY 1970 budget bill) was crushed. Only twenty-two senators sided with Proxmire's anti-SST rebels, as opposed to fifty-eight supporting Jackson and Magnuson. And then—peripeteia—a sudden reversal of fortune. By 1970, the SST, that sleek and gleaming and unloved vehicle of corporate welfare lodged so firmly and squarely and unmoveably in Senator Magnuson's back pocket, started shedding votes like a tree losing leaves in autumn.

On May 27, 1970, the House saved the SST and its $290 million FY 1971 line item by a vote of just 176–162. Fearful that citizen pressure might sway undecideds into the nay column, Senators Jackson and Magnuson succeeded in delaying a Senate vote on the SST until after the 1970 midterm election.

As Joshua Rosenbloom observes, the delaying "tactic backfired, as the SST was turned into an important campaign issue by environmental groups in a number of senatorial races."[94] Citizens groups demanded to know where candidates stood on the SST; fearing the wrath of the voters more than they did the wrath of Scoop and Maggie, senators and senatorial candidates bailed out by the busload. The promise by Senate supporters to federally ban overland supersonic flights was a case of too little, too late. Noise concerns were a distant second to cost in the minds of senators. For once, corporate welfare had become a political liability. The Senate rejected SST funding by a vote of 52–41. A whopping eighteen senators who voted for the SST in 1969 voted against it and its $290 million FY 1971 price tag on December 3, 1970. These voter-changers tended to be Republicans, not only such liberals as Jacob Javits (NY) and Robert Packwood (OR) but also Western Republicans of conservative bent, such as Clifford Hansen (WY), Lee Jordan (ID), and Hiram Fong (HI). (Under pressure from the Nixon White House, Fong switched his vote several months later, in one final showdown.)

The House had approved FY 1971 funding for the SST and the Senate had demurred. So the action shifted to the conference committee. President Nixon termed the Senate vote of December 3 a "devastating mistake."[95] About $700 million had already been spent on the SST over the past decade, said Nixon; he claimed that the cost of ending the program would not be all that much less than the requested $290 million authorization. The two houses were unable to reach an agreement; the House remained marginally pro-SST, while the anti-SST Senate, sparked by Senator Proxmire's filibustering, refused to accept a compromise. The leadership brokered an agreement by which SST funding would be continued until a decisive vote could be taken in March 1971.

On March 24, 1971, the Senate took its long-delayed vote. At issue was continued funding for two SST prototypes. By a margin of 56–41, the SST went down. Almost immediately, Horwitch writes, "the Transportation Department ordered Boeing, General Electric, and their subcontractors to stop all SST work." A post-last-ditch effort by House Minority Leader Gerald R. Ford to revive the SST in May was approved by a vote of 201–197, but it wasn't enough. The Senate finished it off on May 19 by an emphatic vote of 58–37. As Boeing's William Allen said, "People have been dispersed. Subcontracts have been terminated."[96] The federally funded SST was dead—killed by citizen outrage over corporate welfare.

It should be emphasized that the House and Senate did not vote to kill the idea or even the reality of a supersonic jet. It voted to end *federal funding* of such a plane's development. If Boeing or Pan Am or TWA or some other manufacturer or airline wished to pursue the private development of an SST, they were entirely free to do so. But without the artificial stimulus of federal funds, none did.

As David S. Lawrence wrote at the time in the *American Journal of Economics and Sociology*, "Environmental issues notwithstanding, in the final analysis the SST's defeat was a rejection of its economics. . . . The reason the private sector does not build an SST is simply because it is not worth having, at least compared to its alternatives."[97]

Economists Eads and Nelson, marveling at the diversity of American industry, noted that "New products, processes, inputs, and equipment for an industry have come from firms in the industry, suppliers, purchasers, new entrants to the industry, and outside individual inventors. The process certainly was not orderly and planned, and one has the impression that had one tried to impose order and plan the result in many cases would have been much worse." By contrast to this decentralized and free system, federally subsidized development has largely been "dismal."[98] The lesson of the SST is that federal subsidy cannot force technological advancement into preplanned channels—and the political lesson is that under the right conditions, corporate welfare *can* be defeated.

The harsh light of publicity had killed the SST. By 1971, public opinion polls indicated overwhelming—as high as 85 percent—opposition to public funding of the SST. When given the choice, when presented the option, most people will select parsimony, as long as the funding isn't being withdrawn from *their* pet project.

An aide to Senator Magnuson, the champion of Boeing and threatener of recalcitrant senators, said in retrospect:

> Maggie and Scoop [Jackson] called every Senator they thought they could influence this time. They called. They cajoled. They persuaded. They arm twisted. They did everything they could. But you can't

push something down the throats of the Senate. The SST became a big national issue, and it was just beyond the power of the Senators to turn it around.

Vote trading and arm twisting is effective when the issue is not that big, when it isn't a glaring national issue. But it doesn't work when you've got the full focus of national attention on it. Then the pressure is on, as Senators will say, to "vote right."[99]

Putting aside the revealing word choice—Senators will "vote right" only if everyone is watching—the aide's observation is cogent. To kill corporate welfare, you've got to drag it out into the light. Joshua Rosenbloom, assessing the debate in the *Social Studies of Science*, averred that "Only with the development of strong public opposition to the SST did any significant number of Senators change their positions, suggesting that Congress was much more concerned with the political ramifications of the SST than with the technical arguments either for or against it."[100]

So why did the anti-corporate welfare side win the SST fight? In part because it succeeded in shining the harsh light of publicity on a transaction that typically occurs far behind the scenes. Big business solicits and receives governmental favors all the time, but seldom are these the subject of political debate and coverage in the press. Al Smith, the New York governor and first Catholic to gain the presidential nomination of a major party when he ran as the Democratic standard-bearer in 1928, said that nothing un-American can live in the sunlight, and if he overstated matters at least it is true that corporate welfarists *hate* public scrutiny.

As for Boeing, it survived the crash of the SST. It recovered in the 1980s, partly due to government contracts for such vehicles as the space shuttle and the stealth bomber, but also due to its innovations in commercial aircraft. In 1997 it merged with fellow military-industrial complex Bigfoot McDonnell Douglas, though it kept the Boeing name. And it branched out into new areas of corporate welfare: in 2001, Boeing ditched its longtime home of Seattle for Chicago, which won a fierce tax-break-based bidding war against Seattle, Dallas, and Denver.

As of this writing, Boeing employs 172,224 persons, with most of them working in either the commercial airplanes group (83,057) or the defense, space, and security group (58,840). Despite having junked Seattle as its headquarters, about half of Boeing's employees (85,106) are based in Washington State.[101]

And oh, yes, Boeing is still riding high on the corporate welfare sky wagon, as discussed in Chapter 6.

# Notes

1. James T. Bennett, *The Doomsday Lobby: Hype and Panic from Sputniks, Martians, and Marauding Meteors* (New York: Springer, 2010).
2. For a look at how government research and development funding may "crowd out private R&D spending," see Scott J. Wallsten, "The R&D Boondoggle," *Regulation* (Vol. 23, No. 4, 2000): 12–16.
3. T. M. Sell, *Wings of Power: Boeing and the Politics of Growth in the Northwest* (Seattle: University of Washington Press, 2001), p. 14.
4. Ibid., pp. 18–19.
5. Ibid., p. 24.
6. Richard S. Kirkendall, "Two Senators and the Boeing Company: The Transformation of Washington's Political Culture," *Columbia Magazine*, (Vol. 11, No. 4, Winter 1997–98): 38–43; http://www.washingtonhistory.org/files/library/senators-boeing-company.pdf.
7. Paul Dickson, *Sputnik: The Shock of the Century* (New York: Walker & Company, 2001), p. 118.
8. Kirkendall, "Two Senators and the Boeing Company: The Transformation of Washington's Political Culture," *Columbia Magazine*.
9. Sell, *Wings of Power: Boeing and the Politics of Growth in the Northwest*, p. 26.
10. Mel Horwitch, *Clipped Wings: The American SST Conflict* (Cambridge, MA: MIT Press, 1982), p. 2.
11. George Eads and Richard R. Nelson, "Governmental Support of Advanced Civilian Technology: Power Reactors and the Supersonic Transport," *Public Policy* (Vol. 19, No. 3, Summer 1971): 413.
12. Ibid.: 407.
13. David S. Lawrence, "The Initial Decision to Build the Supersonic Transport," *American Journal of Economics and Sociology* (Vol. 30, No. 4, October 1971): 406–7.
14. Ibid.: 404.
15. Horwitch, *Clipped Wings: The American SST Conflict*, p. 12.
16. David Stout, "Najeeb E. Halaby, Former Airline Executive, Dies at 87," *New York Times*, July 3, 2003.
17. *Project Horizon*, United States Task Force on National Aviation Goals (Washington, DC: U.S. Government Printing Office, September 1961; University of California Libraries Reprint), p. iii.
18. Horwitch, *Clipped Wings: The American SST Conflict*, p. 24.
19. *Project Horizon*, p. 3.
20. Ibid., pp. 4–5.
21. Ibid., pp. 14–15.
22. Ibid., p. 77.
23. http://fly.historicwings.com/2012/07/the-soviet-sst/; July 15, 2012.
24. Horwitch, *Clipped Wings: The American SST Conflict*, p. 89.
25. *Project Horizon*, p. 15.
26. Ibid., p. 16.
27. Robert D. Lang, "The SST: Lowering the Sonic Boom on Property Owners," *Albany Law Review* (Vol. 37, 1973): 528.

28. *Project Horizon*, p. 16.
29. Ibid., p. 17.
30. Ibid., p. 80.
31. Eads and Nelson, "Governmental Support of Advanced Civilian Technology: Power Reactors and the Supersonic Transport," *Public Policy*: 405.
32. "Boeing 2707 SST History," www.globalsecurity.org/military/systems/aircraft/b2707.
33. www.nasa.history.ch7.
34. John Fitzgerald Kennedy, "Remarks at U.S. Air Force Academy," June 5, 1963, http://millercenter.org/president/speeches/detail/5763.
35. "Boeing 2707 SST History," www.globalsecurity.org/military/systems/aircraft/b2707.
36. Horwitch, *Clipped Wings: The American SST Conflict*, p. 66.
37. Eads and Nelson, "Governmental Support of Advanced Civilian Technology: Power Reactors and the Supersonic Transport," *Public Policy*: 417.
38. Ibid.: 419.
39. Horwitch, *Clipped Wings: The American SST Conflict*, p. 68.
40. Joshua Rosenbloom, "The Politics of the American SST Programme: Origin, Opposition, and Termination," *Social Studies of Science* (Vol. 11, No. 4, November 1981): 409–11.
41. Lang, "The SST: Lowering the Sonic Boom on Property Owners," *Albany Law Review*: 525.
42. Bo Lundberg "Civil Supersonics: Too Much Hurry?" *Flight*, March 16, 1961, p. 339.
43. Joel Primack and Frank Von Hippel, "Scientists, Politics, and SST: A Critical Review," *Bulletin of the Atomic Scientists*, April 1972, p. 25.
44. Ibid.
45. Ibid.
46. Rosenbloom, "The Politics of the American SST Programme: Origin, Opposition, and Termination," *Social Studies of Science*: 407.
47. www.nasa.history.ch7.
48. Rosenbloom, "The Politics of the American SST Programme: Origin, Opposition, and Termination," *Social Studies of Science*: 407.
49. Primack and Von Hippel, "Scientists, Politics, and SST: A Critical Review," *Bulletin of the Atomic Scientists*, p. 25.
50. Horwitch, *Clipped Wings: The American SST Conflict*, pp. 145–46.
51. Primack and Von Hippel, "Scientists, Politics, and SST: A Critical Review," *Bulletin of the Atomic Scientists*, p. 26.
52. Matthew L. Wald, "William A. Shurcliff, Who Helped Develop Atomic Bomb, Dies at 97," *New York Times*, June 28, 2006.
53. Ian D. Clark, "Expert Advice in the Controversy about Supersonic Transport in the United States," *Minerva* (Vol. 12, No. 4, October 1974): 418.
54. Lang, "The SST: Lowering the Sonic Boom on Property Owners," *Albany Law Review*: 529.
55. Clark, "Expert Advice in the Controversy about Supersonic Transport in the United States," *Minerva*: 428.
56. Horwitch, *Clipped Wings: The American SST Conflict*, p. 236.

57. Clark, "Expert Advice in the Controversy about Supersonic Transport in the United States," *Minerva*: 426.
58. Ibid.: 425, 422–23.
59. Ibid.: 426.
60. Primack and Von Hippel, "Scientists, Politics, and SST: A Critical Review," *Bulletin of the Atomic Scientists*, pp. 26–27.
61. Horwitch, *Clipped Wings: The American SST Conflict*, p. 320.
62. Rosenbloom, "The Politics of the American SST Programme: Origin, Opposition, and Termination," *Social Studies of Science*: 413.
63. Horwitch, *Clipped Wings: The American SST Conflict*, p. 271.
64. Rosenbloom, "The Politics of the American SST Programme: Origin, Opposition, and Termination," *Social Studies of Science*: 414.
65. William J. Broad, "Scientist at Work: Richard L. Garwin," *New York Times*, November 16, 1999.
66. Michael McCloskey, *In the Thick of It: My Life in the Sierra Club* (Covelo, CA: Island Press, 2005), p. 113.
67. Primack and Von Hippel, "Scientists, Politics, and SST: A Critical Review," *Bulletin of the Atomic Scientists*, p. 29.
68. Ibid., p. 28.
69. Ibid.
70. William Proxmire, *The Fleecing of America* (Boston: Houghton Mifflin, 1980), p. 148.
71. Ibid., p. 147.
72. Ibid., p. 148.
73. "The SST Decision," *Wall Street Journal*, September 28, 1970.
74. Horwitch, *Clipped Wings: The American SST Conflict*, p. 215.
75. Milton Friedman, "Statement and Testimony and Answers to Supplementary Questions Submitted Later," *Economic Analysis and the Efficiency of Government, Part 3: Hearings before the Subcommittee on Economy in Government*, U.S. Congress, Joint Economic Committee, 91st Congress, 1st Session, October 6, 1969, p. 21 of Friedman's testimony.
76. http://www.lexic.us/definition-of/Milton_Friedman.
77. Horwitch, *Clipped Wings: The American SST Conflict*, p. 232.
78. Ibid., p. 284.
79. *Congressional Record*, September 15, 1970, Senate, pp. 31680–81.
80. Eads and Nelson, "Governmental Support of Advanced Civilian Technology: Power Reactors and the Supersonic Transport," *Public Policy*: 405.
81. Horwitch, *Clipped Wings: The American SST Conflict*, pp. 219–20.
82. "The SST Decision," *Wall Street Journal*.
83. Primack and Von Hippel, "Scientists, Politics, and SST: A Critical Review," *Bulletin of the Atomic Scientists*, p. 30.
84. McCloskey, *In the Thick of It: My Life in the Sierra Club*, p. 112.
85. Primack and Von Hippel, "Scientists, Politics, and SST: A Critical Review," *Bulletin of the Atomic Scientists*, p. 29.
86. Chapter 7, "SP-4221: The Space Shuttle Decision," http://history.nasa.gov/SP-4221/.htm.

87. "Boeing 2707 SST History," www.globalsecurity.org/military/systems/aircraft/b2707.
88. Horwitch, *Clipped Wings: The American SST Conflict*, p. 321.
89. Ibid., p. 287.
90. Rosenbloom, "The Politics of the American SST Programme: Origin, Opposition, and Termination," *Social Studies of Science*: 418.
91. Horwitch, *Clipped Wings: The American SST Conflict*, p. 328.
92. *Congressional Record*, September 15, 1970, Senate, p. 31681.
93. Primack and Von Hippel, "Scientists, Politics, and SST: A Critical Review," *Bulletin of the Atomic Scientists*, p. 27.
94. Rosenbloom, "The Politics of the American SST Programme: Origin, Opposition, and Termination," *Social Studies of Science*: 416.
95. Horwitch, *Clipped Wings: The American SST Conflict*, p. 305.
96. Ibid., pp. 325–26.
97. Lawrence, "The Initial Decision to Build the Supersonic Transport," *American Journal of Economics and Sociology*: 403, 409.
98. Eads and Nelson, "Governmental Support of Advanced Civilian Technology: Power Reactors and the Supersonic Transport," *Public Policy*: 423–24.
99. Primack and Von Hippel, "Scientists, Politics, and SST: A Critical Review," *Bulletin of the Atomic Scientists*, p. 27.
100. Rosenbloom, "The Politics of the American SST Programme: Origin, Opposition, and Termination," *Social Studies of Science*: 403.
101. http://www.boeing.com/boeing/aboutus/employment/employment_table.page, July 29, 2013.

# 4

# The Great Giveaway: Economic Development, "Incentives," and the Corporate Welfare Wars

Peter K. Eisinger, in *The Rise of the Entrepreneurial State: State and Local Economic Development Policy in the United States*, defines an entrepreneurial state as one in which the government serves "an entrepreneurial function . . . in partnership with private economic actors." Unlike the private entrepreneur whose role has been explicated by, among others, the classical liberal economist Joseph Schumpter, the entrepreneurial state "seeks to identify market opportunities not for its own exclusive gain but on behalf of private actors whose pursuit of those opportunities may serve public ends."[1]

That's the theory, anyway. In practice, influential firms seek to use the "entrepreneurial state" for private gain in the form of public subsidies and favorable tax treatment relative to competitors. The entrepreneurial state, in its operation, is more like the crony-capitalism state. For good or for ill, Eisinger writes that it has "achieved an institutionalized and growing presence in state and local government. For all their modest dimensions and uncertain impact, therefore, they represent the seeds of a genuine transformation in the American political economy."[2]

While agitation for corporate welfare stretches back to Alexander Hamilton, it went national in the 1970s. As Eisinger writes, "No longer a limited regional activity of industrially underdeveloped southern and New England states, economic development is now a universal public function." Moreover, it has moved from the margins "to a central—even pivotal—issue among prevailing concerns."[3] Barely a county or city in the United States today is without an "economic development agency" which funnels subsidies to a fortunate few businesses.

As we have seen, early efforts to encourage industry via subsidy flagged by the 1830s, as Jacksonian laissez-faire triumphed over the Whiggish "American System" of state-sponsored enterprise, and by the latter half of the nineteenth century infrastructure improvements, especially the building of rail lines, were the primary target of state subvention. But by the 1920s, the state governments of Alabama, Florida, Maine, and North Carolina were creating economic development agencies in order to lure industry and investment.

Perhaps surprisingly, the state-level pioneer in subsidizing specific industries was not Massachusetts or New York or any other reputed bastion of progressivism but rather Mississippi, which in the Depression year of 1936 inaugurated the Balance Agriculture with Industry program, or BAWI. This was a melding of progressive ideology, New Deal practicality, and the desperation of an impoverished state.

As James C. Cobb explains in *The Selling of the South: The Southern Crusade for Industrial Development, 1936–1980*, BAWI elevated the Hamiltonian concept of government subsidy of industry from scattered, often one-shot benefactions to an organized statewide program, thus inaugurating "an era of more competitive subsidization and broader state and local government involvement in industrial development efforts."[4]

Other states followed suit. For instance, although the constitution of the state of Tennessee, drawn up in 1870, explicitly forbade corporate welfare—as befits a place called the Volunteer State—by 1937 at least fifty-six recently constructed factories had received such aid, often in the form of the issuance of bonds by state legislative decree.[5] For what is a constitution, the sages of industrial development asked, if not a simple piece of paper?

Robert E. Lowry of the Tennessee Valley Authority investigated this burgeoning form of assistance for a 1941 monograph in the *Southern Economic Journal*. As Lowry explains, in the 1920s, "Industrial promotion became the small town shibboleth" in the South, as "thousands of dollars were raised by private subscriptions and poured into development companies which built factory buildings for the casual occupancy of any operator that could be induced to come in."[6] In such a way did local businessmen, motivated by a combination of community spirit and an understandable regard for their own well-being, assist in the industrialization of the small-town South.

These "privately financed development companies" were the creation of local persons seeking to attract factories to their communities.[7] They were in the "market entrepreneur" tradition described earlier;

to suggest to these investors that the *government* ought to underwrite their campaigns would have smacked of socialism to them. And then along came the Great Depression.

Private subscriptions were not always forthcoming in the 1930s, in those years of dolor and penury. Business capital did not drip like manna from heaven. In Lowry's justifying phrase, "It was only natural under the circumstances for business interests to look to their local governing bodies for assistance in financing industrial promotion." The concept of voluntary economic development took on a coercive cast.

Lowry examined forty-one Tennessee communities whose populations in 1937 ranged from 800 to 25,000. After interviewing municipal leaders and poring over public records, he found that of the forty-one, the vast majority—twenty-nine—had factories that were currently being subsidized by the local government. Another seven had either granted such subsidies in the past or were willing to in the present, four had factories that were entirely unsubsidized, and only one was placed in the category "Without factories, and unwilling to grant inducements."[8]

Lowry found that twenty-seven of the forty-one Tennessee municipalities he studied exempted certain industrial property from local taxation, the most common form of inducement. Typically, the state legislature would authorize the issuance of the bonds to construct the factory and lure the manufacturer. The matter was then placed before the voters of the community, who in every case in Tennessee approved the bond issue. The bonds were then sold and the factories built. The new owner not only had a spanking new building at his disposal, but he was also provided, in many cases, with free or discounted water and utilities in addition to the tax exemption.

The most frequently subsidized factories were those devoted to the manufacture of garments; curiously, factories owned by outside interests were more commonly subsidized than were locally owned concerns.[9] (This pattern is still seen today, as economic development officials in the hinterlands prize outside developers over the local variety, presumably because they suffer from the widespread delusion that an expert is any person living more than one hundred miles from here and carrying a briefcase.)

Communities in Georgia, Arkansas, South Carolina, and Alabama also engaged in such acts as giving free land and even buildings to manufacturers, exempting factories from taxes, and paying for the training of employees. Southern towns and cities often welcomed businesses that were fleeing the north to escape union troubles.[10]

But Mississippi, so often reviled by Northern commentators as a swamp of backwardness, was not only the regional but also the national leader in the establishment of corporate welfare as state policy. The spearhead, as Cobb relates, was Hugh Lawson White, who as mayor of Columbia had attracted a knitting mill, canning plant, and shirt and pajama factory to his city with various community incentives. Some of these efforts relied on private funds; for instance, a garment factory was coaxed to Columbia by an "$80,000 subsidy," writes John E. Moes, "raised through a chamber of commerce campaign among local businessmen."[11] Mayor White took his crusade statewide and was elected governor of Mississippi in 1935 on a pledge to Balance Agriculture with Industry.

Like its neighboring states, Mississippi had a plentiful (and largely nonunion) labor pool and modest manufacturing costs. The state's per capita income was barely one-third ($185 compared to $509) of the national average. But it was not unlike other states of the Deep South, so it needed an edge, and Governor White had just the idea: an act permitting counties and municipalities "to erect, build, purchase, rent or otherwise acquire industries, factories, manufacturing enterprises and buildings and business projects," which were to be financed by city or county-issued bonds backed by the taxpayers of those jurisdictions.[12] A three-member Mississippi Industrial Commission administered the program and assessed potential subsidy recipients. No public assistance could be rendered until at least one-fifth of a muncipality's registered voters signed a petition requesting the provision of alms to the potential recipient.

While Mayor White had relied to some degree on private contributions, Governor White was concerned that "free riders" would profit when other businessmen raised the necessary funds.[13] General taxation mitigates the free rider problem—but it introduces compulsion, favoritism, and market distortions into the mix.

Legal minds figured out an end run around the state constitution's prohibition of expending public monies on private businesses. The relevant language read "No county, city, town or other municipal corporation shall hereafter become a subscriber to the capital stock of any railroad or other corporation or association or make appropriation or loan its credit in aid of such corporation or association."[14] This would seem to bar cities from issuing bonds to construct factories, but the act's preamble said that BAWI was for a "public purpose"; that is, "the present and prospective health, safety, morals, pursuit of happiness, right to gainful employment and general welfare of its citizens demand, as a public purpose, the development within Mississippi of industrial and manufacturing enterprises."[15]

By invoking those magic words, those constitutional talismans *general welfare* and *public purpose*, this act, which plainly violated the state charter of the Magnolia State, became kosher. A test case emerged, involving a $35,000 bond issued by the city of Winona to finance construction of a factory to make bedspreads. By a vote of five to one, and in what James C. Cobb calls "a remarkable departure from the tradition of Mississippi jurisprudence . . . [and] a bit of logical gymnastics suggestive of the manner in which other conservative southern leaders justified federal intervention that benefitted their region," the Mississippi Supreme Court upheld the Balance Agriculture with Industry Act. Dissenting justice W. D. Anderson said this ruling "drove a steam shovel through our constitution," but mere paper charters would mean little if anything to the prophets of subsidized development.[16]

The BAWI act passed, despite significant opposition from farmers who viewed it as giving an unfair advantage to those industries that might lure agricultural workers away from the plow and furrow. In its first four years, the Mississippi Industrial Commission approved twenty-one projects, twelve of which were built. Only one project was approved by the commission and then rejected by local voters (those of Cleveland, Mississippi) in a referendum: as Cleveland's newspaper huffed, "we insist that if a factory concern is not big enough to erect its own building and doesn't want to come to Cleveland that bad, let them stay away."[17]

This was the voice of pre–New Deal America talking: a voice of parsimony in government spending, skepticism of grand schemes, and trust in local wisdom rather than the expertise of outsiders. It was sounding old-fashioned in 1937, but everything that is old becomes new again, and the spirit embodied in that Cleveland, Mississippi, newspaper editorial of 1937 would animate opponents of corporate welfare for generations to come. Though it would acquire different accents—those of Poletown, Michigan, or New York City—it would retain its force.

The verdict on BAWI's effectiveness? Mixed to negative. BAWI did attract businesses to Mississippi: as of 1940, these included "four hosiery plants, three shirt factories, a chenille bedspread concern, a woolen mill, a plywood operation, a tire and rubber plant, and a shipyard." The biggest of these was the factory of the Armstrong Tire and Rubber Company in Natchez, which was built with a $300,000 bond issue.

Yet the total employment due to BAWI projects was 2,691, "less than 5 percent of Mississippi's total industrial labor force," notes Cobb.[18]

"None of the BAWI plants established between 1936 and 1940 paid more than $1,000 per year in rent," writes Cobb, so the promised lessening of the tax burden was not redeemed.[19] Critics stubbornly insisted that BAWI was socialistic, that it encouraged outside investment while discouraging local start-ups, and that it unfairly favored certain industries or firms, especially producers of textiles, above others. On the plus side, Pascagoula "lucked out," in a twisted way, when the shipyard it won in a bidding war with Pensacola, Florida, found itself greatly enlarged by the onset of World War II. Several BAWI plants boomed due to wartime demand.

Despite its provision for the involvement of local registered voters, the BAWI was centralized and bureaucratic, as John E. Moes, an economist sympathetic to industrial development subsidies, has written. It lacked "all knowledge of both entrepreneur and the locality where the plant was to be established," though this ignorance did not prevent the board from categorically ruling out entire classes of business (for instance, those presenting "new hazards").[20]

A more populist Democrat succeeded Governor White in 1940, and the BAWI experiment ended—or, rather, was suspended. But it was revived in 1944 in somewhat different guise. Its administering agency, now the twenty-member Agricultural and Industrial Board, set a pattern that would in time become painfully familiar to observers of public development agencies: it was a credit-claimer. So while, as Cobb notes, other Southern states without BAWI-type programs (e.g., Tennessee and Alabama) enjoyed greater postwar employment increases, the Agriculture and Industrial Board boasted of Mississippi's gains (which, in fairness, exceeded those of Louisiana) and modestly claimed a share of the credit.[21] Between 1944 and 1960, more than $64 million was raised through bond issues that financed 161 new factories and 64 expanded facilities in Mississippi.[22]

The BAWI and its successor would be copied, albeit in various forms, by other states in the years to come. Mississippi—so often ridiculed as the least of states in social, cultural, and economic indices—was the trendsetter. Was BAWI socialist? Progressive? Crony capitalist? Whatever it was, other states wanted in. The irony is that the most fervid supporters of these programs would loudly proclaim their belief in free enterprise, entrepreneurship, and the working of the market. They would, as economic development agencies sprouted across the land, accuse critics of being anti-business and anti-progress, old sticks-in-the-mud who wanted the South (or whatever region they inhabited) to remain poor, primitive, and unwashed. To stand for liberty, for free enterprise without planning, was to be a troglodyte. Even so, the *Richmond News Leader* editorialized against a proposed Virginia Industrial Revenue Bond Act of 1952 by saying that "nothing is to be gained on the weak and rotten crutches of state capitalism."[23]

The forms these Depression-era and midcentury subsidies took are familiar to us today: "gift of building, low rental, tax concession, cash or equivalent, advance of capital."[24] In the decade after World War II, local development agencies, using these varied tools of subsidization, teemed across the country. From the Southwest to New England, luring businesses with taxpayer-endowed carrots became, if not the rage, at least a trend of some vigor. A survey by the US Department of Commerce found that in 1958, about 1,800 local economic development agencies were extant, and more than half of these had been created within the previous five years. The geographic breakdown was 760 in the Midwest, 468 in the Southeast, 223 in the West South Central region, 142 in New England, and 184 in the Middle Atlantic.[25]

Typically, the agency, supported by tax revenue, would purchase land, construct a plant or building for the targeted company, and lease it at a modest rate, with the company taking ownership in, perhaps, ten years. But the whole panoply of corporate welfare was on display in this newly bustling field, as development agencies often exempted the favored industries from taxes paid by competitors, paid utility bills for them, and even gave them outright gifts of money.

It should be noted that some of these development groups were private, often using funds raised from local businesses, and their efforts cannot thus be termed "corporate welfare," since no taxpayer funds were expended. These projects would usually be overseen by the local chamber of commerce. They were still a significant part of the mix in the 1940s and 1950s, though as the idea that economic development was a legitimate function of local and state government became part of conventional wisdom, these private efforts began to fade, as government stepped in.

The most influential academic supporter of Southern efforts to lure industry was the aforementioned John E. Moes, a professor of economics at the University of Virginia. In *Local Subsidies for Industry* (1962), Moes dismisses criticism of subsidies as "fallacious" and argues that "industries can be secured by means of subsidies."[26] This latter remark is unquestionably true; offering the gift of land, a physical plant, and an exemption from local taxation will induce a not inconsiderable number of firms to locate in so generous a jurisdiction. But Moes asserts that what he calls "competitive subsidization" can result in greater "community income" and less unemployment in those areas with significant joblessness. The subsidy, he contends, is "small relative to the total gain in community income" when a plant opens, or a new facility sets up shop in a distressed area.[27] The work of Professor Moes was, as one might imagine, music to the ears of state and local economic development specialists. They now had a scholarly imprimatur on what critics had theretofore complained was a profligate scheme for passing out favors to well-connected businesses.

Yet as Cobb argues, Moes, in proclaiming localized subsidies as an efficient way to boost local wages and employment and expand the tax base, "gave little attention to the indirect costs of industrial growth to the community."[28] These include necessary infrastructure improvements and public safety enhancements, the costs of which are extracted from taxpayers, usually via property taxes or sales taxes (the latter of which are regressive levies which proportionately fall most heavily on the poor, who in the Southern states were disproportionately African American). The costs, as is so often the case, were less visible than the apparent benefits.

* * *

The panoply of breaks and subsidies offered businesses by state and local governments today includes reductions, postponements, or exemptions from property taxes, sales and franchise taxes, and mortgage recording taxes; outright subsidies and grants; low or no-interest loans and loan guarantees; below-market or "free" rent and utilities; infrastructure improvements; the gift of land, including via eminent domain; zoning variances or waivers; and financing through tax-exempt bonds. Putting aside, for the moment, the questions of justice and fairness, do these even work?

Up through the Great Society and its immediate aftermath, the consensus of those who studied industrial location decisions was that the burden of state and local taxes played a distinctly minor role. This seems counterintuitive: surely the size of the government's tax bite matters to those whose job it is to compare bottom lines. Yet the regnant assumptions in the field were that other factors—"labor, markets, transportation, and . . . access to raw materials" as well as the cost of utilities and housing—weighed much more heavily in the decision making. So did other factors, both demographic (education and unionization of the populace) and intangible (quality of life, idiosyncratic personal preferences).

By the 1980s, that earlier judgment had been almost wholly reversed. As John P. Blair and Robert Premus wrote in 1987 in "Major Factors in Industrial Location: A Review," more recent literature had found that "state and local taxes have had an important effect on business location, particularly within metropolitan areas where business property taxes can vary substantially among jurisdictions."[29]

Taxes are not necessarily the prime determinant in location decisions, but they are not negligible or an afterthought, either. So at some level, offering a company a large reduction in taxes (especially a reduction not enjoyed by competitors in the same region) is a significant incentive to move or establish a business in that location. But it seems seldom to be the determining factor, which suggests that economic development monies are, in many cases, wasted; they are thrown at companies that would make the same decision even absent the incentives. Certainly, there is a lack of empirical evidence that targeted incentives are an effective, let alone efficient, way of attracting businesses.

Terry F. Buss, in surveying the literature of firm location decisions in *Economic Development Quarterly*, found that the majority of studies of the effect of tax incentives on firm location reported "negative results." Typical was the state of Washington, which granted favored businesses deferrals, exemptions, and tax credits that were not available to all companies. The State's investigators concluded that there was "little correlation between the amount of tax benefit received by participants in the tax incentive programs and the growth in employment which resulted."[30]

Buss urges that in drawing up incentive packages, governmental entities consider alternative uses of the public monies—opportunity costs. These can and should include leaving the monies in the pockets of taxpayers and consumers. Moreover, location incentives "tend to shift the costs of doing business from the corporation to the individual taxpayer," writes Steven R. Little.[31] Viewed within the framework of most philosophical traditions, this is supremely unfair—even, in the case of natural rights proponents, a violation of the rights of those taxpayers.

From a public-choice perspective, corporate welfare is an egregious match-up of rent seekers—the firms trolling for handouts—and politicians who see in those rent seekers potential supporters and major financial contributors. It is, in that sense, a perfect storm that rains down benefits on both parties, and soaks those on the outside—taxpayers and those firms that do not partake of the incentives.

\* \* \*

The 1980s and 1990s saw a mad interregional tug-of-war as states and cities competed to attract factories and businesses. This was not competition in any free-market sense of the word; it did not feature rival states slashing taxes and regulations and trying to best each other in creating the most conducive climate for enterprise to flourish. No, this was a bidding war centered on "incentives," which was a bland euphemism for subsidies such as grants and outright gifts of money, land, and buildings; infrastructure improvements; loan guarantees; and various below-market-rate financing schemes. A multitude of euphemisms for corporate welfare was employed: *recruitment, job creation,* the dreaded *public-private partnership,* and *extortion.* (Um, actually, no, the last of these four was used by *critics* of these deals.)

This scramble did not reflect any grand overarching macroeconomic strategy or, to use the shibboleth of the day, an industrial policy. It was piecemeal and decentralized. The latter, to be sure, is better, or less pernicious, than the former. A grand national macroeconomic industrial policy is what the Soviet Union implemented for seventy dreary years. Permitting local and state governments to forge their own paths, to experiment with various governing and economic arrangements, is a hallmark of the US system. Supreme Court Justice Louis Brandeis, in his much-quoted dissent in *New State Ice. Co. v. Liebmann* (1932), opined that "a single courageous State may, if its citizens choose, serve as a laboratory; and try novel social and economic experiments without risk to the rest of the country."[32] This concept of the states as "laboratories of democracy" is perhaps the single strongest defense if not of corporate welfare wars then at least of the rights of the states (and cities and counties within) to engage in bidding wars for businesses.

The corporate welfare wars, as they were dubbed, were targeted at specific firms in an attempt to lure them to specific places. In that sense they were blatant handouts: monies transferred from governments, usually local or state, directly to favored companies. This was a fairly bald case of government picking winners, a practice at which it has never distinguished itself, and which reeks of unfairness, both to the unsubsidized competition and to the taxpayers who foot the bill. The unaccountability of the agencies that ladle out these incentive stews is also problematic: unlike governors or state or county legislators or mayors or city councils, members of state and local economic development agencies are insulated from voter pressure. They are typically appointed by political office holders, so they are accountable in only indirect ways. Their loyalty is, perforce, to the politicians who appoint them, not to the voters and taxpayers, so they are both immune to pressure (from voters) but also acutely sensitive to the preferences of the people to whom they owe their jobs—the politicians.

Numerous state constitutions, from Arizona to New York, include prohibitions on government assistance to private corporations or persons. On the surface, these provisions might seem to act as a brake on corporate welfare. For isn't a transfer from the state treasury to an automobile manufacturer an act of government assistance to a private corporation? In practice, these constitutional restrictions are often as effective a hindrance as the posting of the Ten Commandments at an orgy.

Some of the most notable "winners"—or were they losers?—in these tug-of-wars included:

—Alabama, which, in 1993, awarded Mercedes Benz a $253.3 million package to build a plant which the company estimated would employ 1,500 workers at "a staggering $170,000 per job."[33] State officials not only played the siren song of Jobs Jobs Jobs—they also confessed to a rube-like belief that somehow manufacturing Mercedes-Benz sport-utility vehicles would alter Alabama's national image, or what they believed Alabama's national image to be: that of a backwards and impoverished wasteland. This is a common affliction among boosters: they cannot see all the good things in their homes—the wonderful music, literature, cuisine, and even college football that Alabama is known for—and instead dwell on hostile caricatures. In any event, even though the state government of Alabama agreed to purchase 2,500 Mercedes-Benz sport-utility cars as both a subsidy and an attempt to upgrade the image (and the ride!) of state employees, Alabama is still viewed by other Americans much the same as it always was. The comment of Theodore vonCannon, president of the Metropolitan Development Board of Birmingham, is unlikely to lead to a reevaluation of Alabama's reputation. VonCannon said that "as long as we have a free-enterprise system, there is not much you can do" except offer government-funded incentives.[34]

Huh?

Then again, Alabama actually "used National Guard troops to clear the land" it had acquired for Mercedes-Benz.[35] If that's not love. . . .

—Illinois, which in 1989 expended $240 million in incentives and infrastructure improvements to keep Sears, Roebuck in its historic home in the Land of Lincoln.

—Indiana, which in 1992 outbid 92 jurisdictions for a United Airlines airplane rebuilding plant that was projected to employ up to 7,000 persons. The Hoosier State offered United a $294.5 million package consisting of grants, bonds, and road and infrastructure work.

—Kentucky, which in 1986–88 lured Toyota to Scott County with an incentive package of $125 million. The package included a 1,600 acre site for a plant. Some constitutionalist pettifoggers pointed out that Section 177 of the Kentucky constitution read that the "credit of the Commonwealth shall not be given, pledged or loaned to any individual, company or corporation, nor shall the Commonwealth make a donation to any company or corporation." The details of the Kentucky package would seem to explicitly violate Section 177, but a majority of the Kentucky Supreme Court upheld the Toyota deal on the grounds that the projected increase in employment was a "public purpose."[36]

Not stopping at Toyota, in 1993–94, the Bluegrass State also offered a $140 million package to a Canadian company, Dofasco/Co-Steel, which was seeking to build a steel mini-mill.

—North Carolina, which in 1998 provided subsidies totaling $115 million to Federal Express for a "sorting hub" in Guilford County. As William Fulton of the Claremont Graduate University Research Institute wrote in *Governing*, "FedEx is one of America's most successful companies, yet the state was giving the company more than $76,000 per job."[37] That same year, North Carolina convinced Nucor, a steel company, to build a mill in Hertford County. That package was worth $155 million. To which John Hood of the Tar Heel State's John Locke Foundation quipped, "Creating jobs is not the goal of these programs. The goal of these programs is to create job announcements."[38] Mission accomplished.

—Pennsylvania, which in 1997 provided an incentive package worth $307 million so that Kvaerner ASA, a Norwegian concern, could open a shipyard in Philadelphia.

—South Carolina, which in 1992 gave BMW a $150 million package in return for a 2,000 employee, 1.9 million square foot production facility in Spartanburg. Thirty-seven million dollars of that total was used to buy land and homes from neighboring families that were to be displaced by BMW. (So much for the fabled Southern respect for tradition.) The state also paid for road and infrastructure improvements, job training, and tax exemptions. But, boasted defenders of the South Carolina deal, the Palmetto State taxpayers had shelled out only $76,000 per job—about half as much as Alabamans had paid.

—And, Tennessee, which in 1990 won a hotly contested bidding war for a General Motors/Saturn plant for the relative pittance of a $70 million package.

Such deals are "hopelessly unfair" to small businesses, argues John Hood of the John Locke Foundation. The little guys seldom receive the subsidies or tax breaks lavished on the big boys. "There may be no significant difference in economic terms between 100 companies adding 10 new employees each and a single new company adding 1,000 at one site," Hood explains, but "politicians can only negotiate with a limited number of businesses—and, naturally, attend only the most important ribbon-cuttings."[39]

If these deals go sour, well, tough luck. In its special report on corporate welfare, *Time* focused on the sad case of Albert Lea, Minnesota, which in 1990 showered the agribusiness giant Seaboard, Inc., with a $2.9 million low-interest loan as well as tax breaks and infrastructure improvements in return for reopening the former Wilson Foods pork plant. The plant had already consumed over $30 million in local, state, and federal monies, for which Seaboard vice president Rich Hoffman gushed in gratitude: "We're especially grateful to the state of Minnesota and the city of Albert Lea, who together since 1984 have supplied literally millions of dollars in the form of grants, tax incentives, and loans to the facility. They had a lot of confidence in it. . . . Truly this has been a lesson in economic development."

Truly it was. For Seaboard soon began trolling for a better deal, and though the city of Albert Lea offered a $12.5 million incentive package to the company to stay put, Guymon, Oklahoma, bested it with a $21 million sweet pot.[40] Seaboard skipped town. Albert Lea was played for suckers.

Peter S. Fisher and Alan H. Peters of the University of Iowa described one lavish incentive package in the *New England Economic Review*. In 1994, the state of Iowa passed the "Quality Jobs Enterprise Zone" act to benefit a single company: IPSCO, which was to build a steel mill in Muscatine, Iowa. The Quality Jobs Enterprise Zone, combined with other programs already extant in Iowa, was typical of the frenzied giveaways of the era. The features of the package offered IPSCO included:

— exemption from local property taxes on all machinery and equipment;
— exemption from sales taxes on machinery and services;
— $1.5 million for access roads;
— $1.5 million for other infrastructure;
— $1.2 million for job training through the local community college;
— $1 million forgivable loan for Community Economic Betterment;
— $500,000 from Iowa's Economic Development Set-Aside program; and
— the diversion of property taxes on the building (as opposed to machinery and equipment) into a fund to retire the bonds that were issued to finance the construction of the mill.[41]

91

IPSCO, predictably, accepted the offer. It built its plant in Musca-tine. The company was acquired in 2007–2008 by a Swedish concern based in Stockholm, SSAB Svenskt Stal AB. The Quality Jobs Enterprise Zone act was not repealed until 2012, or after IPSCO had reaped all the benefits—benefits that its less favored or more poorly connected competitors did not enjoy. It was good for IPSCO—but what about the other mills in Iowa?

You will notice that a preponderance of the states offering such munificence were Southern or border states. They can be considered heirs of Depression-era Mississippi's Balance Agriculture with Indus-try program—though agriculture is glaringly absent from the biggest corporate welfare packages. This is not to say that this mania is confined to the South or the Midwest, which is also represented on the above list. Corporate welfare knows no bounds, has no particular accent. As documented later, New York has been a leader in the dubious practice of subsidizing development through local agencies. But since the 1930s, the South has been at the forefront of the corporate welfare game. Has it all been a mug's game?

Peter T. Calcagno of the University of Charleston and Henry Thompson of the University of Chicago, writing in *Public Finance Review*, found that states that offered economic incentive packages actually experienced a *decline* in manufacturing value added. The subsi-dized firms, they discovered, "would pull resources from the rest of the state economy," and this reallocation of resources had a negative effect on the state's manufacturing value added.[42] Subsidies are good for the firm subsidized—but bad, it seems, for the rest of the firms in the state.

Terry F. Buss, chair of the Department of Public Management at Suffolk University, is among the leading scholars in the field. With cogency and thoroughness, he has examined the evidence of the efficacy of targeted industry strategies. In a seminal 1999 essay in *Economic Development Quarterly*, after noting, incredulously, that "targeting as a method never has been formally or rigorously evaluated," he proceeds to undertake such an evaluation.[43] Targeting is premised, he observes, on the assumption of market failure in the allocation of resources. Thus subsidies and incentives are necessary to assist new businesses or sustain existing ones. Perhaps Buss cut too close to the bone for some engaged economists. For he remarked that "nearly every university in the country contracts out its research services to states and localities to conduct targeting studies." The contracting entities do not need to spell out to the contractees the findings they desire; those are tacitly acknowledged by both parties. A contractee who concludes that targeted subsidies by the contracting agency will be inefficient, wasteful, politically motivated, or counterproductive will never again receive a contract to conduct such a study. Everyone knows this, yet when the study, inevitably declaring the targeted subsidy entirely salubrious for the local economy, is released, it is almost guaranteed prominent play in the local newspaper and on the local television news broadcasts. That is just how the game is played.

Pointing to the paucity of published research on the subject, Buss, mincing no words, writes that, "Validation is likely impossible because targeting violates basic economic reasoning, uses unsound methodologies and faulty data, and encourages inappropriate political interference, benefitting some at the expense of others." It is smoke and mirrors, and about as empirically verifiable (if a lot less charming) than a fairy tale. This is why, Buss suggests, "targeting studies are not published in professional economic, social science, or policy journals but only appear as unpublished consultant reports, details of which are rarely disclosed."[44]

There is a furtive, embarrassed quality to these reports. The agencies that commission them are interested not in the considered professional judgments of the authors but only in receiving an endorsement from a prestigious source: the imprimatur of the academy, the Good Housekeeping (University Division) Seal of Approval.

Evaluating data on targeted projects in Arkansas, Iowa, Maine, and North Dakota, Buss found gross mathematical and procedural errors, simplistic or deeply flawed models, unverifiable assertions, and fallacious reasoning: in short, a complete and total mess.

Although its statist premises are often camouflaged in jargon-heavy business-speak, at its heart, targeting is just central planning and industrial policy with boosterish bunting. It is, Buss says, rising to the occasion with a series of robust denunciations, "government micromanagement of the economy," and if it were called what is really is—central planning—"it would attract far fewer enthusiasts."[45] But the phrase *central planning* is redolent of Soviet economics, of grey Eastern bloc regimentation, and thus it is spurned by those in the West who actually engage in central planning. Packaging, they have learned, is everything. Or almost everything.

After surveying dozens of the extant studies, Buss concluded that "targeting is based on poor data, unsound social science methods, and faulty economic reasoning and is largely a political activity."[46] As this is exactly what economic development mavens and moguls did not want (or pay) to hear, his conclusions were not trumpeted from the rooftops of economic development agencies.[47]

\* \* \*

In New York, under the governorship of Republican Nelson Rockefeller, who was to unbridled government what Hugh Hefner was to unbridled sex—that is, an unabashed and even gleeful promoter—the Industrial Development Agencies Act of 1969 ushered in a new age of county-level corporate welfare.

The Empire State has led the way in the distribution of corporate welfare via industrial development agencies (IDAs), which the state defines as "public benefit corporations created to facilitate economic development in specific areas by attracting, retaining or expanding businesses." One way to facilitate such development would be through a general reduction of taxation and regulation; this is the course urged by free-market critics of IDAs. But New York's IDAs opt, instead, for what they term "financial assistance."[48] This translates into exempting preferred companies from property, sales, and mortgage recording taxes, as well as offering tax-exempt debt financing. As a rule, about 90 percent of the annual exemptions under IDA agreements are from property taxes, with most of the remaining amount coming from sales tax exemptions. Mortgage recording tax exemptions constitute perhaps 1 percent of the annual total exemptions as measured in dollars.

Decisions about which companies to grant favors to are made by IDA boards of directors, which are usually composed of between three and seven local government officials and businesspeople. These directors are appointed, in most cases, by the mayor, town supervisor, or executive of the affected county. The boards operate with minimal oversight: even the most egregious IDA agreement cannot be overturned by elected representatives of the people in the county legislature or city council. If a project exceeds a certain threshold, the IDA is required to hold a public hearing. In practice, this often means a hearing at, say, 1 PM on a workday, when taxpayers and their advocates are otherwise occupied. IDA directors vote no on proposed projects with approximately the same frequency as the Supreme Soviet used to reject five-year plans. The fix, almost without exception, is in.

Some IDA beneficiaries are required to make payments-in-lieu-of-taxes (PILOTs) to the lead agency, that is, the IDA, which then passes along some or all of the PILOT to selected jurisdictions—but not necessarily *all* of the affected jurisdictions. (This inconsistency is a consistent complaint of local townships in New York.) A PILOT generally lasts from ten to twenty years, after which time the targeted business either competes on the same playing field as its competitors do or it skips town, perhaps in search of another subsidized nest. The amount of these PILOTs is, naturally, considerably less than the tax burden borne by similar companies that do not receive IDA largesse. Whether or not a company makes a PILOT agreement, and the size and duration of the PILOT, is up to the IDA. The details vary widely from project to project and from county to county.

(IDAs may also issue Industrial Revenue Development Bonds, which offer lower interest rates than the subsidized company would get in competitive loan markets. Thomas J. DiLorenzo and I have written about the IDB scam in our 1983 book, *Underground Government: The Off-Budget Public Sector*).[49]

Given that IDAs benefit from fees received from projects that they subsidize, "they have an inherent self-interest in choosing to subsidize applicants," as the leftish authors of "Getting Our Money's Worth: The Case for IDA Reform in New York State" (2007) point out.[50] It's the more the merrier in IDA-land. Sure, every project these entities support increases the tax burden on property owners and disadvantages those companies that compete with the favored business, but that isn't the IDA's problem.

Milton Friedman famously remarked that he was "in favor of any tax cut, under any circumstances, in any way, in any form whatsoever."[51] This is wise policy in general, though not really applicable in this instance. The IDA is not offering tax cuts; rather, it offers targeted tax exemptions to a handful of politically connected firms, leaving the competitors of those firms at a marked disadvantage. Moreover, as New York State Comptroller Thomas DiNapoli noted in a report on IDAs, "When a property is exempt from paying taxes to the local governments in which it is located, the amount that would have been paid generally is shifted to the remaining property taxpayers." In New York, in the most recent year for which the comptroller provided figures, IDA exemptions increased the average property tax bill by $71 per taxpayer; the comparable number for upstate New York taxpayers was $82.[52]

In fiscal year 2011, the last year for which data were available at this writing, 113 IDAs pockmarked New York State. About half (56 of them) were countywide IDAs, 27 were town IDAs, 25 were city IDAs (including the biggest city of them all, New York), and the remainder were village or hybrid city-town IDAs.

Those 113 IDAs financed 4,486 projects with an estimated value of $74.2 billion. IDA-granted tax exemptions totaled almost $1.5 billion. Subtracting $917 million in Payments in Lieu of Taxes (PILOTs), the net exemptions were about $560 million. A plurality of these projects (27.4 percent) was manufacturing-based; the second-most common targets of IDA largesse were services related.[53]

Taking advantage of a window of dubious opportunity, the New York IDAs in FY 2011 subsidized 105 retail projects, which received tax exemptions valued at $41.3 million (or $12.6 million after PILOTs were figured in). State law had prohibited IDAs from sponsoring retail projects before 2008, and that ban was about to be resumed as of 2013–14. Among the reasons for this ban, according to the office of State Comptroller DiNapoli, is that retail "project-related gains often come at the expense of other retail enterprises in the area."[54]

IDAs have gotten around this hardly airtight ban by declaring various retail businesses "tourism destinations" or claiming that the business would not locate in the area—including "highly distressed" areas— absent the subsidy. As a result, companies like Wal-Mart received IDA assistance in New York State. This is the sort of big business crony capitalism that might have warmed the heart of Nelson Rockefeller but it left mom-and-pop shop owners fuming over welfare for the rich. (Wal-Mart is a champion among retailers at extracting subsidies from local economic development agencies. Its 4,170 US stores and 630 Sam's Club sites have consumed well over $1 billion in public subsidies, though exact numbers are hard to pin down, as corporate-welfare muckraker extraordinaire Timothy P. Carney notes.[55])

A county IDA might grant tax favors to, say, a restaurant or clothing store. Other restaurants and clothing stores in the county would receive no such benefit. The unfavored, naturally, howl in protest, only to be informed that such corporate welfare is the way of the world, and too bad for them. This is really no exaggeration: in 2013, the Genesee County (NY) Economic Development Center (GCEDC) granted $1.8 million in tax breaks to COR Development of Syracuse, which in turn lured Dick's Sporting Goods to a site previously vacated by a home improvement chain store. Because of the GCEDC's action, a local mom-and-pop sporting goods store closed its doors, as its owner said it was impossible to compete with an entity receiving almost $2 million in tax breaks that were unavailable to rival stores.

Moreover, the New York State Comptroller's report on IDAs conceded, research suggests that "incentives for retail trade were not effective in increasing the number of retail jobs or amount of retail sales in the region."[56] Without any substantial evidence that the panoply of favors offered by IDAs leads to a net benefit for the local community, even the State of New York—hardly a beacon of laissez-faire, a haven for the free market—frowns on local governments subsidizing retail.

It's not like the typical New York IDA is lavishing its assistance on corner delis, backstreet bodegas, or Al's Hardware Store. In 2011, four of the five largest retail projects supported by New York IDAs were major shopping malls: the Medley Centre in Monroe County (a $260 million project), the Atlantic Terminal Mall in New York City (a $124 million project), the Gallery at Westbury Plaza in Hempstead (a $120 million project), and the Waterfront at Port Chester (a $110 million project.) The fifth project in the quintet was a $90 million CVS distribution center in Chemung County—again, not quite your neighborhood pharmacy.[57]

In recent years, the largest IDA projects in New York have been developments, malls, and energy-related ventures. These have included a $2 billion Chase Manhattan acquisition and construction project in Brooklyn (yes, property taxpayers of New York City, you are subsidizing the ragamuffins of Chase Manhattan); a $501 million General Motors renovation and construction project in Erie County (GM: we take care of the Pontiacs and Chevys, you take care of our tax levies); the $601 million Neptune power transmission project on Long Island; and the $200 million Atlantic Power wind turbine project in Herkimer County.

Going further back into the dim recesses of the 1990s and early twenty-first century, we find such examples of IDA-generated corporate welfare as:

- $1.3 million via the Monroe County (Rochester area) IDA for Cooper-Vision, the manufacturer of contact lenses;
- $20 million from the Westchester County IDA for Lafarge North America (for a gypsum and wallboard plant);
- $78 million from the New York City IDA to NBC—yes, *that* NBC—so that it could "relocate jobs from its MSNBC studios in Secaucus, New Jersey to Rockefeller Center" in Manhattan; and
- $3.3 million from the Saratoga County IDA for Sysco, Inc. the nation's biggest food distributor, which then moved its local offices from Albany County—whose IDA had previously showered Sysco with subsidies—across the border to Saratoga County, fifteen miles away.[58]

Typically, companies on which the IDA bestows its favor promise the creation of X number of jobs and Y amount of economic activity.

The word *promise* is used loosely here, for if in fact the favored company does not create X jobs or generate Y economic activity, it pays no penalty other than, perhaps, a diminution of public esteem. One study found that in 2005, when IDA-sponsored projects in New York received $504 million in tax exemptions and promised 217,000 jobs, the actual number of jobs created was barely a third of that, or 79,000. Moreover, 25 percent of the subsidized companies actually cut employment. And these numbers come from the 52 percent of the 1,907 subsidized projects that provided sufficient data; almost half sent in reports to the state that were too sketchy to mine for information.[59]

Among the subsidy-seekers who failed to meet their employment promises? Wal-Mart, for one. The Arkansas-based behemoth accepted IDA tax exemptions of more than $12 million during the time under review (2002–2005) for stores and distribution centers in five upstate New York counties. In return for the favors, Wal-Mart pledged to create 549 jobs; it actually created 198.[60]

Reformers have suggested "clawback" provisions under which those who receive IDA corporate welfare must repay a percentage of the benefits received should employment or other goals be unmet. This is resisted fiercely by potential alms-getters. Defenders of IDAs argue that they attract new businesses to New York and retain those that are entertaining the idea of decamping for more business-friendly climates. They create *Jobs*, goes the refrain, and those jobs justify the crony capitalism that pervades the program. Local chambers of commerce tend to support IDAs; not coincidentally, their members are sometimes recipients of IDA patronage. And a research institute sponsored by the Business Council of New York has asserted that IDAs have "attract[ed] employers to the Empire State and . . . convinc[ed] New York companies to stay here."[61]

Yet what have the people of New York really gotten for more than four decades of IDA giveaways? Not much, according to Robert G. Lynch of SUNY Cortland, Gunther Fishgold of SUNY Albany, and Dona L. Blackwood of the US Department of the Treasury, who assessed the record for *Economic Development Quarterly* in "The Effectiveness of Firm-Specific State Tax Incentives in Promoting Economic Development: Evidence from New York State's Industrial Development Agencies."

The authors are venturing into uncharted territory, they concede. Their paper was published in 1996, yet in the years since, the available information on IDAs has hardly resembled a landslide. It is nebulous, incomplete, fragmentary, often insubstantial. As Republican former

New York State Comptroller Edward Regan said, "The information that is currently provided on jobs and other activity associated with economic development programs tends to be in press clips and self-laudatory reports released by those who run the programs."[62]

While the data the trio worked with were of necessity, incomplete, they were able to assay information on more than three thousand New York State IDA projects between 1970 and 1992. The sparseness of the data prevents the researchers from making a full evaluation, but they nevertheless reach a definitive conclusion. After evaluating the IDA record, the trio of authors conclude that its labor has been "ineffective in promoting economic development." The reason, they say, is straightforward: "the benefits of IDAs are questionable, whereas their costs, in terms of foregone tax revenues, are clear and substantial."[63]

Lynch, Fishgold, and Blackwood cross-referenced IDA records with information on company relocation. They found that between 1977 and 1986, only 17 of the roughly 150 New York IDAs operating in that decade sponsored companies that relocated to New York. In all, 23 companies received incentives from these 17 IDAs. In 1994, when the researchers undertook their study, fewer than half of these 23 (11) were still in business. Seven of the 11 survivors responded to questions; only two said that IDA "incentives played a role in their decision to relocate to New York State." And both said that they may well have made the move to New York anyway.

This is hardly evidence that IDAs lure businesses with their targeted benefits. But what about the other half of the IDA boast: that they retain businesses that might otherwise flee New York? The authors found "little evidence" that the thousands of projects that had received support from New York IDAs "would not have been undertaken in the absence of IDAs."[64] Hard numbers were especially hard to come by in this study. Most companies would not respond; of the handful that did, fewer than one-third replied that they would not have gone forward with the project in question without subsidy.

One area in which IDAs unquestionably excel is the art of exaggeration. Or hyberbole. Or even outright lying. At best, their motto is "shoot at everything that flies, claim everything that falls." A less charitable rendition might be Pull Numbers Out of Thin Air; No One's Going to Call Us on It. So county by county, IDA by IDA, New York's industrial development agencies profess the creation of thousands upon thousands of jobs, the cumulative figures being nothing more than the sum of projections and estimations made by people who have every reason to inflate the numbers and none whatsoever—except honesty, which is not usually a valued trait in the world of corporate welfare—to come clean.

The absurdly inflated job creation claims are born of a combination of factors. For one thing, "Firms seeking IDA-provided benefits have an incentive to exaggerate."[65] The bestowal of such incentives depends, in part, on the promise of jobs created. So savvy (or unscrupulous) firms pump it up. No one will ever hold you to your pledges. There are no penalties for falling shy of employment projections; no one even verifies the numbers.

Based on the five hundred IDA-sponsored firms whose job claims they were able to investigate, Lynch, Fishgold, and Blackwood estimate that "the actual number of jobs saved and created could not be more than 60% of job projections." They add that in some instances, these jobs were "pirated" from other jurisdictions, as for example in the case of Sysco moving from Albany County to Saratoga County (and sticking each county with an IDA-written due bill). The authors found that 8 percent of the jobs supposedly created by IDAs between 1977 and 1986 were pirated—that is, the firms moved from one part of New York State to another, courtesy of the taxpayers.[66]

And this introduces another question: what might have been had there been no IDAs? What would taxpayers have done with the monies extracted from them to pay for the IDA incentives? What might nonsubsidized companies have done had they not had to contend with competitors enriched by crony capitalism? Lynch, Fishgold, and Blackwood tackle this matter head on:

> When IDAs give tax breaks to some firms, they place all competing firms at a disadvantage: this disadvantage manifests itself in at least two ways. First, IDA-sponsored firms experience reductions in their costs because of the IDA-granted tax breaks. These cost reductions may enable sponsored firms to outcompete their rivals, in terms of prices and profits. Second, non-IDA-sponsored firms may experience a small increase in costs, in the form of higher taxes they must pay to compensate New York governments for the tax losses from IDA-sponsored firms. Hence the increase in output and employment on the part of IDA-sponsored firms is likely somewhat offset or even outweighed by the decreases in output and employment of competing firms.[67]

These are the unseen costs of industrial development agencies, and they are doubly true of retail subsidies. IDA benefits for Wal-Mart, for instance, reduce its cost of doing business relative to its competitors, whether the K-Mart down the road or the mom-and-pop sporting goods store or deli downtown. Jobs are not "created" by such subsidies; they are, instead, reshuffled, transferred from the unsubsidized store to that which receives subsidies. The volume of sales activity in the region is not boosted when a retail store is sponsored by an IDA; it is redistributed.

In the case of New York, as Lynch, Fishgold, and Blackwood explain, there was actually a net loss discovered in three different studies of grocery stores in, respectively, the Albany, Rochester, and Corning/Elmira areas. While the IDAs in these three regions claimed that their sponsorship of new grocery stores resulted in eight hundred new jobs, in fact, as the three studies found, "the end result was a net loss of jobs, not the creation of new ones."[68]

At the end of their IDA study, the trio of researchers conclude, emphatically, that "there is little evidence that IDAs have encouraged firms to relocate to, remain in, or expand within New York State." Nor have they "spurred economic growth or generated many jobs." They have accomplished three things:

- "forced taxpayers to subsidize the intrastate migration of economic activity, which provides no net benefit to the state";
- "provided tax advantages to a few firms at the expense of thousands of other businesses"; and
- cost local governments and the state governments hundreds of millions of dollars in tax revenues, the burden of which was borne by other taxpayers.[69]

This remains the consensus scholarly opinion of industrial development agencies.

IDAs remain a fixture in New York, especially at the county level, evidence be damned. For they are very public symbols of a county's commitment to economic development. No matter, it seems, that they are also symbols of waste and favoritism and the rankest sort of crony capitalism; no matter that they are beacons signaling to other businesses trolling for favors that the light is on and the cash box is open at this particular bazaar. IDAs are by now a well-established vehicle by which politicians and development bureaucrats can show their constituencies that they are earning their money, they are *players* in the game, and the local economy depends on their success.

* * *

The common denominator in all economic development schemes is the claim that they will create jobs. This is, in one sense, true: granting a subsidy or incentive to Business A may very well lead Business A to add X number of jobs. But there is never the slightest acknowledgment that there were alternative uses for those monies: they might have remained with the taxpayers from whom they were mulcted, for instance, or they might have been applied to other public works. The construction workers who labor to build a factory subsidized by taxpayer dollars would, in the absence of that subsidy, have been otherwise engaged. The alternative uses of their labor may have been in more efficient or more profitable enterprises. We do not know. But we do know that these opportunity costs do not show up as line items in the budget of any corporate welfare project.

As the invaluable Terry F. Buss writes, "Communities rarely consider doing nothing as an option; political pressures demanding a response are too great."[70] But sometimes, doing nothing—that is, allowing the actions of consumers and producers, and not government planners, to determine the shape of the marketplace—is precisely the right course. Alas, to do nothing—to refrain from government intervention in the market, to refuse to choose winners and losers and permit consumers to do so instead—earns politicians bad press. Other than outright corruption or, perhaps, involvement in a juicy sex scandal, one of the most damning acts a politician can commit, in the eyes of the media, is *doing nothing*.

Granting favors to high-profile firms, on the other hand, makes it appear as if the political class is laboring hard to bring jobs to the jurisdiction. Its impact is tangible: the factory built, the time clocks punched, the ribbon cutting and handshaking and posing with grateful CEOs. And while it is, at bottom, the ancient practice of taking money from one source and giving to another, it somehow doesn't seem quite so sordid as all that. As Buss writes, "Targeting, cloaked in the legitimacy of what appears to be scientific and economical, provides politicians and practitioners with justification to award political favors without appearing to be political."[71] It's all on the up and up—or so it seems.

Edward A. Zelinsky, the Morris and Annie Trachman professor of law at the Cardozo School of Law at Yeshiva University, has written with great wisdom about the intersection of community, subsidy, and law. Zelinsky not only teaches it, he has lived it: he served as an alderman and later a member of the Board of Finance in New Haven, Connecticut, for almost twenty years. In that time, he writes in the *Case Western Reserve Law Review*, "I shepherded through the legislative process many municipal property tax abatements awarded to developers in return for their promises to invest in the community." Yet, adds Zelinsky, "I now suffer from buyer's remorse as to these deals."

Despite his support for such arrangements while serving as an alderman and member of the Board of Finance, Zelinsky says he is "now intensely skeptical of state and local tax incentive packages designed to stimulate economic development." Yet he pronounces himself "equally skeptical that there is a good way to police such incentives."[72]

Zelinsky is in that position in which honest and intelligent people sometimes find themselves: his policy preferences are, to some degree, in conflict with his interpretation of the rules. He doubts that there are constitutional bars to states and localities that wish to offer subsidies and tax abatements to favored industries. And he admits to mixed feelings about the subsidies and tax abatements, too.

On one hand, writes Zelinsky, "I find compelling the argument that tax competition among states and localities is healthy because such competition disciplines political officials and allows taxpayers to sort themselves among jurisdictions." Competition tends to foster excellence, or at least improvement. It can encourage a locality to moderate (or even slash) tax rates in order to attract businesses.

But on the other hand, "targeted tax incentives are generally inefficient and unfair." For one thing, they suffer from an "inherent and irremediable information asymmetry" between the local development officials and the companies they are trying to lure. The latter know what they want; the former are fishing in the dark. And the targeted companies "have every reason to hide their true choices and preferences." They may well have decided already on a particular locality, but why reveal their hand if playing it coy could bring them additional millions in incentives?[73]

There is always an implied threat in these negotiations—give us what we want or we won't site our plant in your town/city/county/state. And the negotiators for the town/city/county/state really have no way of knowing if these threats are credible or just hot air. What they *do* know is that voters will probably blame them, and blame the local politicians, if the business or factory chooses to locate elsewhere. For that will be the implication left hanging: if only the politicos and the economic development bureaucrats had offered a better package, the Smith Widget Company and its three hundred jobs would have moved here instead of to Timbuktu. The negotiators therefore have every reason to give away the store.

This is compounded by the variation in time horizons: short for voters and politicians, and long for the smaller number who care about the jurisdiction's economic health. Edward Zelinsky notes that "the political calculations strongly favor the granting of tax incentives since the apparent benefits are immediate and visible—the decision of corporations or developers to build and invest—while the costs in the form of reduced tax revenues fall heavily in the future when others will be in office."[74] And those "reduced tax revenues" will, in all probably, be *shifted* tax revenues: the greater burden will simply fall on competitor businesses or property owners—people and firms that were not lucky or well connected enough to receive an incentive package. This in turn distorts their economic choices; the higher taxes that the unsubsidized must pay are supremely unfair.

In many cases, as we see in the handful of scholarly research studies of the subject, companies would have made the same location decisions regardless of the subsidies. In the words of Professor Richard D. Pomp, "tax incentives probably reward corporations for doing what they would have done anyway."[75] They are, as one executive confided, "a little extra cream on top."[76] Thus the inefficiency Zelinksy mentions. The company benefits, and so do local officeholders and bureaucrats, who have another feather to put in their caps, another notch on their economic development belts, but the taxpayers of the region are saddled with the bill. And no one is any the wiser for the fact that the company would have come or stayed anyway.

One problem is that it is devilishly hard to measure the projected benefits when putting together an incentive package. The would-be recipient of the incentives will paint a picture of almost blinding brightness in the matter of potential jobs created, but even the most credulous bestowers of benefits must realize that this contains an element of smoke and mirrors.

Edward Zelinsky, who not only studied but lived this issue, concludes that the best solution is to support general "tax competition among jurisdictions" but not targeted tax incentives.[77] If, say, Lincoln, Nebraska, or Lancaster County, or the state of Nebraska reduce certain tax rates across the board in order to attract or retain businesses, that is all to the good. This kind of jurisdictional competition improves the climate for both new and existing businesses. It lowers tax rates for all businesses, not just for the favored few (or even the favored one).

It gets the government out of the dubious job of picking winners. It leaves that to the market, or to the market's constituents: consumers.

Zelinsky opposes targeted incentives, but he is highly skeptical, indeed outright oppositional, of proposed legislation at either the state or federal level to outlaw such incentives. For the cure, he fears, would be worse than the disease. State and federal lawmakers would not be satisfied merely to prohibit targeted incentives, he argues. Under pressure from higher tax counties and states, lawmakers would go the next step and outlaw *all* jurisdictional tax competition. The anti-decentralist philosophy underlying the movement to permit higher levels of government to ban development incentives by lower levels of government would slide easily into legislation banning salutary tax competition.

Zelinsky writes: "By the time legislation curtailing tax competition emerges from the state or federal legislative process, it would likely wind up inhibiting healthy, as well as undesirable, tax competition."[78] Well-meaning attempts to end the latter would swallow up the former in the process. For there is *good* tax competition—a general lowering of rates or outright abolition of certain taxes—as well as bad, and the powerful constituencies for the bad would, if they could, wipe out the good.

He is also skeptical that legislators can come up with workable definitions of "targeted" tax incentives that would not subsume healthy tax competition, too. Again, jurisdictions with high tax rates would seek to punish neighbors with lower rates by drawing definitions so loosely as to include general tax reductions. In the end, Zelinsky says, it may be unrealistic to look to legislatures for the cure, for "not all problems have acceptable solutions."[79]

There is one solution, however, that is not only acceptable but, given sufficient political will, achievable: a taxpayer-led movement to end business subsidies, aka corporate welfare, in whatever guise, and at all levels of government.

Alas, the level of political will necessary to effectuate a voluntary end to the interstate corporate welfare wars seems far beyond our current crop of solons. For as observers (among them Matthew Schaefer of the University of Nebraska College of Law) have noted, the states are in the classic "prisoners' dilemma" situation. The prisoner's dilemma is here described by Avinash Dixit and Barry Nalebuff, coauthors of *Thinking Strategically*:

> In the traditional version of the game, the police have arrested two suspects and are interrogating them in separate rooms. Each can

either confess, thereby implicating the other, or keep silent. No matter what the other suspect does, each can improve his own position by confessing. If the other confesses, then one had better do the same to avoid the especially harsh sentence that awaits a recalcitrant holdout. If the other keeps silent, then one can obtain the favorable treatment accorded a state's witness by confessing. Thus, confession is the dominant strategy for each. But when both confess, the outcome is worse for both than when they keep silent.[80]

States and localities in competition for potentially relocating businesses are in the position of the prisoners. The competing jurisdictions are in separate rooms; they don't know what the other will do. Ideally, each would remain silent—that is, offer no incentives. But without a binding agreement, each fears that the other will offer an incentive package and tilt the playing field. So both parties bundle up as much corporate welfare as they can in an effort to outdo the other. The firm so wooed is better off; the taxpayers of the competing jurisdictions are not.

Matthew Schaefer elaborates: "Each state would be better off if constraints were placed on all states regarding the amount of investment attraction subsidies they could grant. However, because states are unable to receive sufficient assurances that other states will not grant investment attraction subsidies, they avoid the 'heavy sentence' that would be imposed on them by maintaining, enacting or enforcing unilateral state constitutional constraints."[81]

This heavy sentence, he writes, is defeat for the politicians who are seen as insufficiently devoted to luring industry to their district, or it is the loss of industry to other jurisdictions that are more forthcoming with the proffered subsidies. Of course there is a strong case, as volumes of academic research have shown, that the "winners" in corporate welfare wars are not really winners, and that losing, when it means not having to cough up millions or even hundreds of millions of dollars in incentives, is really winning.

The prisoners in the corporate welfare dilemma almost always rat each other out. They would be better off keeping silent, but given the uncertainty over what the other party may do, and the high cost of keeping silent while he squeals, it is almost inevitable that both will play their assigned parts in the prisoners' dilemma. Which is one reason why, despairing of any voluntary cessation of the corporate welfare wars, some academics and politicos began searching for a national solution to the problem.

As mentioned earlier, in the 1990s, the mayfly-like attention of the national news media was focused, for a time, on the new War Between the States: that is, the contest among states to outbid each other in subsidies and tax breaks in trying to lure major corporations to within their borders. States like Alabama and Kentucky and South Carolina—mostly but not exclusively in the South—found themselves in a kind of national auction, though it was an auction in which the auctioneer and the item being bid on were one and the same. Mercedes-Benz, Toyota, United Airlines, Nissan: major corporations, many of them transportation related, had put their headquarters or their plants on the auction block. The states, or at least those with aggressive (or aggressively unhinged) economic development agencies, kept upping the ante, putting together lavish packages consisting of outright subsidies, infrastructure improvements, gifts of land, tax abatements, low or no-interest loans, and every other form of corporate welfare known.

Only the good sense of the economic development people and the politicians to whom they answer acted as a brake on the runaway train of escalating bids, which is to say it acted as no brake at all. When the dust cleared, the midsection and the southland of the United States were pimpled with vast monuments to corporate welfare.

Governors and state legislators across the fruited plain cried: "Stop Me Before I Subsidize Again!" and so was born the idea of a multistate, or even all-fifty-state, pact, through which the signatories would agree to limiting the size, shape, and extent of their corporate welfare packages.

In August 1993, the National Governors Association approved "voluntary guidelines" (in political parlance, no guidelines at all) on subsidies. These guidelines were proposed by Illinois Republican Governor Jim Edgar, one of the few recent Illinois governors who has not come under indictment. Governor Edgar spoke of the need to "de-escalate the bidding wars" and forge a "non-aggression" pact among the states.[82]

The NGA recommended that "states focus economic development on roads and other infrastructure that only governments typically build," and disdain outright gifts as well as targeted tax incentives.[83] This was, in itself, a loophole big enough to drive a Mercedes-Benz through. Multimillion-dollar infrastructure improvements had become common features of corporate welfare packages. But the idea of a truce, as it was called, was a start.

Edgar told a reporter at the time that his proposal was the result of complaints from "good corporate citizens" who were sick and tired of seeing their competitors rake in corporate welfare.[84] Those punished by the corporate welfare regime, he said, were the small businesses who lacked the access and clout to win targeted incentives, and those large corporations which tried to play by the rules of our (relatively) free market system. Poor Governor Edgar had very bad timing. Less than a fortnight after the NGA truce had been proclaimed, Alabama announced its $253 million deal with Mercedes-Benz.

Governor Edgar's somewhat naïve proposal never had a chance. Edgar himself had engaged in the very practice he was deriding. Other governors might give lip service to the notion of a truce or a pact against corporate welfare, but their resolve would melt like a snowflake in August the first time a Mercedes-Benz or a United Airlines hinted that they might be persuaded to move their corporate offices or factories in exchange for certain considerations.

Edgar had run into the prisoners' dilemma. True, in the case of the states, unlike those of the theoretical inmates, the parties in this dilemma are permitted to speak to each other. But nothing binds them to their word, and without such compulsion their word is as good as, well, a politician's promise.

A flurry of interstate battles had already given the lie to any promises of non-aggression. In October 1991, New York State, New York City, New Jersey, and Connecticut agreed to a tristate-plus-city pact, which New Jersey Governor James J. Florio later broke wide open when he "unveiled a $234-million recovery fund to provide incentives to businesses crossing the Hudson."[85] There have been mobsters' pacts that lasted longer and were signed by more trustworthy men.

The problem with regional compacts is that states outside the compact, or the region, are free to dangle incentive packages before the businesses being pursued. Even if New York, New Jersey, and Connecticut sign a blood oath not to engage in a corporate welfare war, adjacent non-signers of the pact—Pennsylvania, Delaware, Massachusetts—are free to launch a bidding war of their own. Politicians and economic development activists are likely to see voluntary regional compacts as acts of unilateral disarmament in the corporate welfare war. (Not that unilateral disarmament isn't a good idea in a self-destructive war.)

The next step beyond a voluntary interstate pact is a national ban on state and local subsidies and targeted tax preferences when these are used to either lure businesses from other jurisdictions or to keep them from abandoning one's own jurisdiction. Such proposals entered the academic literature in the 1980s and 1990s. They tended toward the coercive and the comprehensive, for as Steven R. Little notes in the *Hamline Law Review*, "Unless a nationwide agreement was binding and enforceable, it would be meaningless."[86]

The feeling seemed to be that if the states were unable to control themselves, then the feds should restrain them. It was something of a "Stop Me—Stop Them—Before I—Before They—Subsidize Again!" strategy; it did not exactly show the states to their best advantage.

For instance, Mark Taylor, in the *Texas Law Review*, proposed an "Industrial Relocation Incentive Prohibition Act." Taylor rehearses the litany of problems with relocation incentives—"misallocation of resources, unnecessary concentration of economic and political power, corruption of the system by special interest lobbying, needless competition between local governments, and erroneous identification of proper candidates"—and concludes that a blanket ban is called for. This, he says, "would be the choice of strict free market economists," though in his assertion he overlooks the respect most free-market economists have for the federalist system, and their skepticism of national-government solutions to what are regional or localized problems.[87] A basic strength of the US system is its decentralized (at least in theory) distribution of power. A national stricture against state or municipal incentives and subsidies, however wasteful or unwise or counterproductive those incentives and subsidies may be, would run counter to a long tradition of respect (again, at least in theory) for local autonomy.

Taylor does call for a certain flexibility, lest impoverished districts be left without any means of attracting industry. He evaluates three possible methods of enforcement: judicial, bureaucratic, and legislative. Under the first of this trio, the statute would leave enforcement of the ban to the courts. Suits would be brought by private parties or the federal government against agencies or governments that offer illegal relocation incentives. The courts would decide whether or not the subsidy in question violated the act. This would result, says Taylor, in uncertainty and an inconsistent application of the law.

In the bureaucratic model, the determination of whether or not an incentive package violated the national prohibition would be assigned to a federal agency. This would eliminate the uncertainty that would plague the judicial model, says Taylor, since states and localities would submit their proposals to the agency before officially tendering them. It would also be more consistent than the judicial model. Finally, "the agency would acquire expertise in national economic planning," though this is, perhaps, not quite the kind of recommendation that warms hearts and inspires confidence.[88]

Its disadvantages are weighty, however, and they are embedded in the model's very name: bureaucracy. This would be expensive, unpopular, and it would entangle hundreds if not thousands of local and regional economic development entities in the briar patch of procedures and regulations. Even the most dedicated statists might—*might*—blanch at the prospect of a new gargantuan on the Potomac. And if no party chooses to sue the state or local entity that is offering the incentive package, then it will continue unimpeded. The result would be great irregularities and significant uncertainty in enforcement.

Under the third of these models, the legislative, Congress would enact a ban on relocation subsidies and incentives. This would be enforced via the federal tax code. The cost of implementation would be considerably lower than under a judicial or bureaucratic model; indeed, much of it would fall on those being subsidized. But it would be inflexible, argues Taylor, and invite political manipulation. As a practical matter, one can almost guarantee that every member of Congress would seek an exemption for the interests in his or her own district.

Taylor's preference is for the bureaucratic model, which, he says, "holds the prime advantage of developing a sophisticated method of analysis that can be applied consistently over time."[89] (Steven R. Little, too, concludes that "the only viable option for constraining the corporate welfare war is a federal legislative response based on an administrative model."[90]) Taylor's proposed statute defines relocation incentives in such a way as to include property tax breaks, subsidized infrastructure improvements, employee-training programs tailored to a specific business, the gift of land or buildings, and free or below-market rent and loans. It prohibits states and political subdivisions thereof from offering such incentives unless they are "equally available to private commercial enterprises already operating within the boundaries of the states or political subdivision," though exceptions may be made for regions suffering acute levels of unemployment.[91]

On their face, as Philip P. Frickey, professor of law at the University of Minnesota, wrote in a 1996 publication of the Federal Reserve Bank of Minneapolis, national restrictions on interstate corporate welfare wars seem "to run afoul of two American traditions: free enterprise and local control."[92] But do they accord with the US Constitution? The relevant section is the Commerce Clause, Article 8, Section 3, which grants the Congress the power "To regulate Commerce with foreign Nations, and among the several States, and with the Indian tribes." The commerce clause was primarily intended to put an end to discriminatory acts by the states against each other—to create, in effect, a national common market. The architects of the Constitution wanted to prevent a war of all against all in which rivalrous states imposed tariffs or even banned outright the goods of other states. In the words of Supreme Court Justice Cardozo's opinion in *Baldwin v. G.A.F. Seelig, Inc.* (1935), the commerce clause was a guard against "the mutual aggressions and jealousies of the States, taking form in customs barriers and other economic retaliation."[93]

Alexander Hamilton, writing in *Federalist* 7, explained that "Competitions of commerce" could be a "fruitful source of contention" among the states. Absent the coercive mechanism of the Constitution, Hamilton detailed, "Each state . . . would pursue a system of commercial policy peculiar to itself. This would occasion distinctions, preferences, and exclusions, which would beget discontent."[94] Thus the need for a national government strong enough to prevent states from practicing this kind of favoritism. Or so Alexander Hamilton believed.

Yet while it affirmatively grants power to the Congress, the federal courts have long interpreted the clause as barring "state actions that intrude upon, or interfere with, federal authority over interstate commerce."[95] This is known as the "dormant" commerce clause, or "negative" commerce clause, and it prevents states from enacting legislation that unduly burdens interstate commerce. It may even prohibit certain forms of state-generated corporate welfare.

Outnumbered critics of dormant commerce clause jurisprudence wonder: Whither the Tenth Amendment? That capstone of the Bill of Rights provides that "The powers not delegated to the United States by the Constitution, nor prohibited by it to the States, are reserved to the States respectively, or to the people." This would seem a formidable obstacle to the existence of any "dormant" aspect of the commerce clause, as the Tenth Amendment makes plain that powers not expressly delegated under the Constitution are reserved to the states or the people. Justice Clarence Thomas, for instance, has opined that the "negative Commerce Clause has no basis in the text of the Constitution, makes little sense, and has proved virtually unworkable in application."[96]

Be that as it may, the dormant commerce clause is a legal doctrine of long standing, and it impinges on the debate over the interstate corporate welfare wars. As Professor Frickey notes, the US Supreme Court has interpreted the Commerce Clause with such latitude over the years that "there is little doubt that the power to regulate 'commerce among the states' includes virtually unlimited authority to regulate any economic transaction even remotely affecting interstate markets."[97] This suggests that a national legislative ban on the weapons used in interstate economic development bidding wars would pass constitutional muster. It also suggests that the states themselves or injured parties therein could mount potentially successful constitutional challenges to specific relocation incentives.

But there is a countertradition in American jurisprudence as well. The courts have generally found that subsidies and tax preferences granted by state and local governments are permissible as long as they are not intended to penalize out-of-state parties. This was affirmed, somewhat paradoxically, in a case in which the Court struck down a state law by applying the Commerce Clause. *West Lynn Creamery v. Healy* (1994) concerned a Massachusetts levy on all fluid milk dealers. Although most of the milk sold in Massachusetts is produced outside the Bay State, the revenue from the assessment was distributed to Massachusetts dairy farmers only. Thus, out-of-state milk producers were required to subsidize Massachusetts dairy farmers.

Justice Stevens, writing for the majority (Rehnquist and Blackmun dissented), declared that the order was "clearly unconstitutional under this Court's decisions invalidating state laws designed to benefit local producers of goods by creating tariff like barriers that neutralized the competitive and economic advantages possessed by lower cost out-of-state producers." He went on to say that "Preservation of local industry by protecting it from the rigors of interstate competition is the hallmark of the economic protectionism that the Commerce Clause prohibits."[98]

So far, so good, at least for advocates of a strenuous application of the Commerce Clause. Economic protectionism by the states is clearly and unequivocally banned by the Constitution. But Justice Stevens makes clear that this prohibition does not extend to state subsidies to in-state businesses. He writes that "A pure subsidy funded out of general revenue ordinarily imposes no burden on interstate commerce, but merely assists local business." To this form of assistance the Court has no objection. But "The pricing order in this case, however, is funded principally from taxes on the sale of milk produced in other States." It benefits in-state economic interests by punishing out-of-state interests, and thereby runs afoul of the Commerce Clause. Its "purpose and its undisputed effect are to enable higher cost Massachusetts dairy farmers to compete with lower cost dairy farmers in other States."

In a footnote, Stevens observes that "We have never squarely confronted the constitutionality of subsidies, and we need not do so now.

We have, however [in *New Energy Co. of Indiana v. Limbach* (1988)], noted that '[d]irect subsidization of domestic industry does not ordinarily run afoul' of the negative Commerce Clause." (In *New Energy Co. v. Limbach*, the Court struck down a state of Ohio tax credit for ethanol that was granted only to Ohio-based dealers or dealers in states that offered similar credits to Ohio dealers. Yet the dictum quoted suggests strongly that had Ohio simply doled out state monies to its gasohol dealers, all would have been constitutionally well.) The Court has never suggested that creating conditions conducive to economic health, whether in the form of low taxation or infrastructure improvements, comes anywhere close to being a violation of the Commerce Clause. Nor has it denied states the right, when they are market participants, to give preferential treatment to in-state providers of goods or services.

In a concurring opinion, Justice Scalia stated that "subsidies for in-state industry . . . would clearly be invalid under any formulation of the Court's guiding principle."[99] But would they? Professors Walter Hellerstein and Dan T. Coenen of the University of Georgia School of Law, writing in the *Cornell Law Review*, point to Stevens's aforementioned statement that a "pure subsidy funded out of general revenue ordinarily imposes no burden on interstate commerce, but merely assists local business." This refutes Scalia, they argue: the subsidy to Massachusetts milk producers is clearly constitutional (whether it is advisable is another matter), but the method of raising the revenue for the subsidy is not. Contra Scalia, *West Lynn Creamery* is not, Hellerstein and Coenen say, "a vehicle for attacking all business subsidy programs."[100]

In *Metropolitan Life Ins. Co. v. Ward* (1985), in which the High Court, in a 5–4 decision, struck down an Alabama statute that taxed out-of-state insurance companies at a higher rate than Alabama insurance companies, the Court nevertheless observed that "a State's goal of bringing in new business is legitimate and often admirable." In a stinging dissent, Justice O'Connor wrote:

> This case presents a simple question: Is it legitimate for a State to use its taxing power to promote a domestic insurance industry and to encourage capital investment within its borders? In a holding that can only be characterized as astonishing, the Court determines that these purposes are illegitimate. This holding is unsupported by precedent and subtly distorts the constitutional balance, threatening the freedom of both state and federal legislative bodies to fashion appropriate classifications in economic legislation. Because I disagree with both the Court's method of analysis and its conclusion, I respectfully dissent.

(As I wrote at some length in *Mandate Madness* (2014), Justice O'Connor was the Court's foremost contemporary defender of federalism.[101])

The Court has frequently used the Commerce Clause to "strike down state regulations that discriminate against out-of-state economic actors."[102] In *Boston Stock Exchange v. State Tax Commission* (1977), the Supreme Court unanimously struck down a New York tax law that cut the tax rates on stock transfers if they were made on a New York exchange. The goal of the law was to retain the exchanges in New York and boost the state's (or, rather, its largest city's) brokerage industry, but in discriminating against out-of-state brokers it ventured into unconstitutionality. In his opinion, Justice White wrote that the tax-rate differential violated "the fundamental purpose of the [Commerce] Clause," which, he said, "is to assure that there be free trade among the several States. This free trade purpose is not confined to the freedom to trade with only one State; it is a freedom to trade with any State, to engage in commerce across all state boundaries."[103]

Similarly, in *Bacchus Imports, Ltd. v. Dias* (1984), the Court struck down a Hawaii law, enacted in 1939, that exempted locally produced liquors from the state's 20 percent excise tax on liquor. The purpose of the law was to encourage the growth of the Hawaiian liquor industry, particularly such products as okolehao, a Hawaiian brandy, and pine-apple wine. One might think that under federalist principles, Hawaii had a perfect right to favor its domestic industry, but in this case, the nationalist Commerce Clause trumped federalism. Regardless of the law's motivation, it discriminated against out-of-state producers.

Referencing his decision in *Boston Stock Exchange v. State Tax Commission*, Justice White, again writing for the Court, opined that "a cardinal rule of Commerce Clause jurisprudence is that 'no State, consistent with the Commerce Clause, may impose a tax which discriminates against interstate commerce . . . by providing a direct commercial advantage to local business.'" (Unlike the *Boston Stock Exchange* case, *Bacchus* was not unanimous: Justices Stevens, Rehnquist, and—naturally—O'Connor dissented.) "No one disputes that a State may enact laws pursuant to its police powers that have the purpose and effect of encouraging domestic industry," stated Justice White, but discriminating against out-of-state products is beyond the bounds of those powers.[104]

So in the matter of taxation, a state must be neutral between in-state and out-of-state businesses and their activities. With respect to subsidies, however, the Court has taken a more benign view. We know that under the negative Commerce Clause, Maryland, for instance, could not impose a tariff on goods from Delaware, and Wyoming could not slap a higher sales tax rate on Montana-made goods than goods made within the state. That much is clear. What is murkier is whether an incentive package offered by Alabama to lure a company away from South Carolina passes constitutional muster. Certainly on its face it does: nowhere does the Constitution empower the national government to strike down such an arrangement. But then "dormant" powers tend to lurk under surfaces, not on the document's face.

Exploring the "ill-defined distinction" between constitutional and unconstitutional state subsidy, incentive, and tax cases, Professors Hellerstein and Coenen conclude that according to the Supreme Court, "discriminatory subsidies, unlike discriminatory tax breaks, are almost always constitutional." However, states, in this admittedly nebulous doctrine, may not "impos[e] greater burdens on out-of-state goods, activities or enterprises than on competing in-state goods, activities, or enterprises."[105]

Is the Commerce Clause, then, the instrument by which the dragon of corporate welfare might be slayed, judicially? Professor Peter D. Enrich of the Northeastern University School of Law, writing in the *Harvard Law Review*, contends that the Commerce Clause "provides a solid basis for constitutional attacks on many common forms of business tax breaks." The Supreme Court, he notes, has consistently used the Commerce Clause to strike down state-level taxes that disfavor out-of-state concerns. Moreover, he argues, the Commerce Clause is intended to protect the states from the pernicious effects of "competitive exercises of their sovereignty."[106]

Enrich believes that numerous business location incentives may stand on the foul side of the Commerce Clause. After all, they "relieve businesses locating in-state from tax burdens to which out-of-state competitors remain subject."[107] Yet there is a serious obstacle to using the dormant Commerce Clause to strike down state incentive packages: difficulty in finding a party who has standing to bring a suit. Enrich considers parties that might have both a stake in the matter and also the motivation to pursue it: his preliminary list includes "out-of-state businesses, which, because of their decision to locate elsewhere, are not permitted to make use of a particular incentive; second, ordinary citizens and taxpayers, who must ultimately pay the cost of the incentives;

and third, the states themselves, whose autonomy and fiscal capacity is undermined by the competitive actions of other states."[108]

This first party in Enrich's list is unpromising, in his judgment, for out-of-state businesses that do not take advantage of a relocation incentive are not injured by their failure to do so; they are merely not benefitted. Moreover, since these incentives are targeted to businesses, even those that do not wind up with the golden tickets may be reluctant to call the cops on the scam. After all, at some future point *they* may be the recipient of such favors. And while citizens and taxpayers unquestionably have a direct interest in the cost of relocation incentives, their interest is "attenuated."[109] It is nowhere near as strong as the interest of a business competitor.

The states, however, Enrich finds to be "the most attractive and plausible candidates to bring challenges to other states' location incentives." They are the "most direct losers" in interstate bidding for business. Enrich pronounces them the "logical" and "suitable" candidates to raise the Commerce Clause flag in defiance of corporate welfare.[110] But the case envisioned by Professor Enrich has yet to materialize. It will eventually materialize, one suspects, though how the Court will rule is a matter beyond the ken of even the most skilled seer of the future.

In the meantime, Congress shows no inclination to reconsider the matter. The idea of a national prohibition on interstate corporate welfare wars that entered the policy conversation in the 1990s died there, too, unable to make the transition to the new millennium, even as corporate welfare strode merrily along. (Though, admittedly, the most high-profile bidding wars belonged to the 1990s, not the new century.)

The proposed national solution to state bidding wars never got even a toehold in Congress. For one thing, the states that were winning these bidding wars had no interest in handcuffing themselves. For another, the states would take such a law as a gross imposition on their rights. It flies in the face of federalism, it violates decentralist tenets, and while decentralism has few adherents in the US Congress—the notion of returning power from Washington to the states and localities is about as popular in Washington as theosophy and phrenology—politicians do not like to be seen running roughshod over the fifty states. Moreover, these measures implied that the states are as children, unable to exercise any self-restraint whatsoever. (This is not to say that there isn't more than a grain of truth to that characterization.)

Thus we are left with a dilemma that admits of no obvious and achievable solution. The voters—the taxpayers—the small businesspeople who are the great unsubsidized—hold the key that could lock the corporate welfare drawer . . . but they currently show no real inclination to use it.

## Notes

1. Peter K. Eisinger, *The Rise of the Entrepreneurial State: State and Local Economic Development Policy in the United States* (Madison, WI: University of Wisconsin Press, 1988), p. 9.
2. Ibid., p. 342.
3. Ibid., pp. 11–12.
4. James C. Cobb, *The Selling of the South: The Southern Crusade for Industrial Development, 1936–1980* (Baton Rouge: Louisiana State University Press, 1982), p. 5.
5. Ibid., p. 6.
6. Robert E. Lowry, "Municipal Subsidies to Industries in Tennessee," *Southern Economic Journal* (Vol. 7, No. 3, January 1941): 317.
7. Ibid.: 320.
8. Ibid.: 318.
9. Ibid.: 319, 323.
10. See also Lester Tanzer, "Dixie Dilemma: Bond Buyers Frown on Public Money Lure for Southern Plants," *Barron's National Business and Financial Weekly*, August 18, 1952, p. 33.
11. John E. Moes, *Local Subsidies for Industry* (Chapel Hill: University of North Carolina, 1962), p. 72.
12. Cobb, *The Selling of the South: The Southern Crusade for Industrial Development, 1936–1980*, pp. 22, 12.
13. Moes, *Local Subsidies for Industry*, p. 73.
14. Cobb, *The Selling of the South: The Southern Crusade for Industrial Development, 1936–1980*, p. 20.
15. Ibid., p. 14.
16. Ibid., pp. 20–21.
17. Ibid., p. 19.
18. Ibid., pp. 23–24.
19. Ibid., p. 21.
20. Moes, *Local Subsidies for Industry*, pp. 76–77.
21. Cobb, *The Selling of the South: The Southern Crusade for Industrial Development, 1936–1980*, p. 30.
22. Moes, *Local Subsidies for Industry*, p. 80.
23. Ibid., p. 74.
24. Ibid., p. 69.
25. Ibid., pp. 115, 121.
26. Ibid., pp. 3, 100.
27. Ibid., pp. 196–97.
28. Cobb, *The Selling of the South: The Southern Crusade for Industrial Development, 1936–1980*, p. 60.
29. John P. Blair and Robert Premus, "Major Factors in Industrial Location: A Review," *Economic Development Quarterly* (Vol. 1, No. 1, 1987): 80.

30. Terry F. Buss, "The Effect of State Tax Incentives on Economic Growth and Firm Location Decisions: An Overview of the Literature," *Economic Development Quarterly* (Vol. 15, No. 1, February 2001): 99.

31. Little, "Corporate Welfare Wars: The Insufficiency of Current Constitutional Constraints on State Action and the Desirability of a Federal Response," *Hamline Law Review*: 857.

32. *New State Ice Co. v. Liebmann* 285 U.S. 262 (1932).

33. Wim Wiewel, Joseph Persky, and Daniel Felstenstein, "Are subsidies worth it? How to calculate costs and benefits of business incentives," *Government Finance Review*, October 1, 1995, http://www.thefreelibrary.com/Are+subsidies+worth+it%3F%3A+How+to+calculate+costs+and+benefits+of-a017586506.

34. John Hood, "Ante Freeze," *Policy Review*, Spring 1994.

35. Bartlett and Steele, "Corporate Welfare," *Time*.

36. Matthew Schaefer, "State Investment Attraction Subsidy Wars Resulting from a Prisoner's Dilemma: The Inadequacy of State Constitutional Solutions and the Appropriateness of a Federal Legislative Response," *New Mexico Law Review* (Vol. 28, Spring 1998): 317.

37. William Fulton, "The endless subsidy cycle," *Governing*, February 1999, p. 101.

38. Bartlett and Steele, "Corporate Welfare," *Time*.

39. Hood, "Ante Freeze," *Policy Review*.

40. Bartlett and Steele, "Corporate Welfare," *Time*.

41. Peter S. Fisher and Alan H. Peters, "Tax and Spending Incentives and Enterprise Zones," *New England Economic Review* (March/April 1997): 109.

42. Peter T. Calcagno and Henry Thompson, "State Economic Incentives: Stimulus or Reallocation?" *Public Finance Review* (Vol. 32, No. 6, November 2004): 651.

43. Terry F. Buss, "The Case Against Targeted Industry Strategies," *Economic Development Quarterly* (Vol. 13, No. 4, November 1999): 339.

44. Ibid.: 340.

45. Ibid.: 346.

46. Ibid.: 339.

47. For a refutation of Professor Buss, see Wim Wiewel, "Policy Research in an Imperfect World: Response to Terry F. Buss, 'The Case Against Targeted Industry Strategies,'" *Economic Development Quarterly* (Vol. 13, No. 4, November 1999): 357–60. Wiewel charges that Buss's "ideological bias causes him to attack any tinkering with the free market; on that basis, all economic development efforts are inappropriate" (Wiewel: 357).

48. "Annual Performance Report on New York State's Industrial Development Agencies," Office of New York State Comptroller Thomas P. DiNapoli, May 2013, p. 1.

49. James T. Bennett and Thomas J. DiLorenzo, *Underground Government: The Off-Budget Public Sector* (Washington, DC: Cato Institute, 1983).

50. "Getting Our Money's Worth: The Case for IDA Reform in New York State," New York Jobs with Justice, May 2007, p. 17.

51. Peter Robinson, "Milton Friedman and the Moral Argument for Tax Cuts," www.nationalreview.com, October 17, 2007.

52. "Annual Performance Report on New York State's Industrial Development Agencies," Office of New York State Comptroller Thomas P. DiNapoli, May 2012, p. 1.
53. "Annual Performance Report on New York State's Industrial Development Agencies," May 2013, pp. 4–5.
54. Ibid., pp. 8, 2.
55. http://corporate.walmart.com/our-story/our-business/locations/.
56. "Annual Performance Report on New York State's Industrial Development Agencies," May 2013, p. 8.
57. Ibid., p. 9.
58. "Getting Our Money's Worth: The Case for IDA Reform in New York State," pp. 9, 15.
59. Ibid., pp. 2–3.
60. Ibid., p. 6.
61. Robert G. Lynch, Gunther Fishgold, and Dona L. Blackwood, "The Effectiveness of Firm-Specific State Tax Incentives in Promoting Economic Development: Evidence from New York State's Industrial Development Agencies," *Economic Development Quarterly* (Vol. 10, No. 1, February 1996): 62.
62. Ibid.: 57–58.
63. Ibid.: 57.
64. Ibid.: 62.
65. Ibid.: 63.
66. Ibid.: 64.
67. Ibid.: 63.
68. Ibid.: 65.
69. Ibid.: 66.
70. Buss, "The Case Against Targeted Industry Strategies," *Economic Development Quarterly*: 349.
71. Ibid.: 351.
72. Edward A. Zelinsky, "Tax Incentives for Economic Development: Personal (and Pessimistic) Reflections," *Case Western Reserve Law Review* (Vol. 58, No. 4, 2007–2008): 1146.
73. Ibid.: 1147–49.
74. Ibid.: 1149.
75. Quoted in ibid.: 1151.
76. Peter D. Enrich, "Saving the States from Themselves: Commerce Clause Constraints on State Tax Incentives for Business," *Harvard Law Review* (Vol. 110, No. 2, December 1996): 392.
77. Zelinsky, "Tax Incentives for Economic Development: Personal (and Pessimistic) Reflections," *Case Western Reserve Law Review*: 1151.
78. Ibid.: 1153.
79. Ibid.: 1155.
80. Avinash Dixit and Barry Nalebuff, "Prisoners' Dilemma," *Concise Encyclopedia of Economics*, http://www.econlib.org/library/CEEBiographies.html.
81. Schaefer, "State Investment Attraction Subsidy Wars Resulting from a Prisoner's Dilemma: The Inadequacy of State Constitutional Solutions and the Appropriateness of a Federal Legislative Response," *New Mexico Law Review*: 303.

82. E. J. Dionne Jr., "It's time to call off bribery for jobs," *Austin American-Statesman*, August 31, 1993.

83. Cathy Collins and Sherry Watson, "The New War Between the States: Economic Policy or Corporate Welfare," *Journal of State Taxation* (Vol. 15, No. 11, 1996–97): 18.

84. Dionne Jr., "It's time to call off bribery for jobs," *Austin American-Statesman*.

85. Steven Prokesch, "Cuomo Calls for New York and New Jersey to End Rivalry," *New York Times*, December 3, 1992; Collins and Watson, "The New War Between the States: Economic Policy or Corporate Welfare," *Journal of State Taxation*: 18.

86. Little, "Corporate Welfare Wars: The Insufficiency of Current Constitutional Constraints on State Action and the Desirability of a Federal Response," *Hamline Law Review*: 888.

87. Mark Taylor, "A Proposal to Prohibit Industrial Relocation Subsidies," *Texas Law Review* (Vol. 72, 1993–94): 702.

88: Ibid.: 706.

89. Ibid.: 708.

90. Little, "Corporate Welfare Wars: The Insufficiency of Current Constitutional Constraints on State Action and the Desirability of a Federal Response," *Hamline Law Review*: 851.

91. Taylor, "A Proposal to Prohibit Industrial Relocation Subsidies," *Texas Law Review*: 711.

92. Philip P. Frickey, "The congressional process and the constitutionality of federal legislation to end the economic war among the states," June 1, 1996, www.minneapolisfed.org/publications.

93. *Baldwin v. G.A. F. Seelig, Inc.*, 294 U.S. 511 (1935) http://www.law.cornell.edu/supct/html/historics/USSC_CR_0294_0511_ZS.html.

94. James Madison, Alexander Hamilton, and John Jay, *The Federalist Papers* (New York: New American Library, 1961), pp. 62–63.

95. Enrich, "Saving the States from Themselves: Commerce Clause Constraints on State Tax Incentives for Business," *Harvard Law Review*: 424.

96. *Camps Newfound/Owatonna, Inc. v. Town of Harrison et al.*, 520 U.S. 610 (1997), http://www.law.cornell.edu/supremecourt/text/520/564.

97. Frickey, "The congressional process and the constitutionality of federal legislation to end the economic war among the states," www.minneapolisfed.org/publications.

98. *West Lynn Creamery v. Healy* 512 U.S. 186 (1994), http://www.law.cornell.edu/supct/html/93-141.ZS.html.

99. Ibid.

100. Walter Hellerstein and Dan T. Coenen, "Commerce Clause Restraints on State Business Development Incentives," *Cornell Law Review* (Vol. 81, No. 4, May 1996): 837.

101. *Metropolitan Life Insurance Co. v. Ward*, 470 U.S. 869 (1985), http://scholar.google.com/scholar_case?case=16467267132220576092&hl=en&as_sdt=6&as_vis=1&oi=scholarr.

102. Enrich, "Saving the States from Themselves: Commerce Clause Constraints on State Tax Incentives for Business," *Harvard Law Review*: 378.

103. *Boston Stock Exchange v. State Tax Commission* 429 U.S. 318 (1977), http://www.law.cornell.edu/supremecourt/text/429/318.

104. *Bacchus Imports, Ltd. V. Dias* 428 U.S. 263 (1984), http://www.law.cornell.edu/supremecourt/text/468/263.

105. Hellerstein and Dan T. Coenen, "Commerce Clause Restraints on State Business Development Incentives," *Cornell Law Review*: 792–93.

106. Enrich, "Saving the States from Themselves: Commerce Clause Constraints on State Tax Incentives for Business," *Harvard Law Review*: 378, 381.

107. Ibid.: 439.

108. Ibid.: 408.

109. Ibid.: 413.

110. Ibid.: 418.

# 5

## Corporate Welfare as Theft: How Detroit and General Motors Stole Poletown

If the great corporate welfare programs of the nineteenth century were directed at transportation, in particular the nurturing (or artificial stimulation of) the railroad industry and canals, the corporate welfare complex of our era has seen the automobile industry park itself in a prominent position. The previous chapter surveyed the sweetheart deals that state and local economic development agencies sealed with, among others, Toyota, Mercedes-Benz, BMW, and Saturn. Although these agreements met some opposition within the affected states, their critics were drowned out by the chorus of hosannas from local boosters. Fiscal conservatives and populist leftists railed against these giveaways, but their voices did not come close to carrying the day, perhaps because the issues lacked an emotional component. They seemed too buttoned down, too cut and dried: a handshake deal between the commercial and political establishment and the captains of multinational industry.

That missing emotional edge has been present, in heartbreaking fashion, in a handful of corporate welfare episodes, most notoriously that of "Poletown," the Michigan neighborhood that was demolished by the city of Detroit at the imperious request of General Motors and over the anguished protests of some of its longtime residents. An in-depth look at the Poletown case, among the most outrageous—because it was so clearly an act of theft—instances of government favoritism to a powerful corporation in American history, is clearly warranted. A less well-known and, because eminent domain did not cut nearly so wide a swath, less controversial sequel of sorts, involved Chrysler and was centered to the south of Detroit, in Toledo, Ohio.

These cases did not appear in a vacuum. All throughout the land of the free at the end of the twentieth century, municipal governments were condemning private property for the benefit of corporate interests. And it seemed that in each case, those whose property was taken had to endure sanctimonious lectures about how their loss was society's gain, the imputation being that only a selfish brute could object to government transferring his property to another owner.

In East St. Louis, Illinois, it was a metals-recycling business that was seized by a government-created entity and given to a motor speedway (which used the razed property for a parking lot). In Port Chester, New York, the land on which a cosmetics packaging company sat was taken from its owners and given to a shopping-center developer. In Merriam, Kansas, a Toyota dealership was condemned and transferred to . . . a BMW dealership! In East Harlem, New York, a cabinetmaker had his property taken to make room for a Home Depot and Costco.

The justification was always the same. In the words of the attorney for the developer that received the land in Port Chester, "It's the greater good vs. one individual interest." A spokesman for the developer that received the cabinetmaker's land said, "This project brings a sense of faith and a sense of improvement to an area that has sorely lacked self-confidence." As these quotes indicate, those who benefit from eminent domain are not excessively punctilious when it comes to the moral dimensions of the act. The pleas of those whose property is taken fall on deaf ears. As one Kansas attorney who defended a hotelier being booted off his property to make way for yet another motorway said, "I call it the marriage of big business and big government. The little property owners get creamed."[1]

But these episodes, brazen and shameless as the thievery may have been, were trifles compared to what happened in Detroit over several months stretching from 1980 into 1981. For in the neighborhood of Poletown, the city of Detroit and General Motors pulled off an act of corporate welfare as vast in scale as it was breathtakingly audacious.

The story of Poletown, in the words of Ralph Nader, one of the very few American political figures who had the guts to stand up for the place, "is the story of the spirited, integrated, lower-middle-class urban community in Detroit that refused to die until the bulldozers of corporate socialism destroyed its physical being."[2]

Poletown was a racially, ethnically, religiously, socially, and economically mixed neighborhood—not a paradise, but a genuine neighborhood nevertheless. As its nickname suggests, it was built on an Eastern European base.

The neighborhood known since the late nineteenth century as Poletown is, or was, found in the northeastern part of Detroit up to and including parts of the City of Hamtramck, which incorporated as a separate city rather than throw in with Detroit. The Polish population of the eastside of Detroit exceeded 22,000 by 1885 and approached 50,000 by 1900. It was large enough to support three Polish parishes of the Roman Catholic Church—the religious pillars on which the community rested, and which would prove a source of support but also abandonment a century later. The area was not ethnically homogeneous, however, as Russians, Eastern Europeans of other-than-Polish extraction, and African American and poor white migrants from the South and Appalachian states, respectively, also made their homes in Poletown.

Although it was home to five cigar factories, the auto industry would become a primary employer of the people of Poletown. As John J. Bukowczyk writes in "The Decline and Fall of a Detroit Neighborhood: Poletown vs. G.M. and the City of Detroit," the Dodge Main Works, site of a famous 1937 sit-down strike, had a heavily Polish workforce, and several other carmakers (Cadillac, Detroit Electric, and E-M-F) also had nearby plants.

Dodge Main was built in 1910. By the Second World War, Dodge Main employed forty thousand workers. Roman Catholic churches continued to spring up, as did a complex and interdependent network of small shops, bars, barbershops, and fraternal organizations. Undergirding Poletown, writes Bukowcyzk, was "a deep attachment to family and neighborhood and a pride in home ownership doubtless linked to the cultural legacy of peasant land-hunger carried over from the Polish countryside."[3]

After the Second World War, the Polish character of the neighborhood eroded somewhat as new arrivals took their place in Poletown. Postwar economic readjustments altered Poletown, too, as factories moved to the suburbs, where rent was cheaper and land was more plentiful. The workforce of Dodge Main also diminished. And, Bukowczyk reminds us, federal government policy nudged people out of Poletown: "Upwardly mobile second generation Polish-American veterans, sometimes using GI-Bill benefits, often sought better jobs and larger, newer homes in the burgeoning suburbs. The availability of federally financed home mortgages encouraged this movement, as did postwar federally funded road and highway construction which made these suburban areas more accessible."[4] Federally financed urban renewal in other parts of Detroit uprooted residents, many of them African American, who moved into Poletown.

And there was more. From the mid-1950s through the mid-1960s, especially, the National System of Interstate and Defense Highways— the military-sounding title given to what was popularly known as the Interstate Highway System—cut a merciless path through many large cities. Detroit was no exception. Poletown bore its share of the destruction. Interstate 94, or the Ford Freeway, "cut a broad swath through Poletown and had a catastrophic effect on the life-chances of the district."[5] (The GM plant site was in that section of Poletown that had been cut off from the rest of the neighborhood by the Ford— Edsel Ford, that is—Freeway.) Due to highway construction, writes Jeanie Wylie in her moving and valuable book, *Poletown: Community Betrayed* (1989), "An estimated 1,400 families had to be resettled between 1953 and 1955." I-94 even cut off many parishioners from Immaculate Conception Church; in battles between church and state, especially when the state interest is in transportation, always bet on the state to win.

Interstate 75, or the Chrysler Freeway, took out another chunk of the neighborhood, in this case a largely African American section that lost an estimated three thousand housing units.[6] Ford, Chrysler: the very names that had built Detroit into an economic powerhouse were now being applied to public-works projects that were tearing the place down. Government, in the guise of the defense industry of the 1940s and the highway industry of the 1950s, had given to Poletown, and now government was taking away.

Still, Poletown endured, through the freeways, the ethnic tensions of Detroit, the blight, and the aging of the Polish population as the children of Poletown left for the suburbs. It was certainly not a fashionable address or a mecca for hip young Detroiters, but it was a neighborhood. As David R.E. Aladjem wrote in the *Ecology Law Quarterly*, Poletown was "a rare commodity in an urban environment: a stable, integrated area that in many ways harkened back to the close-knit ethnic communities that characterized Detroit's past."[7] A 1980 University of Michigan study opined that "this area may be one of the most continuously racially integrated areas in Michigan."[8] But with urban renewal and freeway construction and public housing, Detroit had spent a good deal of time, energy, and money knocking down that past. Poletown was next on the wrecking list.

In 1979, Chrysler, which since 1928 had owned Dodge Main, decided to close the plant. Though its workforce of three thousand was far smaller than it had been in the booming years of midcentury, the announcement was still a blow. Chrysler, coincidentally, would soon be the recipient of one of the most famous bailouts in US history, the Chrysler Corporation Loan Guarantee Act of 1979, which put American taxpayers on the hook for $1.5 billion.[9] General Motors chairman Thomas Murphy called the bailout for his company's rival "a basic challenge to the philosophy of America." This from a man who a year and change later would be an architect and beneficiary of Poletown! Irony and self-awareness were not, apparently, Chairman Murphy's strong points.[10]

(This was hardly the first instance of Detroit's titans feasting on corporate welfare. In 1974, the Michigan legislature enacted the Plant Rehabilitation and Industrial Development Districts Act, which permitted industrial development districts, created by municipalities, to grant property-tax exemptions for up to a dozen years to plants that promise to "create employment, retain employment, prevent a loss of employment, or produce energy in the community." As Mark Taylor notes in the *Texas Law Review*, the act was passed in response to Chrysler's claim that it required such assistance to save its Mack stamping plant in Detroit, but other large corporations rushed in to take advantage. For instance, between 1975 and 1990, "General Motors received tax abatements of more than $1.3 billion" on its Ypsilanti plants.[11])

No one disputes that Detroit was in a bad way. Unemployment hovered around 18 percent (and over 14 percent in the state of Michigan), and unemployment among African Americans in Detroit ran to 30 percent. Chrysler was being fed by the lifeline of federal loans, and the other major automobile manufacturers (Ford, American Motors, and General Motors) were bleeding red ink.

In 1980, General Motors announced that by 1983 it would be closing its Cadillac and Fisher Body plants in Detroit. Six thousand jobs would be lost in the plants alone; thousands more in dependent or supporting fields (such as sales) would vanish as well. This was part of a comprehensive retooling plan for GM involving the renovation and construction of plants across the Michigan industrial trail, from Flint to Warren.

The automotive Goliath proposed a deal, however. GM would build a new plant in Detroit if four criteria could be met. They were: a site of 450–500 acres; a rectangular shape of 3/4 mile by one mile; and access to both the freeways and a long-haul rail line. Moreover, General Motors demanded title to the property by May 1, 1981. That wasn't all. GM also demanded that Detroit make the land shovel ready—that is, cleared of all signs of previous human existence—and available for purchase by General Motors at a bargain-basement price. And while we're at it, suggested the auto giant, how about a tax abatement as well?

The city came up with nine possible sites, though only one fit GM's bill: the Poletown site, which comprised 465.5 acres in Detroit and bordering Hamtramck, including the land on which Dodge Main had stood. (About a third of the site was in Hamtramck, though it was the residents of Detroit who were to be displaced, as the Hamtramck segment had long been given over to Dodge Main and a sea of parking spaces.) To execute the deal, the Central Industrial Park (CIP) was created by the state legislature under the Economic Development Corporations Act of 1974. (That act provided for the creation of the so-named corporations, which were given the power to acquire property "by gift or purchase"— not by eminent domain, a power reserved to the municipalities—and to issue revenue bonds and lease or sell projects.) The actual plant would occupy only about 70 acres; the other 395.5 acres would be devoted to parking lots, landscaping, and rail yards and tracks.[12]

It would cost the city $200 million to assemble and clear the site. GM then bought it for $8 million. Even the skinflints of legend would call that a bargain. The breakdown of that $200 million was $62 million for land acquisition, $25 million for relocation, $35 million for demolition, $23.5 million for roads, $12 million for rail, $38.7 million for other site preparation, and $3.5 million for professional services.[13] GM explained that it was "much less costly to build a new plant than to try to retrofit an old plant."[14] The new plant, which would be more energy efficient, was necessary in part due to federal hydrocarbon emission control standards, which the old plant designs made very difficult and expensive to meet.

The entire project was estimated to cost GM $500 million. The chairman of General Motors, Thomas Murphy, explained to Detroit Mayor Coleman Young and Hamtramck Economic Development Corporation chairman Howard Woods in a letter of October 8, 1980, that "I firmly believe the prospect of retaining some 6,000 jobs, and the attendant revitalization of these communities is a tremendous challenge. But it is also an opportunity and a responsibility which none of us can ignore."[15]

This sounded awfully noble and high-minded of Mr. Murphy. He was willing to take on the "responsibility" of revitalizing "these communities," which presumably included Poletown. Just how one revitalizes something by knocking it down is a mystery, though GM, he was sure, was up to the job. And inveigling 465 acres of cleared city land out of that city, and its residents, was indeed a "tremendous challenge." But General Motors would prove to be up to that one, too.

The CIP, a bloodless acronym for the about-to-be-vanquished section of Poletown, began to cut its bloody swath across the neighborhood. The project was officially approved by the Detroit City Council on Halloween 1980, with only one dissenting vote, that of Kenneth Cockrel, an African American leftist who later gave this sage advice to the people of Poletown: "Don't rely on elected politicians. Don't count on us. All we want is to get re-elected and keep driving our free cars."[16]

The eight supporters of the resolution were evenly split between whites and blacks: the dispossession of Poletown had biracial political support. In later years, Detroit vandals would turn Halloween Eve into "Devil's Night," an evening of arson and conflagration, but the City Council might be said to have put its own stamp on Devil's Night when it condemned Poletown on Halloween 1980.

The Council, in its resolution, stated that "said project constitutes a public purpose."[17] These were the magic words opening the Pandora's box of eminent domain. (One reason the City Council was so unresponsive to Poletown is that progressives had earlier succeeded in abolishing representation by wards and substituting the "at-large" system, whereby all members of the council are elected on a citywide basis. Thus there was no one to look out for the interests of specific neighborhoods and localities.)

On November 3, 1980, Mayor Coleman Young signed the resolution. The battle of Poletown was on. The city's job: "the most massive and rapid relocation of citizens for a private development project in US history."[18] Mayor Coleman Young, as Ralph Nader reminds us, was a "former socialist and civil rights advocate."[19] Several historians of American communism contend that Young, who served twenty years as mayor (1974–94), had his political birth in the Communist Party USA.[20] Be that as it may, what is not in dispute is that Young presided over the economic dissolution of Detroit, though some of that was due to factors beyond his control, such as the shrinking of the US auto industry.

Young's ally, Congressman George Crockett, also had ties to the Communist Party USA, yet he was just as deep into GM's pocket as was Mayor Young. Representative Crockett told Poletowner Bernice Kaczynski, "I believe it is vital to the future economic condition of our city that projects such as the GM plant be encouraged. The shrinking tax base, increasing unemployment, and reduction of federal support for Detroit have jeopardized our economy. We must act for the economic survival of the entire Detroit community."[21]

A Chamber of Commerce shill couldn't have said it better than this putative leftist. Crockett was in the pocket of General Motors, and as for Mayor Young, he was acting like a "petty dictator," Ralph Nader charged.[22]

Although Mayor Young had a socialist, perhaps even communist, past, he was, in the Poletown dispute, acting in the interests, as Ralph Nader said, of corporate socialism. For throughout the process, Detroit was working hand in glove with General Motors. Indeed, as Michigan Supreme Court Justice James L. Ryan wrote in his extraordinary dissent in *Poletown Neighborhood Council vs. City of Detroit* (1981), which is examined later, "what General Motors wanted, General Motors got."[23]

There were charges that Young was happy to sacrifice Poletown because elderly Poles were not, to put it mildly, his strongest supporters. And there were countercharges, as Bukowczyk notes, that white elites considered Poletown "blighted" because it contained a significant black population. There is likely more than a grain of truth to both charges. Poletown was not a fashionable neighborhood, it had few if any yuppies or hipsters, and its ethnic blend of older Polish persons and non-affluent African Americans is not a marketer's idea of a hot demographic. What these people had, though, was a neighborhood. And what the City of Detroit and General Motors failed to understand were "the cultural values that underlay the attachment of the Polish residents to their parish and the rootedness of the Poles and others to their homes and neighborhood."[24]

To city officials and GM honchos, the residents were making a big deal out of nothing. After all, wasn't the city (backed by the US Department of Housing and Urban Development) paying the Poletowners for the land it was taking? Sure, homes were being seized and then knocked down, but it's not like the homeowners were getting nothing in return. The city even claimed that it was offering above-market prices for the homes. So what was the Poletowners' beef? Those in charge of the clearances could not figure out why the people being cleared didn't just take the money and run. After all, isn't one house pretty much the same as the next? Isn't one neighborhood more or less like all the others?

To those people of Poletown who resisted the CIP, the befuddlement of the authorities was in itself a cause for befuddlement. Didn't they understand that the people of Poletown had worked hard for these homes? In many cases, they had grown up in the homes in which they now lived, or they had raised families, even multiple generations, within those four walls. One house was *not* pretty much the same as the next. And for a city government to come along and take the house—even if it paid a sum of money for the taking—and then give it to General Motors was nothing less than theft. It was a violation of that commandment—Thou Shalt Not Covet Thy Neighbor's Goods—whose teaching was a responsibility of the churches that Detroit and GM were also in the process of razing. The whole thing just seemed *wrong*; it was an act of theft on a massive scale, and yet the institutions that these people were raised to respect—government, the automobile industry, even the church—were either masterminding the theft or condoning it. The world, it seemed, was turning upside down. From beginning to end, GM called the shots: "The corporation conceived the project, determined the cost, allocated the financial burdens, selected the site, established the mode of financing, imposed specific deadlines for clearance of the property and taking title, and even demanded 12 years of tax concessions."[25]

Mayor Young's political alliance with the Carter administration paid dividends. The federal Department of Housing and Urban Development paid upfront acquisition costs, with the city later reimbursing it for half the expenditure. HUD loaned the city $100 million, or half the total cost of the clearance, with the other $100 million coming from "outright grants from or payments by the federal and state governments that were earmarked for the Poletown project."[26] This was, for all intents and purposes, a federal government venture.

Indeed, William A. Fischel, professor of economics at Dartmouth, speculated in the *Michigan State Law Review* that "it is unlikely the city of Detroit would have undertaken the project if it was required to raise its own funds to finance it or if the money had been given to the city by the federal government to do with as it pleased."[27] In other words, *the federal government was an essential partner in the destruction of Poletown*. Without its subvention—without its *targeted* subvention—Detroit would not have razed the neighborhood for GM. It would have been fiscally incapable of doing so. And, with respect to the second part of Professor Fischel's assertion, had Detroit been given the money with no strings attached, it likely would have used (or wasted) those funds on different projects. Though Poletown was planned and executed at Detroit City Hall and in the boardroom of General Motors, it was made possible by Jimmy Carter and the Department of Housing and Urban Development.

The City of Detroit, "unmoored by financial constraints"—after all, this binge was on the feds—had no reason to carefully weigh what it was about to do.[28] No reason, that is, apart from a scrupulous respect for the rights of property owners, which was not a notable concern of Coleman Young's. Now, the theft and destruction of Poletown may have been planned in the waning days of the Carter administration, but it didn't actually occur until the early weeks of the presidency of Carter's successor, Ronald Reagan. One might think, given Reagan's rhetorical defenses of individual liberty, that his HUD would have cut off the flow of money to Detroit. But it did not. All it did, as Fischel notes, was insist that the Republican governor of Michigan, and not the Democratic mayor of Detroit, got to announce the delivery of federal funds.

The operation—the assault—the clearance—was done in blitzkrieg style. The city moved with astonishing alacrity. Goaded by GM's ultimatum and a fear that the window of opportunity would close it if didn't act fast, the city moved the CIP along at breakneck speed. This required, as Justice Ryan wrote, "sweeping away a tightly-knit residential enclave of first- and second-generation Americans, for many of whom their home was their single most valuable and cherished asset and their stable ethnic neighborhood the unchanging symbol of the security and quality of their lives."[29]

But what did such intangibles matter to a city government and a corporation united in the pursuit of 465 acres of land? After all, claimed General Motors, six thousand jobs would be created on the ruins of Poletown. Add in the preternaturally dubious multiplier effect, which permits economic development hucksters to claim several times as many spinoff jobs, and you've got a virtual rebirth of Detroit embedded in the CIP.

To achieve the CIP, GM and Detroit had to roll over 1,362 homes, about 4,200 people, 143 businesses, 16 churches, a hospital, and 1,176 buildings. (Yes, sixteen churches. Parishioners of Immaculate Conception, a Polish Roman Catholic Church, carried signs outside the General Motors headquarters reading "G.M. Desecrates Churches."[30] One would think that desecrating, desanctifying, even tearing down churches would gnaw at the conscience of most men, but those guiding GM were made of sterner, or maybe that should be sinister, stuff.) This was a vast displacement of people of a magnitude more commonly found in countries with totalitarian governments. Demographically, those displaced were fairly evenly split (about 40 percent each) between black and Polish, with another 5 to 10 percent Albanian, and the remainder a smattering of Yemeni, Ukrainians, Filipinos, and southern whites.

The announcement of the creation of the Central Industrial Park "left the area's residents numbed," writes John J. Bukowczyk.[31] It seemed as if the entire world—certainly the entire city, and even the institutions on which the people of Poletown had depended—was against them. Their property, they were told, was no longer theirs. It was being condemned. It would soon to belong to GM. They could accept the city's offer of what the city claimed were above-market prices for their homes and property, or they could refuse, and be sure, they were told, to lose later down the line.

Appraisers went door to door. The only question left, it seemed, was how much each homeowner would get for his property. So many homes were being condemned that the required condemnation hearings were held in Cobo Hall, the giant convention center at which the Detroit Pistons of the NBA had played. (The hall was named after former Mayor Albert E. Cobo, who had presided over the orgy of freeway building and consequent displacement of Detroiters in the 1950s, so this was a symbolically apt place in which to hold the hearings.)

Justice James L. Ryan spoke of "the overwhelming psychological pressure which was brought to bear upon property owners," especially the elderly and retired Poles of the neighborhood.[32] Dodge Main, for so many decades a symbol of the district's industrial history, was being demolished by late 1980. Other buildings and properties were falling to the wrecker's ball. The mass media, the labor unions, the politicians, and the business community seemed solidly behind the project, which was hailed as the savior of Detroit.

By March 1981, "eighty percent of the residents of the C.I.P. site had been persuaded, or subtly pressured, to accept the City's offer."[33] Those who hadn't, as Bukowczyk notes, were threatened with "quick take," an accelerated form of eminent domain in which the city can condemn and take a property in weeks, even before compensation for the taking has been determined. The quick-take law had been hurried through the Michigan legislature weeks before GM and the city unveiled the Poletown project. An expeditious transfer of property from private owner to corporate beneficiary of the government was the intention.

Not everyone caved in and took the money. Residents, particularly those with strong ties to the neighborhood, protested at public meetings held at local schools and churches. Jeanie Wylie, who chronicled the Poletown saga firsthand in her affecting *Poletown: Community Betrayed*, quotes sixty-eight-year-old John Saber, who challenged city council members who had shown up at a meeting at a local school:

> I been living in this neighborhood for over forty-six years, and I don't intend to move because you con artists are trying to pull a rip off.

> Nobody can tell me up to eighty percent of the value of my house, how much that house is worth. To me it is a million dollars. My house has a brand new bathtub, and I don't intend to move to a clunker, God-damned cockroach-infested house that you pick out. I want to live on Kanter and I love every rotten board in that house.[34]

The Detroit establishment, when it wasn't helping GM and Coleman Young steal Poletown from its property owners and residents, wouldn't give Poletown the time of day. The United Auto Workers was solidly behind the company. Many citizen activists, "muzzled by the grants machine that Washington provided city governments, looked the other way," says Ralph Nader. The federal government was solidly lined up behind the clearance. The news media, while sometimes presenting heart-rending images of older people sobbing at the prospect of losing their homes, generally took the position that, well, this is the price of progress, and the needs of the many outweigh the rights of the few, and although it's only natural to feel compassion for those poor souls who are being evicted from the only neighborhood they have ever known, hey, that's the price you pay for progress. What's good for General Motors is good for Detroit, and anything that hampers or hinders General Motors is bad for the Motor City.

The Catholic Church, the faith of most of the old-time Poletown residents, refused to defend its parishioners. Michigan's US senators, Democrats Carl Levin and Don Riegle, and the Democrat who "represented" Poletown in the US House of Representatives, "refused even to meet with [Poletowners], much less represent their pleas for help in any way."[35] Governor William Milliken, a Republican, was all for this instance of Big Government with a vengeance. Senator Riegle went so far as to say that opposition from Poletowners to the project "borders on the irresponsible."[36]

The city's economic, political, and journalistic establishment was ecstatic and cheered on the GM project with all the vigor of amphetamine-amped high-school cheerleaders. Six thousand jobs! A new investment in the ailing city of Detroit! Who cared about the four thousand–plus residents who would have move? After all, as the communists were once fond of saying, you can't make an omelet without breaking a few eggs.

It was all happening so fast.

The courts, too, seemed in league with GM and the city establishment. A lawsuit filed by the Poletown Neighborhood Council was heard by the circuit court from November 17 to December 2, 1980, and dismissed on December 9. The case was argued before the Michigan Supreme Court (as residents of Poletown filled the courtroom) on March 3, 1981, and the opinions were filed on March 15. Justice Ryan complained that "the crushing burden of litigation which this Court must address daily did not afford adequate time for sufficient consideration of the complex constitutional issues involved" in the case.[37] Submission, consideration, and decision all happened within the span of just twelve days—not even two weeks.

The skids were greased.

The plaintiffs in *Poletown Neighborhood Council v. City of Detroit* (Mich. 1981) were the aforementioned council and ten residents of Poletown. The nub of the case was this: Did the city of Detroit, in condemning the properties in Poletown via eminent domain, violate the Michigan constitution, which prohibits the taking of private property for private use? The state constitution and precedent had firmly established the impermissibility of taking private property for private use. In the Michigan case of *Berrien Springs Water-Power Co. v. Berrien Circuit Judge* (1903), the Michigan Supreme Court had ruled that "Land cannot be taken, under the exercise of the power of eminent domain, unless, after it is taken, it will be devoted to the use of the public, independent of the will of the corporation taking it."[38] (The sole exceptions were the usual ones: railroads, canals, and highways.) The Wolverine State's Constitution does permit the taking of property, with just compensation, for public use. And that, the city asserted, is just what it had done in Poletown.

The 5–2 majority, in its decision, gives away the game in its opening sentence. It asks if a municipality, using the power of eminent domain under Michigan's Economic Development Corporation Act, may "condemn private property for transfer to a private corporation to build a plant to promote industry and commerce, thereby adding jobs and taxes to the economic base of the municipality and state?"

Intercalating the phrase that begins "thereby adding jobs and taxes" suggests strongly that the writer is about to defend the depredation in question. After all, who can possibly *oppose* jobs and taxes? "There is no dispute about the law," declares the court's majority. "All agree that condemnation for a public use or purpose is permitted. All agree that condemnation for a private use or purpose is forbidden." The challenge, then, is to somehow, by an act of judicial legerdemain, make it appear that General Motors is *not* a private interest with a private purpose.

The *Poletown* plaintiffs claim that "General Motors is the primary beneficiary of the condemnation," a claim that would seem beyond dispute—indeed, it would seem incontrovertible.

But the five learned justices of the majority controvert it. They cite testimony by city officials of Detroit's economic straits. City representatives, they say, "presented substantial evidence of the severe economic conditions facing the residents of the city and state, the need for new industrial development to revitalize local industries, the economic boost the proposed project would provide, and the lack of other adequate available sites to implement the project."

Nothing in the language above can possibly annul the fact that General Motors is the primary beneficiary of the condemnation. Yet the justices annul this fact just the same. Condemning private property in Poletown and transferring this property to General Motors is, according to the Michigan Supreme Court, not primarily an act to benefit General Motors. Rather, it is "primarily to accomplish the essential public purposes of alleviating unemployment and revitalizing the economic base of the community." The Court adds: "The benefit to a private interest is merely incidental."

*Merely incidental*! This, all must concede, is a hell of an incident. A total of 1,362 homes and 143 businesses are being taken from their private owners and given to General Motors by the governmental authorities. And the benefit to GM is *merely incidental*?

"We hold this project is warranted on the basis that its significance for the people of Detroit and the state has been demonstrated," concluded the Court.[39] Seizing private property from more than a thousand owners and handing it over to a corporation that was promising to create 6,000 jobs (which it did not do, by the way) satisfied the definition of public use, ruled the Michigan Supreme Court. The decision staggered many observers. It was an unusually brutal and raw ratification of the tyranny of the well connected; of corporate welfare in its most naked form. The powerful, said the Michigan Court, could take property from the powerless, and there was nothing the latter could do about it. Ralph Nader called the Michigan Supreme Court's ruling "perhaps the most extreme judicial sanction behind corporate power against individual property rights" in the nation's history.[40]

Two justices dissented from *Poletown*: Justice John Warner Fitzgerald and Justice James L. Ryan. Their dissents were spirited, strongly worded, and serve as classic protests against eminent-domain-based corporate welfare. Justice Fitzgerald's dissent, to which Justice Ryan concurred, surveys previous instances in which the court ruled on attempts to transfer private property to private interests. "In each case," he writes, "the proposed taking was held impermissible." In defense of the Poletown taking, the city had adverted to slum clearance cases—of the notorious urban renewal program—in which property was condemned and then resold. But the resale, as the Michigan court had emphasized in a 1951 case, was "incidental and ancillary" to the purpose of slum clearance. The receipt by General Motors of the takings in Poletown was anything but incidental. It was the primary purpose of this act of eminent domain.

Thus, avers Justice Fitzgerald, "Our approval of the use of eminent domain power in this case takes this state into a new realm of takings of private property; there is simply no precedent for this decision in previous Michigan cases."

Justice Fitzgerald's conclusion roundly condemned the majority ruling. "The decision that the prospect of increased employment, tax revenue, and general economic stimulation makes a taking of private property for transfer to another private party sufficiently 'public' to authorize the use of the power of eminent domain means that there is virtually no limit to the use of condemnation to aid private businesses."

The ruling was a carte blanche to government agencies that would appropriate the property of the less powerful and give it to the more powerful, in particular major corporations. After all, said Justice Fitzgerald, "Any business enterprise produces benefits to society at large." If all that is needed is for the government to demonstrate that a piece of private property might generate more wealth, or "public benefits," if it happened to be in other hands, then "no homeowner's, merchant's or manufacturer's property, however productive or valuable to its owner, is immune from condemnation for the benefit of other private interests that will put it to a 'higher' use."[41] The ruling meant that it was open season on private property in Michigan.

Justice Ryan's lengthy dissent was, if anything, even more powerful. It was one of those relatively rare pieces of judicial writing that was positively suffused with outrage. "This is an extraordinary case," he begins. "The reverberating clang of its economic, sociological, political, and jurisprudential impact is likely to be heard and felt for generations. [This prophecy was not entirely accurate, as shown below.] By its decision, the Court has altered the law of eminent domain in this state in a most significant way and, in my view, seriously jeopardized the security of all private property ownership."

The Michigan Supreme Court had sanctioned "municipal condemnation of private property for private use." In so doing, it had demonstrated, in a shocking way, "how easily government, in all its branches, caught up in the frenzy of perceived economic crisis, can disregard the rights of the few in allegiance to the always disastrous philosophy that the end justifies the means."

The case could be boiled down to one fundamental issue: "the right of government to expropriate property from those who do not wish to sell for the use and benefit of a strictly private corporation." After a lengthy and often impassioned recital of precedent and the details of Poletown, Justice Ryan declared, "There may never be a clearer case than this of condemning land for a private corporation. . . . I can discern no principled ground on which [the majority's] decision can be reconciled with the body of law interpreting the state taking clause."

This was unusually condemnatory language. But there was more. Justice Ryan assessed the human cost of this gigantic exercise in corporate welfare. The damage, he said, was not measurable in mere dollars, nor even in lost liberties, though it was considerable on both scores, and entailed "a significant diminution of constitutional rights." There were intangible losses, too, he said: the "severance of personal attachments to one's domicile and neighborhood and the destruction of an organic community of a most unique and irreplaceable character."

Given that eminent domain is reserved for sovereign powers, and that in this case it was exercised on behalf of a private corporation, "one is left to wonder who the sovereign is." Justice Ryan's peroration was powerful and worth quoting at some length:

> What has been done in this case can be explained by the overwhelming sense of inevitability that has attended this litigation from the beginning; a sense attributable to the combination and coincidence of the interests of a desperate city administration and a giant corporation willing and able to take advantage of the opportunity that presented itself. The justification for it, like the inevitability of it, has been made to seem more acceptable by the "team spirit" chorus of approval of the project which has been supplied by the voices of labor, business, industry, government, finance and even the news media. Virtually the only discordant sounds of dissent have come from the minuscule minority of citizens most profoundly affected by this case, the Poletown residents whose neighborhood has been destroyed.
>
> With this case the Court has subordinated a constitutional right to private corporate interests. As demolition of existing structures on the future plant site goes forward, the best that can be hoped for,

jurisprudentially, is that the precedental value of this case will be lost in the accumulating rubble.[42]

*That's* telling them.

Justice Ryan's hope that the opinion of his five eminent colleagues should be buried in the rubble would, in a way, come true—though not nearly in time to save the people of Poletown. Ryan, by the way, was a Republican who was nominated to the state Supreme Court by Republican Governor William Milliken. In 1985, President Reagan appointed him to the US Court of Appeals for the Sixth Circuit.

* * *

But even while it was losing in the courts, Poletown was fighting in the court of public opinion. The Poletown Neighborhood Council, whose name graces the notorious opinion of the Michigan Supreme Court, began life as the Roman Catholic organization known as the Poletown Inter-Parish Council. It met in the basement of Immaculate Conception Roman Catholic Church—ground zero of the battle of Poletown. Four hundred angry Poletowners attended its first meeting.

Even after the organization was no longer Catholic in name, it retained a distinctly Catholic flavor. Immaculate Conception, designed by architect Gustav Mueller in the Romanesque Revival style, took seven years to build (1928–1935) and was much praised for its beauty. Its raising was the work of the largely working-class people of Poletown, whose donations made possible its construction. The *Historic American Buildings Survey* described it as of "architectural significance. It displays an austere Romanesque Revival exterior and an elaborate interior, reflecting the traditions of Polish church architecture. The building is of historic significance for its over fifty years of service to a largely Polish-American parish."[43]

Yet Immaculate Conception, whatever its aesthetic qualities and religious purpose, and however much it meant to its parishioners and the life of the community, was slated for demolition. To add insult to injury, as Jeanie Wylie writes, "The land on which the Immaculate Conception Church stood was designated for shrubbery."[44] Shrubbery!

If ever the people of Poletown had wondered just how important they were to city officials or the big shots at General Motors, the blueprint for the new plant informed them, bluntly as could be, that they meant nothing in the grand scheme of things. The spiritual center of their lives and their community, the rock on which their parish was built, could be taken by the city over the objections of parishioners and just knocked down, reduced to rubble, the cleared land then to be transferred to General Motors, which would use the land on which Immaculate Conception once sat not even for the well-paying auto assembly jobs it had promised but instead for mere . . . shrubbery.

This did not, as you might guess, sit well with the people who occupied the pews of Immaculate Conception. These people—patriotic working Americans, the kind who are often idealized, ironically, in automobile commercials—were being taught the rude lesson that they and their private property and even the church in which they had been baptized, confirmed, married, and would, they assumed, someday be given a funeral service, counted for nothing if a city government and major corporation wanted what they had. All those shiny shibboleths about life, liberty, and property meant nothing when corporate welfare was on the table.

Many of the men of Poletown had served in the US armed forces in Europe, the Pacific, Korea, and Vietnam. They had been told that they were fighting for freedom, for the American Way, and yet in the battle of Poletown they discovered that such pretty phrases did not describe what was happening to them, in their homes, at the instigation of their local government, and with the complicity, indeed the essential subsidy, of that same federal government for which they had taken up arms and fought overseas.

The women of Poletown who rose up to protest the GM deal were often devout Catholics, older women who provided the heart and soul of the protests. They were not the demographic from which protesters are usually drawn, which made them more photogenic and striking: elderly women wearing symbols of their faith and challenging a united establishment in defense of their homes.

Father Joseph Karasiewicz of Immaculate Conception R.C. Church became a leading figure in the anti-corporate welfare battle, and his church was a center of the Save Poletown movement. Father Karasiewicz, fifty-nine, son of a Ford Motor Company janitor, was a native Detroiter, a product of St. Hyacinth's Church and St. Mary's Polish Seminary. He was hardly a firebrand; by all accounts, he was a kindly, even quiet neighborhood priest. But he was outraged by what the city, General Motors, and even his archdiocese were doing to his parishioners. He spoke up—and it cost him his life.

Said Father Joe: "This is worse than the Communists in Poland. To go down to a very basic definition of stealing, it is simply taking other people's property against their will, and this was taken away from

them, the people, against their will."[45] Father Karasiewicz and Thomas
Olechowksi, the president of the Poletown Neighborhood Council,
reacted to the Michigan Supreme Court's ruling with indignation:
"The use of eminent domain by Multi-National, private, Corporate
powers, turns democracy into a sham and working people's property
deeds into meaningless papers; lends sovereign state police power to
secretive, anti-democratic, profit-centered corporations, who use the
tax structure as just another vehicle and the government as its willing tool and accomplice."[46] For good measure, the priest called the
ruling "diabolic," though even the tools of a good exorcist may not
have been up to the task of defeating Detroit and GM in the Michigan
Supreme Court.[47]

To be sure, some residents of the CIP area were more than willing
to be bought out. They took the money and moved, perhaps also hoping that they would be in line for jobs in the new plant. The average
buyout price was $13,000, with an extra $3,500 in incentives for those
who moved by a deadline. In addition, they could access up to $15,000
more if the price of their new home exceeded the buyout.

The result of this compensation, which was often above market
value, was to "undermin[e] organized resistance by the Poletown community," writes William A. Fischel. Young people, less rooted to the
neighborhood, were more likely to take the money and run than were
older residents who had deep roots in Poletown. Those who stayed
were more likely old and Polish than those who departed, which "made
resistance look like a racial issue when it was not."[48]

Ralph Nader organized a Poletown Support Team, complete with a
trio of lawyers, to lend outside assistance to the beleaguered locals. To
Nader, Poletown was a classic case of corporate welfare. He explained:
"Once upon a time in American economic history, companies established production facilities by purchasing a parcel of land and building
a factory with their own money. Times have changed for corporations
who used to believe in free enterprise. Now, even the wealthiest multinational corporations such as General Motors prepare a prospectus
for building a plant and then dangle it before various municipalities and
states to ascertain how large a subsidy the taxpayers will be compelled
to provide if they want the plant in their area."[49]

Nader was berated by Mayor Young as a carpetbagger, an outsider
interfering in the affairs of Detroit, a fanatical hater of General Motors.
Young welcomed the Michigan Supreme Court's decision—he had
never been mistaken for an ardent fan of private property anyway—and

exclaimed, "We have to be able to find some way of rearranging our people in order to be able to attract and accommodate new plants."[50]

This was a revealing locution. "Rearranging our people" is the kind of thing a totalitarian might say: a Soviet commissar, perhaps, or a North Korean bureaucrat for whom people are means to an end who can be rearranged with as little concern as one might rearrange chairs on a patio. If Michigan's congressional delegation scorned Poletown and chose GM, a handful of national political figures tried to speak up for its residents. Senator William Proxmire, the Wisconsin Democrat who had taken on corporate welfare for years, most notably the SST, questioned the sense of subsidizing Cadillacs when smaller and more fuel-efficient cars seemed to be the wave of the future.

Although Nader and his activists had reputations as people of the "Left," precious few other liberal or leftist groups stood in solidarity with the people of Poletown. In part this was because the issue at hand—property rights—is not one that has traditionally been high on the agenda of the institutional left. Populists such as Nader might stand with embattled small-property holders, but ideologues of the Left have tended toward a suspicion of small-property owners, whom they see as a reactionary force. Nor did many activists on the "Right" rally to defend Poletown. In part this may have been due to the identity of the "villain": General Motors, a venerable American company. Conservatives more concerned about appearances than principles may not have wanted to sharply criticize a major US corporation. After all, isn't criticism of corporations more typically an act of the Left?

To be fair, a handful of national observers, such as conservative columnist William Safire of the *New York Times*, liberal columnist Colman McCarthy of the *Washington Post*, and muckraking syndicated reporter Jack Anderson, did write pieces sympathetic to Poletown or condemning of GM and Detroit. And Richard Wilcke, president of the Council for a Competitive Economy, a DC-based free-market organization, visited Detroit to give libertarian support to the people of Poletown. He called the actions of Detroit and GM a

> shameful . . . violation of property rights and repudiation of free enterprise. Eminent domain, government subsidies and loan guarantees do not constitute voluntary exchange, but its very opposite. Our organization is unalterably opposed to their use in the procurement of plant sites, or for any other purpose, "public" or private. . . . The right to own homes or a business should not be subordinated to the political or economic gain of others. This is not an issue of business

versus the people, but rather of liberty versus political power. We condemn anyone who aspires to use that power for any purpose. . . . As this case clearly and dramatically demonstrates, if property rights are not respected, there can be no rights at all.[51]

There is another reason for the relative paucity of outsiders of who came to the defense of Poletown, and that is ethnic. Mayor Young was black; and while Poletown was a racially integrated neighborhood—indeed, the black population may have slightly exceeded that of the Polish-American population—many liberals and probably some conservatives did not want to publicly take the side of Poletown against Young. Ronald Reosti, the labor lawyer who served as counsel for the Poletown Neighborhood Council in its lawsuit against the City of Detroit, complained, with exasperation, that many of his fellow left-wing Detroit lawyers took him to task for "facilitating racism," as Wylie quotes him, by siding with the people of Poletown against Mayor Young.[52]

Perhaps the greatest disappointment to Poletown's Poles was the acquiescent posture of the Catholic Church. The church never came out and said "Blessed Be the CIP," but Cardinal John F. Dearden, whose chums at the Bloomfield Country Club included GM honcho Thomas Murphy, complied with the city's request that Immaculate Conception and St. John the Evangelist be sold and razed, with their congregations then subjoined to other parishes. The Archdiocese won the goodwill of city leaders and GM, but the bitter enmity of those Catholics (and others) who were deemed expendable by the powers that be. The Archdiocese received a bit more than the biblical mess of pottage for the churches: the city bought the right to reduce St. John's to rubble for $1.09 million, while Immaculate Conception went for $1.3 million.

The faithful were incensed by this display of faithlessness. Hard-working Catholics had built these churches with sweat and blood and weekly contributions, and now the Archdiocese was pocketing millions by handing them over to the city to be destroyed. As Jeanie Wylie wryly notes in *Poletown: Community Betrayed*, the same week that Father Joe was saying the final mass at Immaculate Conception, Cardinal Dearden was blessing a Gucci store at a tony suburban mall. You had to say this for the Cardinal: he was oblivious to irony and unrestrained by shame or good taste.[53]

Perhaps the most outrageous—dare we say un-Christian?—remark uttered by a church potentate came from Auxiliary Bishop Thomas Gumbleton, who was to achieve a certain notoriety soon thereafter as a crusader for liberal causes. Gumbleton had been made a bishop in 1968 at the age of thirty-eight, thereby becoming the youngest

American priest to have attained such a rank. Thirty-eight years later, in 2006, Gumbleton would be retired by the pope. Speculation was that Gumbleton had strayed too far afield from Catholic teachings.[54] Be that as it may, in 1980, as members of his flock were fighting to save their homes and churches, Auxiliary Bishop Gumbleton defended not the poor and the powerless, the meek and the voiceless, but the power structure and two of its main components: the city government and General Motors. Bishop Gumbleton said: "The overall good of the city is achieved by cutting away a certain part. When you're trying to make something grow, you prune."[55]

That is a chilling remark for anyone to make, let alone a putative man of God. He had likened the people of Poletown to dead branches that one might cut away so that the vigorous parts of a plant or tree might flourish. This is the language one associates with history's monsters. And to magnify the insult, Gumbleton had the nerve, in December 1980, as the wrecking ball was starting to swing in Poletown, and its elderly residents were looking to their church for sustenance and support, to cofound an organization called the Michigan Coalition for Human Rights. The lofty goal of this organization, according to another cofounder, was to challenge those who "neglected unemployment, sexism, racism, militarism, and economic justice." It engaged in such high-stakes battles as persuading local restaurants and groceries not to sell South African lobsters.[56] But while the Michigan Coalition for Human Rights occupied itself with symbolic acts protesting injustices on the other side of the world, it had nothing whatsoever to say about what was happening in an unfashionable neighborhood in Michigan's largest city. These people, it seems, were dead tree branches, and we all know that they must be pruned so that the rest of the tree can grow. Immaculate Conception church just was not as sexy an issue as South African lobsters.

Immaculate Conception did not go down without a fight. The final mass was held, appropriately for a church so named, on Mother's Day, May 10, 1981. More than 1,500 worshippers packed Immaculate Conception. Father Joe Karasiewicz said the final mass (as well as an earlier one that Sunday); he sermonized that what was happening to his church was sinful. Father Joe, parishioners, and supporters began a vigil after that last mass. They would not abandon the church voluntarily. Under the press of harsh publicity, GM now offered to move the church to another site. The corporation was not completely deaf to community outrage. The Archdiocese, to the surprise of the people of Immaculate Conception, said no. Father Joe was given a move-out date of June 17. Father Karasiewicz offered GM chairman Roger Smith a personal tour of Immaculate Conception. Chairman Smith did not take him up on the offer.

Father Joe, beloved to the end by his congregation, obeyed the hierarchy and left on that day, but he was mindful that a number of holdouts, some church members and some sympathizers, intended to stay. Their numbers would vary over the next month, as they staged what turned into a twenty-nine-day sit-in. Utilities were shut off, statues removed from the church, and on July 14, 1981, the Special Weapons Attack Team (SWAT) descended on Immaculate Conception in the predawn hours. Sympathetic cops had alerted those inside of the impending raid. The protesters inside the church had bolted the doors of Immaculate Conception closed; the SWAT Team pried them open with the help of a tow truck. Sixty policemen poured in to remove the twenty or so protesters, among them a half-dozen "little old Polish ladies" who prayed the Hail Mary.[57] A dozen of those who had kept vigil at Immaculate Conception were arrested by police officers who were obviously uncomfortable with the assignment. Those arrested were later released, but the task had been accomplished: Immaculate Conception was empty. The church was razed, as hundreds of Poletowners, including Father Joe, watched in horror and in tears. Poletown was officially dead. (The last holdout, the neighborhood eccentric John Saber, had fortified his home and was defending it with a .22 caliber rifle. He was evicted March 22, 1982.)

Father Karasiewicz died of a heart attack on December 14, 1981. After the demolition of Immaculate Conception he had been without a church. The archdiocese, it seemed, was punishing him. His heart was, quite literally, broken.

The human toll of Poletown was tragic. A year after Poletown was stolen, razed, and presented to GM on a silver platter, former residents spoke of the cost to them. Ann Locklear had "lost my faith in the Church, the city and General Motors"—the Holy Trinity of the Motor City. Walter Jakubowski, who lived with his wife Josephine for forty-six years on Poletown's Kanter Street, and was one of the plaintiffs in *Poletown Neighborhood Council v. City of Detroit*, said that the event had "destroyed our roots, our homes, everything."[58] Josephine had earlier vowed, "This is America, not Russia. We're not going to let you do this. We're going to fight like hell."[59] But fighting City Hall is tough enough; when you throw in General Motors, the entire business and commercial establishment of Detroit, and the court system of Michigan, people like the Jakubowskis didn't stand a chance.

Louise Crosby told the story of her husband, George, after their forced removal: "He kept saying, 'I want to go home, I want to go home.'" He tried to go home, but wound up wandering in a snowstorm. He never made it back to Poletown, ending up in a nursing home instead.[60]

There is a bittersweet coda to *Poletown*. The decision was widely criticized even at the time as a case of "majoritarian tyranny" run wild.[61] Libertarians and conservatives viewed it as a sad instance of Big Government run wild; some liberals and leftists saw it as evidence that corporations were really running things. This is not to say that the Michigan Supreme Court didn't have its defenders. For instance, Thomas Ross, associate professor of law at the University of Vermont Law School, argued in the *George Washington Law Review* that Justice Ryan's concerns about how the decision heralded an open season on private property were "not valid" and that the "public use" which justified eminent domain had not so much expanded as simply evolved, from the nineteenth-century accommodations for roads and canals to twentieth-century uses such as urban renewal.[62] In either case, property had been seized from private owners and transferred to other private interests in order to achieve a "societally desired result."[63] (The potential for mischief concealed within these three words is enormous.)

*Poletown*'s immediate influence was pernicious and not limited to Michigan. As Timothy Sandefur noted in the *Harvard Journal of Law & Public Policy*, *Poletown* instantly "became the most well-known instance of economic redevelopment eminent domain" [a distinction it was to turn over to the 2005 *Kelo v. New London* case in Connecticut, in which the US Supreme Court upheld that city's taking of homes for a development project benefitting Pfizer] and was cited by courts in nine other states.[64] Within Michigan, *Poletown* was used to justify the city of Center Line's condemnation of apartments and shops for the benefit of a Toyota dealer. (There's something about the automobile industry that brings out the tyrant in Michigan politicians.) But as Sandefur explains, in 1987 the state's Court of Appeals blocked Center Line from condemning the property.[65] The state's lower courts sniped at *Poletown* and the precedent it set. Like the properties it had condemned, *Poletown*'s days were numbered.

The case that overturned *Poletown* was *County of Wayne v. Hathcock* (2004). Using federal funds (a $21 million grant from the Federal Aviation Administration), Wayne County determined to promote commercial development in the area surrounding Detroit's Metropolitan Airport. The plan was to build a business and technology park consisting of a mall, a motel, a conference center, and other facilities. The justification, or delusion, depending on one's point of view, was that the so-called Pinnacle Park would be an economic boon to the area. The roseate projection was that thirty thousand jobs would be created. (Industrial-sized grains of salt had to be taken with that prediction.)

The county bought 1,000 acres from owners of the desired land, but nineteen owners whose property totaled about 1,300 acres refused to sell. In a pre-*Poletown* world, this might have presented the County with two options: 1) increase its offers to the nineteen holdouts; or 2) draw up a new plan that did not include those 1,300 acres. But the Michigan Supreme Court, in *Poletown*, had engendered a third option: Just take the land, and that is exactly what Wayne County did.

A trial court and the Michigan Court of Appeals found that this commercial development constituted a public use. However, two of the three appellate judges explained, in the Supreme Court's formulation, that although precedent required them to rule as they did, they believed that *Poletown* "was poorly reasoned, wrongly decided, and ripe for reversal by this Court."[66] "This Court," it appeared, agreed.

So more than two decades after *Poletown*, the Michigan Supreme Court revisited the case. Amicus briefs were filed by a range of organizations and persons ranging from libertarian-conservative groups such as the Institute for Justice and the Mackinac Center for Public Policy of Michigan to Ralph Nader and the American Civil Liberties Fund of Michigan.

This time, the Michigan Supreme Court ruled unanimously. With what appeared as a gigantic judicial sigh of relief, the Court overturned the lower courts' rulings in *Hathcock* and in the process consigned *Poletown Neighborhood Council v. Detroit* to the precedental dump heap.

Wayne County, said the Court, "intends to transfer the condemned properties to private parties in a manner wholly inconsistent with the common understanding of 'public use' at the time our Constitution was ratified."[67] Throughout the eighty-five-page decision, the justices commended the hearty dissent from *Poletown* of Justice Ryan. They noted that the *Poletown* decision was the only instance in Michigan jurisprudence that lent support to the plaintiff's position in *Hathcock*. By every other case and precedent and measure, seizing land from private owners to transfer to the developers of a business park was a violation of the Michigan Constitution. "The majority opinion in *Poletown*," said the Court, "is most notable for its radical and unabashed departure from the entirety of this Court's pre-1963 eminent domain jurisprudence."[68]

The *Hathcock* Court saw *Poletown* as a license for almost unmitigated governmental tyranny:

> Every business, every productive unit in society, does . . . contribute in some way to the commonweal. To justify the exercise of eminent domain solely on the basis of the fact that the use of that property by a private entity seeking its own profit might contribute to the economy's health is to render impotent our constitutional limitations on the government's power of eminent domain. *Poletown's* "economic benefit" rationale would validate practically *any* exercise of the power of eminent domain on behalf of a private entity. After all, if one's ownership of private property is forever subject to the government's determination that another private party would put one's land to better use, then the ownership of real property is perpetually threatened by the expansion plans of any large discount retailer, "megastore," or the like.[69]

Justice Ryan's hope that "the precedental value of this case will be lost in the accumulating rubble" came to fruition—too late to save Poletown, it is true, but perhaps in time to save other Poletowns from the juggernaut of corporate welfare. So *Poletown*, like Poletown, died. The plant that took its place sputters on. The area surrounding the plant has not exactly experienced a renaissance. While the plant "is sealed off from the rest of the community by berms and fences and is accessible by gates that make it clear that the general public is not welcome," the adjacent streets do not hum with new urbanist activity.[70] There has been no spillover effect. This should not be surprising, given that the effect of the CIP was to rip the heart out of a historic neighborhood. Rejuvenation is exceptionally unlikely when the heart is gone.

Today, the Detroit-Hamtramck Assembly Plant employs only 1,600 workers, or 27 percent of the number it had promised all those years ago, when Poletown still stood as a living, if not quite vibrant or prosperous, neighborhood. It assembles Chevrolet Volt, Malibu, Impala, and the Opel Ampera automobiles.[71] And despite the gift thirty-plus years ago of a $200 million cleared site for just $8 million, General Motors is still rattling the tin cup. In September 2013, GM requested from the City of Detroit a $1.8 billion tax abatement over fifteen years for construction of a logistics center at the Detroit-Hamtramck site.

The company predicted that two hundred jobs would be created at the new center. Once on the gravy train, it's devilishly hard to jump off.

And how can Detroit, once having sacrificed not only mere dollars but even the houses and lives of its residents, ever again say no? Well, it couldn't. The city council approved the tax break on a 5–1 vote. The council estimated the abatement at $600 million over twelve years, which would seem less generous than the deal General Motors had sought, though a GM spokesman explained that the disparity was the result of different calculations of the tax burden GM would face over the period in question.[72]

* * *

The automobile industry, whose glamour and sway convinced states, especially those in the South, to put together lucrative corporate welfare deals to lure manufacturers throughout the 1980s and '90s, continued to exert an almost hypnotic influence over desperate economic development functionaries into the new millennium. So powerful was its lure that as the new century dawned, the State of Mississippi condemned twenty-three acres in an African American neighborhood in Canton, Mississippi, even though Nissan, the beneficiary of the condemnation, did not need the land for its plant.

Mississippi had lured Nissan to within its borders with a $400 million-plus package that included a $17 million building, $60 million in new roads and improvements to existing roads, an $80 million job-training program, and 1,500 acres of land that the state would either purchase or take by eminent domain from its rightful owners and transfer to Nissan.

Two deep-rooted African American families, the Archies and the Bouldins, spurned the state's offer of a buyout and brought suit when the state attempted to take their land via eminent domain. The Archies owned twenty-three acres of land that were not essential to the project. But as James C. Burns Jr., executive director of the Mississippi Development Authority, told the *New York Times*, "It's not that Nissan is going to leave if we don't get that land. What's important is the message that would send to other companies if we are unable to do what we said we would do. If you make a promise to a company like Nissan, you have to be able to follow through."[73] Even at the expense of Mississippians.

(Timothy Sandefur notes that Burns's explanation is "startlingly similar" to that offered by Larry Brown, who was the principal development economist for the Poletown project.[74] Jeanie Wylie quoted Brown as saying, "We'd do it again. There's no question about it. The city didn't have a choice. . . . If we had not been able to accommodate General Motors in the city, then we would have had no credibility with any other companies in terms of being able to deliver buildable land or financing."[75])

As *New York Times* reporter David Firestone pointed out, neighboring Alabama did not use eminent domain in assembling its 1993 package for Honda. Mississippi legislators were showing, in their view, that they would go the extra mile for the corporation. For his part, Mississippi Development Authority Executive Director Burns was unconcerned about any possible abuse of eminent domain. "How can you imagine this as anything but a public good?" he asked the *New York Times*. "This project gives us an opportunity to change the destiny of this state."[76]

There is such a thing as bad publicity, however, and the state soon dropped its attempt at condemnation. The plant was built and today employs about 5,200 workers. Whether it changed the destiny of the state is another question.

The GM-Poletown case set a new standard, or nadir, in extreme instances of corporate welfare. But for all the bad publicity the company got, for all the heart-wrenching images of elderly Polish women sobbing as their homes and churches were taken from them and demolished, GM and the city won. They seized the land; they executed the gifts and subsidies and tax abatements entailed by the project; they built the new plant. From the joint governmental-corporate point of view, Poletown was a success.

Despite the fears of corporate-welfare critics, Poletown did not serve as a model for a nationwide spree of similar projects. It was, perhaps, too outrageous, too offensive to too many people, and it carried the whiff, even, of fascism—of a partnership of big government and big business combined with a contemptuous disregard for everyday citizens.

This is not, however, to say that large corporate welfare projects involving vast subsidies and eminent domain and servicing the transportation industry ceased. For about fifteen years later, just sixty miles south of Detroit, the city of Toledo undertook, with gusto and a fine lack of concern for the niceties of private property, a Keep Jeep campaign of which Coleman Young might have approved.

\* \* \*

Jeeps—probably a slurred contraction of "General Purpose" vehicles, a military term—have been manufactured in Toledo since 1941.

As is so often the case with subsidized methods of transport, their paternity was partially governmental. The Army wanted small, or "bantam," four-wheel-drive vehicles for general purpose usage. The Army chose the design submitted by Willys-Overland, an automobile company founded by John Willys and located in Toledo since 1911. (Theretofore, Toledo had been the center spoke of American bicycle production. In the 1890s and early 1900s, several bicycle manufacturers called Toledo home.[77])

The company had success with its name brand auto, the Overland, though by the late 1920s the Overland had been supplanted by a smaller vehicle called the Whippet. The Whippet failed, and Willys-Overland flirted with bankruptcy in the 1930s. But it would meet its savior in the form of the Jeep. Willys-Overland profited from the Second World War. It churned out about 360,000 Jeeps for the Army. Production was humming; government contracts kept the factory busy.

After the war, Willys-Overland transitioned into the manufacture of Jeeps for the civilian market, though it also produced them for the Army. The company was purchased by Kaiser Motors in 1953. The Jeep was a popular vehicle, and Kaiser opened a second manufacturing plant five miles away. As geographers Jay D. Gatrell of Indiana State University and Neil Reid of the University of Toledo write in the journal of the Royal Dutch Geographical Society, this was a decision with ramifications down the years. Dividing production between these two sites inaugurated "an inefficient and expensive manufacturing process that would influence all future location decisions associated with Toledo Jeep."[78] Body frames were assembled at one location (Jeep Parkway), and those frames had to be trucked to the other location (Stickney Avenue) for the addition of engines, brakes, wheels, and other parts. Production costs were, understandably, boosted.

Kaiser sold out to American Motors, and AMC in turn was purchased by Chrysler, which merged with the German automotive giant Daimler AG in 1998. Jeep remained a mainstay of the local economy. In fact, the Jeep plant was "the oldest continuously-operating automobile assembly facility in the United States." In the late 1990s, the majority of manufacturing jobs in Lucas County, home of Toledo, were in manufacturing. Leading the pack was DaimlerChrylser AG, producers of Jeep Cherokees and Wranglers, which employed 5,600 workers.[79]

But production costs were high, aggravated by the bifurcated nature of the Toledo plants. Chrysler began casting about for alternatives. In August 1996, the company announced that it needed a larger plant, and it was open to leaving Toledo. In an eerie echo of General Motors, Chrysler declared that it was looking for five hundred acres on which to build the new plant. In order to take advantage of the existing transportation and business infrastructure and the experienced regional workforce, Chrysler would be investigating potential sites within fifty miles of Toledo: that is, within the industrial area of the northern Ohio/southern Michigan region. Thus the current workers at Toledo Jeep would be permitted to keep their jobs, as long as they didn't mind the commute. The prize: a Jeep plant and an estimated 4,900 jobs (which was later repegged at 3,900 jobs).

The competition was on. As was the case with Mayor Young and Detroit in the Poletown episode, Toledo Mayor Carty Finkbeiner and the city's entire establishment mobilized behind a "Keep Jeep" campaign. (Mayor Finkbeiner, who served three separate terms as Toledo's helmsman, left behind him a long line of missteps, contretemps, and strange actions, ranging from confrontations with constituents and other public officials to parking in handicapped spots to his admittedly entertaining suggestion that the owners of homes near the Toledo Airport, who had complained of noise levels, should sell their houses to deaf people.[80])

Mayor Finkbeiner, whatever his personal foibles, was a good politician. His first step: organize. He came up with a hokey title—Keep Jeep—for the nascent campaign to prevent Jeep from leaving Toledo. He picked a thirty-nine-member team for the project. The majority of its members (twenty) were employees of the City of Toledo, while the rest represented Lucas County, the office of the Governor of Ohio, the United Auto Workers, the Chamber of Commerce, and various economic development organizations and even Jeep itself.

As is often the case, Toledo and the other localities vying for Jeep—they included Oregon, Monclova, and Wood County, Ohio, and Dundee and Detroit (no, it hadn't learned its lesson), Michigan—had no real idea of the contours of the package necessary to keep or lure Jeep.[81] For the company, it was a matter of Make Your Best Offer. The fact that Jeep was born in Toledo, was the city's largest employer, and had been the backbone of the local economy may have been a minor consideration to Chrysler, but sentiment only goes so far—not nearly as far as does the gift of free land and generous tax abatements.

Because Chrysler wished to keep Jeep somewhere in the Ohio/Michigan industrial corridor, some observers expressed the hope that perhaps the states and municipalities involved in the pursuit of Jeep might forswear the usual bidding game for a more cooperative venture. This did not have to be an all-or-nothing contest, for the employees of Jeep, whether in Toledo or some city or county less than fifty miles distant, would be drawn from the region. Perhaps, hoped some optimists, a form of regional taxation might distribute revenues across the area and lessen inter-municipal competition.

That, anyway, was the theory. In practice, as geographer Linda McCarthy of the University of Wisconsin-Milwaukee writes in the publication of the Royal Dutch Geographical Society, "Toledo and other governments within the region, particularly across the state line in Michigan, entered into the typical cutthroat contest that occurs when a transnational corporation solicits incentive offers from localities across the United States and abroad."[82] Cooperate? Never! Let the incentives roll!

Professor McCarthy interviewed the major players in those jurisdictions bidding for Jeep. To put it mildly, she did not find a cohort of skeptical stewards of the taxpayers' money. Rather, these economic development specialists were inordinately eager to offer lavish packages to Jeep—even if they did not think that their city or county was in the running.

"Companies, especially international ones, need to feel welcome and wanted, and incentive offers do that," remarked one official. It doesn't so much matter whether or not the incentive package makes economic sense for the city; what matters is flattering the free-agent corporation and demonstrating that your city is a serious participant in the game. In a commendably frank admission, another economic development official, says McCarthy, "volunteered that because his jurisdiction did not expect to 'win,' it bid high to drive up the cost for the winning locality—in his opinion, 'the new plant was Toledo's to lose.'"[83]

Not terribly neighborly of him, but then all is fair in love and corporate welfare wars. And decades of subsidies had habituated both giver and receiver to these unnatural acts. Another economic development official told McCarthy: "We have fed these businesses and nurtured them with all of our packages and bragged about all of our incentives for all these years and now they are all conditioned to ask for them, so we've dug our hole and here we are."[84]

How to climb out of the hole? Well, that question was not asked by Toledo, Jeep, or any of the other principals in this story. The Jeep project came up with an incentive and land package centered on the Stickney Avenue location and valued at $259.8 million, though recalculations later pegged it at $332.35 million. This worked out to about $57,142 per job. Of this total, about $75 million would be borne out of pocket by the taxpayers of Toledo. These costs included $35.8 million to relocate—that is, raze—eighteen businesses, and $5.9 million to relocate—that is, raze—eighty-three households (the ghosts of Poletown make regular visits in the industrial Midwest), $18.5 million for road building and modification, $3.6 million to relocate a rail yard, $7.8 million for environmental work, and $2.9 million for the installation of water and sewer lines. The 190 acres to be cleared were to be conveyed to Chrysler free of charge.[85]

The remainder of the package was in the form of a ten-year property tax exemption—that is, a 100 percent property tax exemption—worth $92 million, and state of Ohio Manufacturing Machinery & Equipment Investment Tax Credits, which would become the subject of a later lawsuit. Toledo City Councilman Gene Zmuda said, "It basically was a Christmas wish list for DaimlerChrysler." A Libertarian political activist and Jeep employee, Dave Domanski, remarked, "From the get-go, I think Carty [Finkbeiner] rolled over and played dead."[86]

As was the case in Detroit, the local media giddily led the cheers for the Jeep package. As Gatrell and Reid note, Valentine's Day 1997 dawned with readers of the Toledo *Blade* finding 170,000 heart-decorated "Toledo Loves Its Jeep" posters inserted in the daily paper. Readers were instructed to paste them in their windows at home or in their automobiles as part of a massive vehicular love-in, as the city sought to enlist Cupid's help in convincing Chrysler to stay. This was a harmless display of boosterism, though the *Blade* seemed willing for the city to pay any price, bear any burden to keep Jeep. As it editorialized:

> What Toledo wants, what Toledo must have, is the Jeep plant right here. It's an issue of jobs and tax revenue, of course. But, it's also about pride and identity. This is the city that builds Jeeps. The 5,575 people who build 777 Cherokees and 398 Wranglers a day construct vehicles that are inextricably linked in the mind of the nation with the Glass City. That must not change. Toledo is Jeep's home. It is city leadership's greatest challenge to ensure it stays that way.[87]

There is an almost adolescent insistence to that editorial. Toledo not only *wants* Jeep, it *must have* Jeep. And if Toledo must have Jeep, then price is no object. As the ineffable Mayor Carty Finkbeiner later said, "Had we lost Jeep, it would be like Detroit losing the Tigers. It would be like the Yankees leaving New York. We don't have a major-league sports team. Jeep is a major part of our identity."[88] The Toledo Mud Hens, it seems, were not enough for Carty.

City officials chased Chrysler bigwigs all the way to Seattle, site of the company's 1997 annual meeting, where they were greeted with a billboard reading "Toledo Loves Its Jeep."[89] The auto giant relented. Or it allowed itself to be caught. In July 1997 the company announced that Toledo had won the Jeep sweepstakes, and for its approximately $300 million (depending on whose numbers one believed) package the city would remain the home of Jeep. Chrysler's investment in its Toledo facilities would total $1.2 billion. The agreement was made final the next year.

Chrysler chairman Robert Eaton made it sound like Toledo was the choice all along, and that the corporation just wanted to feel a little love—that love being in the form of eminent domain, the gifts of land and infrastructure, and tax abatements. Eaton said: "The entire Corporation was touched by the outpouring of support displayed by the people of Toledo. With historical roots going back to the early part of this century, the brand-name Jeep always has been and will continue to be synonymous with the City of Toledo."[90]

The package was executed. Those home and business owners who stood in the way of Jeep were displaced. Some took the money and ran, while others were forcibly ousted by eminent domain. These latter were aided by Ralph Nader, who said that the city should "shame" Jeep into paying the costs of relocation.[91]

In *Cutting Corporate Welfare*, Nader explained:

> The most outrageous element of Toledo's Jeep deal is that it requires the displacement of a community near the plant. As it turns out from DaimlerChrysler's plans, the company does not even genuinely intend to use the land that the city will transfer to it from 83 homeowners. In its public explanations, Jeep identifies the community's parcel as a potential truck waiting area; but in its map, the area is to be used for landscaping—a truck waiting area is designated for another parcel of land.[92]

To Nader, the Toledo Jeep deal smacked of Poletown-style corporate welfare. It combined the brazen theft of private property with massive layouts from the taxpayers for the benefit of a giant corporation.

Herman and Kim Blankenship, owners of Kim's Auto and Truck Service, were among those losing their land to the city and Jeep. "Our property was just a strawberry on the corner for them," said Herman

Blankenship.[93] As David Cay Johnston writes in his book *Free Lunch: How the Wealthiest Americans Enrich Themselves at Government Expense (and Stick You with the Bill)* (2007), the Blankenships were partners in business as well as in life: Kim was a welder, and her husband Herman was a mechanic. They had launched their business in 1991 and, by the time Jeep came beeping at their door, employed six people.

As their neighbors gave up, selling their homes for what they could get from a city that was determined to clear this patch of Toledo just as thoroughly as Detroit had cleared Poletown, business started to dry up. Their street was being torn up, and at odd times "electricity would abruptly go off." Kim Blankenship lamented, "Our business has gone from $25,000 a month to $1,500, maybe $2,000, but we are still paying taxes to support Chrysler."[94]

As in the case of the assault of Detroit and GM against Poletown, a lawsuit, which eventually bore the name *Cuno v. DaimlerChrysler*, was filed against the Toledo-Jeep package. Unlike *Poletown*, however, *Cuno* was not fought on the eminent domain front. Rather, it took on corporate welfare as a violation of the dormant Commerce Clause. The catalyst was Ralph Nader, longtime and indefatigable foe of special favors for corporations. Nader had read Professor Peter D. Enrich's seminal 1996 *Harvard Law Review* article "Saving the States from Themselves: Commerce Clause Restraints on State Tax Incentives for Business." He saw in it the germ, or the slingshot, that might bring down the corporate welfare Goliath, and Nader "encouraged [Enrich] to litigate the question."[95]

The target: Ohio's Manufacturing, Machinery & Equipment Investment Tax Credit, which was part of the package that kept Chrysler and its Jeeps from leaving Toledo. This tax credit was enacted in 1995. It provided for a nonrefundable credit for the purchase of "new manufacturing machinery and equipment during the qualifying period" as long as "the new manufacturing machinery and equipment are installed" in the Buckeye State. This tax credit, which was pegged at either 13.5 or 7.5 percent, depending on the economic condition of the area where the machinery or equipment is used, is applied against the state's franchise tax, which it levies on any corporation doing business in the state.[96]

Now, it might seem that the fairest and most fruitful way of encouraging business would be to repeal or reduce the franchise tax, but that's not what the 1995 Ohio tax credit did. Hence the lawsuit.

The lawsuit bears the surname of Charlotte Cuno of West Toledo. Cuno, a paralegal and grandmother of three, became the face of anti-corporate welfarism in 2006, when *DaimlerChrysler v. Cuno* reached the US Supreme Court. Cuno was one of eighteen individuals and small business proprietors who challenged the constitutionality of Ohio's investment tax credit. "Corporate welfare is what's happening," she explained.[97]

She and the other plaintiffs argued that Ohio's investment tax credit and the property-tax exemption had the effect of increasing taxes on Ohio citizens and businesses that did not receive the tax credit or exemption.

The United States Court of Appeals for the Sixth Circuit ruled that the tax credit was indeed a violation of the dormant Commerce Clause in that it discriminated against out-of-state commerce. (The property-tax exemption was not unconstitutional, in its judgment.)

The State of Ohio had argued, as S. Mohsin Reza writes in the *University of Richmond Law Review*, that precedent had established that "tax incentives were unconstitutional only if they either imposed a higher tax on out-of-state products or businesses or factored both a business's out-of-state and in-state activities to calculate the business's tax rate." By this agreement, the investment tax credit was not penalizing out-of-state firms; thus it did not violate the dormant Commerce Clause. But the appeals court read the clause, or its dormant implications, more broadly. Because Ohio's ITC "coerced companies to conduct more business in the state," reckoned the appellate court, it discriminated against other interstate commerce and was a form of protectionism.[98]

The case went on for review to the US Supreme Court. It cut a high profile; subsidy- and incentive-dependent companies and economic development agencies across the country watched warily, for a decision in favor of *Cuno* and her fellow taxpayers might have occasioned a significant rollback of countless incentive packages from Maine to California, and probably would have brought a constitutional challenge to state and municipal subsidies as well. The stakes were potentially in the hundreds of billions of dollars.

The decision was something of an anticlimax. On May 15, 2006, the High Court ruled unanimously that Cuno and her fellow taxpayers and businesspeople did not have standing. According to Chief Justice Roberts's opinion, "State taxpayers have no standing under Article III to challenge state tax or spending decisions simply by virtue of their status as taxpayers."[99]

Thus the question of whether or not such incentives as Ohio's investment tax credit run afoul of the dormant Commerce Clause was pushed off till another day. The substantive constitutional arguments against corporate welfare in *Cuno* did not get their day in court, although Chief Justice Roberts, adverting to the plaintiffs' plaint that incentives boosted their tax burdens, did note that the "very point of the tax benefits is to spur economic activity, which in turn *increases* government revenue."[100] (As a side note, the Ohio tax incentives were being phased out as the case wended its way through the court system.)

As Morgan L. Holcomb and Nicholas Allen Smith explain in their survey of the "Post-*Cuno* Litigation Landscape" in the *Case Western Reserve Law Review*, contemporaneous taxpayer lawsuits in Minnesota and North Carolina also came a cropper. In Minnesota, which the authors call "The Land of 10,000 Subsidies," *Olson v. State* was a challenge by taxpayers to the cheesily acronymed JOBZ program—that is, the Jobs Opportunity Building Zone law. JOBZ provided for a whole raft of exemptions from property, income, sales, and motor vehicle taxes for favored businesses. Olson, who was a former lieutenant governor, claimed that as a result of JOBZ, he paid higher property taxes and was "forced to bear a disproportionate burden of supporting government functions of all types."[101]

As with *Cuno*, the *Olson* plaintiffs argued that the incentive program in question violated the dormant Commerce Clause (as well as the Constitution of the State of Minnesota, which mandates uniform taxation). And also as with *Cuno*, *Olson* was dismissed, in this case by the state Court of Appeals, because a mere taxpayer lacks standing. The appellate court stated, "The proper party to challenge an exemption on behalf of the public and in the public's interest is a government official, not a private citizen. . . . Here, appellants are private citizens with no injury-in-fact and no evidence of an expenditure made as a result of the challenged statutes. Because appellants lack an injury-in-fact and can point to no illegal expenditure or waste of tax monies, the limitations on taxpayer standing support the district court's dismissal of appellant's claims."[102]

In North Carolina, meanwhile, the subject of taxpayer ire was a package of tax credits and incentives estimated at somewhere around $300 million shelled out by the City of Winston-Salem and the County of Forsyth to Dell Inc. in 2004. Robert F. Orr, a former associate justice of the Supreme Court of North Carolina, filed suit on behalf of the North Carolina Institute for Constitutional Law. The suit, which bore the title *Blinson v. State*, was based in part on the dormant Commerce Clause. Orr also asserted that Delma Blinson and her fellow plaintiffs faced higher tax bills as a result of the Dell package.

And as was the case with *Cuno* and *Olson*, the court, in this case the North Carolina Court of Appeals, gave no relief to the taxpayers. In what Holcomb and Smith judge a puzzling ruling, in 2007 the appellate court denied that the plaintiffs had standing to pursue the Commerce Clause claim. As a footnote, Robert F. Orr, the ex-justice who was seeking justice for Tar Heel taxpayers, launched a campaign for the 2008 Republican nomination for governor of North Carolina; one of his platforms was opposition to corporate welfare. Stated Orr: "Despite what some politicians would like you to believe, the answer is not for state and county governments to take your tax dollars and give them to a few giant global corporations, hoping for the outsourcing of a small part of their operation in North Carolina, creating a few hundred jobs with profits flowing out of state."[103]

Justice Orr had dissented from the North Carolina Supreme Court's 5–2 ruling in *Maready v. Winston-Salem* (1996) that subsidies and tax breaks given to two dozen businesses in Forsyth County were constitutional. He was thus one of the very few modern political figures to have as a central concern corporate welfare.[104]

Orr's North Carolina Institute for Constitutional Law also fought, unsuccessfully, against a $260 million incentive package to Google. A conservative Republican, Orr has been praised by free-market conservatives, libertarians, and populist leftists for his steadfast opposition to corporate subsidies. According to an admiring profile in the Raleigh *News & Observer* that bore the title "Robert Orr, legal warrior, fights corporate welfare," Justice Orr has even tangled with his son, a financial analyst in the state, over the issue. Father called son a "greedy businessman" for his support for corporate subsidies and asked him, "Don't they teach ethics in business school?"[105] If only every state had a Justice Robert Orr. . . .

And as for Kim's Auto and Truck Service, David Cay Johnston notes that it isn't even part of the factory for which the targeted Toledoans were told they would have to sacrifice; rather, the site of the erstwhile auto shop "is now a lawn at the factory's edge."[106] It's almost as if the city, in exercising its power of eminent domain, just wanted to show everyone who's boss.

# Notes

1.  The aforementioned examples may be found in Dean Starkman, "Take and Give: Condemnation is Used to Hand One Business Property to Another," *Wall Street Journal*, December 2, 1998.

    The late and much-lamented federal Urban Renewal program, which demolished entire neighborhoods in numerous American cities before it was demolished by widespread public protest (and works like Martin Anderson's lacerating study *The Federal Bulldozer: A Critical Analysis of Urban Renewal, 1949–1962*), was also a form of corporate welfare. First and foremost, urban renewal was an act of theft and destruction; it erased whole neighborhoods, historic buildings, and the character of its targeted communities. To satisfy the "public use" standard, structures and neighborhoods which the powers-that-be wished to knock down were defined as "blighted," a hazily defined term that gave states and localities wide berth in their urban renewing activities. One man's blight, it turned out, was another man's lively working-class neighborhood or charming historic street. Yet because so-called blight was said to pose a danger to the public health, its eradication satisfied the requirements of "public use."

    "Slum" properties (though just how blighted these were was often an open question; in many cases they were desirable to those who did not own them but wished to) were condemned by pliant local governments. The properties were then sometimes sold "at deep discounts" to private interests. The resultant development was well "below the hopes and expectations of its proponents." Michael H. Schill, "Deconcentrating the Inner City Poor," *Chicago-Kent Law Review* (Vol. 67, 1991): 808–809.

2.  Ralph Nader, Foreword, *Poletown: Community Betrayed*, by Jeanie Wylie (Urbana: University of Illinois Press, 1989), p. ix.

3.  John J. Bukowczyk, "The Decline and Fall of a Detroit Neighborhood: Poletown vs. G.M. and the City of Detroit," *Washington and Lee Law Review* (Vol. 41, 1984): 56.

4.  Ibid.: 58.

5.  Ibid.: 59.

6.  Wylie, *Poletown: Community Betrayed*, p. 19.

7.  David R.E. Aladjem, "Public Use and Treatment as an Equal: An Essay on *Poletown Neighborhood Council v. City of Detroit* and *Hawaii Housing Authority v. Midkiff*," *Ecology Law Quarterly* (Vol. 15, 1988): 673–74.

8.  Wylie, *Poletown: Community Betrayed*, p. 7.

9.  For a summary of the argument against the Chrysler bailout, see David R. Henderson, "A Step toward Feudalism: The Chrysler Bailout," *Cato Institute Policy Analysis* No. 4, January 15, 1980.

10. Quoted in "Chrysler's Crisis Bailout," *Time*, August 20, 1979, http://content.time.com/time/magazine/article/0,9171,947356,00.html.

11. Taylor, "A Proposal to Prohibit Industrial Relocation Subsidies," *Texas Law Review*: 676–77.

12. Wylie, *Poletown: Community Betrayed*, p. 51.

13. *Poletown Neighborhood Council v. City of Detroit* (1981), 410 Mich. 616, http://scholar.google.com/scholar_case?case=10677990641940457475&hl=en&as_sdt=6&as_vis=1&oi=scholarr.
14. Ibid.
15. Letter from Thomas A. Murphy to Coleman A. Young and Howard Woods, October 8, 1980, in *Poletown Neighborhood Council v. City of Detroit*.
16. Wylie, *Poletown: Community Betrayed*, p. 165.
17. *Poletown Neighborhood Council v. City of Detroit*.
18. Wylie, *Poletown: Community Betrayed*, p. 52.
19. Nader, *Poletown: Community Betrayed*, p. ix.
20. See "Childs at Play," Harvey Klehr, John Earl Haynes, and Ronald Radosh, *The Weekly Standard*, September 5, 2011, http://www.weeklystandard.com/articles/childs-play_591433.html?nopager=1.
21. Wylie, *Poletown: Community Betrayed*, p. 90.
22. Jenny Nolan, "Auto plant v. neighborhood: The Poletown battle," *Detroit News*, January 26, 2000.
23. *Poletown Neighborhood Council v. City of Detroit*.
24. Bukowczyk, "The Decline and Fall of a Detroit Neighborhood: Poletown vs. G.M. and the City of Detroit," *Washington and Lee Law Review*: 66–67.
25. *Poletown Neighborhood Council v. City of Detroit*.
26. William A. Fischel, "The Political Economy of Public Use in *Poletown*: How Federal Grants Encourage Excessive Use of Eminent Domain," *Michigan State Law Review* (Winter 2004): 943–44.
27. Ibid.: 930.
28. Ibid.: 944.
29. *Poletown Neighborhood Council v. City of Detroit*.
30. Bukowczyk, "The Decline and Fall of a Detroit Neighborhood: Poletown vs. G.M. and the City of Detroit," *Washington and Lee Law Review*: 65.
31. Ibid.: 62.
32. *Poletown Neighborhood Council v. City of Detroit*.
33. Bukowczyk, "The Decline and Fall of a Detroit Neighborhood: Poletown vs. G.M. and the City of Detroit," *Washington and Lee Law Review*: 64.
34. Wylie, *Poletown: Community Betrayed*, p. 63.
35. Nader, *Poletown: Community Betrayed*, p. x.
36. Wylie, *Poletown: Community Betrayed*, p. 90.
37. *Poletown Neighborhood Council v. City of Detroit*.
38. Ibid.
39. Ibid.
40. Nader, *Poletown: Community Betrayed*, p. x.
41. *Poletown Neighborhood Council v. City of Detroit*.
42. Ibid.
43. http://www.loc.gov/pictures/item/mi0157/.
44. Wylie, *Poletown: Community Betrayed*, p. 51.
45. Ibid., p. 199.
46. Bukowczyk, "The Decline and Fall of a Detroit Neighborhood: Poletown vs. G.M. and the City of Detroit," *Washington and Lee Law Review*: 69.

47. Wylie, *Poletown: Community Betrayed*, p. 134.
48. Fischel, "The Political Economy of Public Use in *Poletown*: How Federal Grants Encourage Excessive Use of Eminent Domain," *Michigan State Law Review*: 951–52.
49. Wylie, *Poletown: Community Betrayed*, p. 113.
50. Ibid., p. 134.
51. Ibid., p. 137.
52. Ibid., p. 75.
53. Ibid., p. 151.
54. "Pope retires liberal Bishop Gumbleton," *Christian Century*, February 21, 2006, http://www.christiancentury.org/article/2006-02/pope-retires-liberal-bishop-gumbleton.
55. Wylie, *Poletown: Community Betrayed*, p. 105.
56. "History," Michigan Coalition for Human Rights, http://www.mchr.org/history/.
57. George Corsetti, "Poletown Revisited," www.counterpunch.com, September 18–20, 2004.
58. Nolan, "Auto plant v. neighborhood: The Poletown battle," *Detroit News*.
59. Wylie, *Poletown: Community Betrayed*, p. 59.
60. Nolan, "Auto plant v. neighborhood: The Poletown battle," *Detroit News*.
61. Aladjem, "Public Use and Treatment as an Equal: An Essay on *Poletown Neighborhood Council v. City of Detroit* and *Hawaii Housing Authority v. Midkiff*," *Ecology Law Quarterly*: 677.
62. Thomas Ross, "Transferring Land to Private Entities by the Power of Eminent Domain," *George Washington Law Review* (Vol. 51, 1983): 356.
63. Ibid.: 368.
64. Sandefur, "A Gleeful Obituary for *Poletown Neighborhood Council v. Detroit*," *Harvard Journal of Law & Public Policy*: 664.
65. Ibid.: 666.
66. *County of Wayne v. Hathcock*, Michigan Supreme Court, July 30, 2004, p. 9 http://www.michbar.org/opinions/supreme/2004/073004/24048.pdf.
67. Ibid., p. 4.
68. Ibid., p. 41.
69. Ibid., p. 45.
70. Fischel, "The Political Economy of Public Use in *Poletown*: How Federal Grants Encourage Excessive Use of Eminent Domain," *Michigan State Law Review*: 937.
71. Melissa Burden, "GM seeks $1.8 million tax abatement for Detroit-Hamtramck plant project," *Detroit News*, September 23, 2013, http://www.detroitnews.com/article/20130923/AUTO0103/309230111.
72. Melissa Burden and Christine Ferretti, "Detroit council approves $600K tax break for GM," *Detroit News*, September 24, 2013, http://www.detroitnews.com/article/20130924/AUTO0103/309240098.
73. David Firestone, "Black Families Resist Mississippi Land Push," *New York Times*, September 10, 2001.
74. Sandefur, "A Gleeful Obituary for *Poletown Neighborhood Council v. Detroit*," *Harvard Journal of Law & Public Policy*: 675.

75. Wylie, *Poletown: Community Betrayed*, p. 218.

76. Firestone, "Black Families Resist Mississippi Land Push," *New York Times*.

77. Nick Shultz, "Toledo, from bicycle giant to the automobile," *Toledo Free Press*, November 6, 2008, http://www.toledofreepress.com/2008/11/06/toledo-from-bicycle-giant-to-the-automobile/.

78. Jay D. Gatrell and Neil Reid, "The Cultural Politics of Local Economic Development: The Case of Toledo Jeep," *Tijdschrift voor Economische en Sociale Geografie* (Vol. 93, No. 4, 2002): 403.

79. Linda McCarthy, "The Keep Jeep in Toledo Campaign: A Lost Opportunity for the Wheels of Change?" *Tijdschrift voor Economische en Sociale Geografie* (Vol. 95, No. 4, 2004): 392.

80. "Ohio Mayor Regrets Remark on Deafness," *New York Times*, November 6, 1994.

81. McCarthy, "The Keep Jeep in Toledo Campaign: A Lost Opportunity for the Wheels of Change?" *Tijdschrift voor Economische en Sociale Geografie*: 397.

82. Ibid.: 393.

83. Ibid.: 397.

84. Ibid.: 400.

85. Julie M. McKinnon, "Is Toledo Paying Too Much to Keep Jeep? Many Factors Involved in Size of Aid Packages," Toledo *Blade*, September 12, 1999.

86. Ibid.

87. Gatrell and Reid, "The Cultural Politics of Local Economic Development: The Case of Toledo Jeep," *Tijdschrift voor Economische en Sociale Geografie*: 405.

88. Reza, "*DaimlerChrysler v. Cuno*: An Escape from the Dormant Commerce Clause Quagmire?" *University of Richmond Law Review*: 1236.

89. Gatrell and Reid, "The Cultural Politics of Local Economic Development: The Case of Toledo Jeep," *Tijdschrift voor Economische en Sociale Geografie*: 405.

90. McCarthy, "The Keep Jeep in Toledo Campaign: A Lost Opportunity for the Wheels of Change?" *Tijdschrift voor Economische en Sociale Geografie*: 398.

91. John Seewer, "Toledo takes on criticism for cost of Jeep plant deal," *Bryan* [Ohio] *Times*, December 9, 1998.

92. Nader, *Cutting Corporate Welfare*, p. 37.

93. Amity Shlaes, "When Chrysler's Jeep Runs Over the Little Guy," *Bloomberg News*, March 1, 2006, http://www.bloomberg.com/apps/news?pid=email_us&refer=&sid=aYbnXJNIe0VA.

94. David Cay Johnston, *Free Lunch: How the Wealthiest Americans Enrich Themselves at Government Expense (and Stick You with the Bill)* (New York: Penguin, 2007), pp. 87–88.

95. Morgan L. Holcomb and Nicholas Allen Smith, "The Post-*Cuno* Litigation Landscape," *Case Western Reserve Law Review* (Vol. 58, No. 4, 2008): 1159.

96. Reza, "*DaimlerChrysler v. Cuno*: An Escape from the Dormant Commerce Clause Quagmire?" *University of Richmond Law Review*: 1235.

97.  Sharon Silke Carty, "High court case hinges on tax breaks," *USA Today*, February 28, 2006.
98.  Reza, *"DaimlerChrysler v. Cuno*: An Escape from the Dormant Commerce Clause Quagmire?" *University of Richmond Law Review*: 1246.
99.  *DaimlerChrysler et al. v. Cuno et al.*, 547 U.S. 332 (2006).
100. Ibid.
101. Holcomb and Smith, "The Post-*Cuno* Litigation Landscape," *Case Western Reserve Law Review*: 1172–73.
102. *Olson v. State*, Minnesota Court of Appeals, 2007, http://injurylawstpaul. com/messages/318.htm.
103. Holcomb and Smith, "The Post-*Cuno* Litigation Landscape," *Case Western Reserve Law Review*: 1182.
104. "Bob Orr: Under the Dome," Raleigh *News & Observer*, http://projects. newsobserver.com/dome/profiles/bob_orr.
105. John Murawski, "Robert Orr, legal warrior, fights corporate welfare," Raleigh *News & Observer*, December 12, 2010.
106. Johnston, *Free Lunch: How the Wealthiest Americans Enrich Themselves at Government Expense (and Stick You with the Bill)*, p. 93.

# 6

# A Reverse Robin Hood: The Derring-Do (on Behalf of Transnational Corporations) of the Export-Import Bank

The anti-corporate welfare coalition of libertarians, anti-corporate leftists, free-market economists, and good-government activists who abhor the pork barrel achieves a state of virtual apoplexy when the subject turns to the Export-Import Bank, the notorious "reverse Robin Hood" that takes from the poor—or, more accurately, the poor beleaguered taxpayer—and gives to the richest corporations in the world. It is their bête noire: a slush fund for corporations that is so over-the-top in its unabashed subsidy of the largest US companies that socialist US Senator Bernie Sanders of Vermont, Tea Party conservatives such as Senator Mike Lee of Utah, and activist Ralph Nader are united in their full-throated denunciations of the bank known colloquially as Ex-Im. Former Texas congressman and presidential candidate Ron Paul speaks for them all when he says, "This is naked corporate welfare. It never ceases to amaze me how members of Congress who criticize welfare for the poor on moral and constitutional grounds see no problem with the even more objectionable programs that provide welfare for the rich."[1]

There is a full range of programs that subsidize US exports. These include such excrescences as the Market Access Program of the US Department of Agriculture, which helps advertise the products of such corporations as McDonald's, Nabisco, Welch's, Sunkist, and Blue Diamond in foreign markets to the tune of over $200 million a year. (How in the world would the hamburger eaters of Asia know about McDonald's without the US Department of Agriculture to spread the word?) According to Taxpayers for Common Sense, the two largest recipients of Market Access funding between FY 2006 and 2012 were Cotton Council International (to the tune of $140.58 million) and the US Meat Export Federation ($114.74 million).[2]

Or consider the Overseas Private Investment Corporation (OPIC), which provides loans and loan guarantees for US corporations prospecting in unpredictable markets. OPIC claims to assist "US businesses gain footholds in emerging markets, catalyzing revenues, jobs and growth opportunities both at home and abroad." It also helps "solve critical development challenges and in doing so, advances US foreign policy."[3] In practice, it acts to protect the foreign investments of Fortune 500 corporations by offering low-interest financing and insurance for risky investments by major financial institutions. As *Time*'s special report on corporate welfare explained, "For every buck you put up, the government in the form of . . . OPIC puts up two bucks. Best of all, if the deal goes sour because of a crumbling economy, currency devaluation or some other unforeseen event, you won't have to pay back the government's share."[4]

Again, Ralph Nader asks the pertinent question: Why should "overseas marketing and lending and other export assistance . . . be a government rather than a private business function"?[5] Analyst Stephen Slivinski notes, "Citibank is consistently the top beneficiary of OPIC programs."[6] OPIC's publicists may boast that the entity is an instrument of US foreign policy, but in fact it has served as a tool of the party in power. The late Ron Brown, the ethically challenged wheeler-dealer who served as chairman of the Democratic National Committee and President Clinton's Secretary of Commerce, doled out low-interest OPIC loans as chits. According to a *Boston Globe* investigation, a "massive amount of OPIC support [was] given to companies that traveled with Brown and donated money to the Democrats."[7] Shocking!

But OPIC, the Market Access program, and other subsidies that follow US companies beyond US borders play distinct second fiddles in the export subsidy band to the Export-Import Bank. While Ex-Im is not the only federal agency whose portfolio includes the boosting of exports, it is the most prominent, the most self-promoting, and the most audacious.

\* \* \*

The Ex-Im Bank, born in the Depression, was conceived by New Dealers who believed that banks were incapable of or unwilling to loan monies to firms needing credit to do business internationally.

As James S. Olson, author of *Saving Capitalism: The Reconstruction Finance Corporation and the New Deal, 1933–1940*, notes, "by early in the 1930s commercial credit for manufacturers selling in foreign markets dried up, just as it had for domestic business."[8]

There is no constitutional authorization for the federal government to subsidize or guarantee exports, but the prevailing mood in the mid-1930s among those with access to the levers of power was that the Constitution was a relic of horse-and-buggy days. A new era demanded a new Constitution, or at least a Constitution interpreted in light of Depression-era realities instead of late eighteenth-century philosophies.

Those seeking credit for transactions abroad turned to Washington, and the Roosevelt administration was happy to oblige them. (As Olson notes, the previous administration, that of Republican Herbert Hoover, father of the Reconstruction Finance Corporation, made tentative steps in the direction of loaning sums to agricultural commodity exporters. It didn't start with FDR, though his Brain Trust surely accelerated the process.) And of course *Jobs!* was the shibboleth used to sell the program to the public. Subsidizing exports meant more jobs for Americans, the claim went, and a people mired in a Great Depression were unlikely to object to a seemingly anodyne attempt to alleviate joblessness.

But the desire to establish trade relations with the Soviet Union was also at play. The administration had formally recognized the communist state in its first year in office, and on February 2, 1934, via Executive Order 6581, FDR decreed the existence of the Export-Import Bank of Washington, whose stated purpose was "to aid in financing and to facilitate exports and imports and the exchange of commodities between the United States and other Nations or the agencies or nationals thereof."

At first, "other Nations" meant the Soviet Union exclusively. (That would soon change.) The preamble to Executive Order 6581 explains the reason that the Bank is being created by executive order rather than the legislative process:

> Whereas the Congress of the United States had declared that a national emergency exists by reason of widespread unemployment and disorganization of industry; and has declared it to be the policy of Congress to remove obstacles to the free flow of interstate and foreign commerce which tend to diminish the amount thereof, to provide for the general welfare, by promoting the fullest possible utilization of the present productive capacities of industries, to reduce and relieve unemployment, to improve standards of labor, and otherwise to rehabilitate industry."[9]

Given that such is the policy of Congress, one might think that enabling legislation would naturally originate in Congress, but in "national emergencies," such niceties tend to fall by the wayside.

Its certificate of incorporation sketched an Export-Import Bank whose powers were those of, well, an actual bank. It had the ability

> to do a general banking business (except that of discount or circulation [the former power was soon granted]); to receive deposits; to purchase, sell and negotiate, with or without its endorsement or guarantee, notes, drafts, checks, bills of exchange, acceptances, including bankers' acceptances, cable transfers, and other evidences of indebtedness; to purchase and sell securities, including obligations of the United States or of any State thereof, but not including the purchase with its funds of any stock in any other corporation; to accept bills or drafts drawn upon it; to issue letters of credit; to purchase and sell coin, bullion, and exchange; to borrow and to lend money; and to do and perform the necessary functions permitted by law to be done or performed in conducting said enterprise or business.[10]

The expectation, as Gardner Patterson wrote in a 1943 monograph in the *Quarterly Journal of Economics*, was that in due course, and thanks in part to the Ex-Im Bank, trade between the US and the USSR "would reach great dimensions following our diplomatic recognition of that country."[11] It didn't happen. The bank never did finance any exports to the Soviet Union, since Soviet and US negotiators were unable to agree on just how much of the $200 million debt to the US that the Russians had incurred during World War I should be paid off. (The Roosevelt administration was hamstrung by a prohibition on making loans to those nations that had outstanding World War I debts to the United States.) In fairness to the communists, the $200 million debt had been incurred by the interim Kerensky government that Lenin and his Bolsheviks had overthrown. Negotiations between the Soviets and the Roosevelt administration dragged on for years, as the Soviets offered between $50 and $75 million while the president's men insisted that any repayment not containing nine digits would be politically impossible.[12]

The trustees of the Bank refused to approve any actions vis-à-vis the Soviet Union until the Soviet debt matter was settled. As it was not, the dreams of mutually profitable US-USSR trade were deferred. But the idea of a lending institution created by the federal government in order to facilitate trade was a durable one. The impasse with the Soviets was hardly serious enough to dissipate that dream. In fact, the progenitors of the Ex-Im Bank envisioned a whole series of banks whose purpose would be to subsidize trade with various favored nations.

Cuba was next. On March 9, 1934, the Second Export-Import Bank of Washington, DC, was created so that the US might extend credits to its island neighbor. Both banks had been conjured from thin air by an executive order rather than through the arduous but democratic and constitutional legislative process. (The orders were later ratified by the Congress.)

Organization and reorganization proceeded at what, for Washington, was breakneck speed. On June 30, 1934, the Second Bank's portfolio was extended to all nations except that which was covered by the First Bank, the Soviet Union. Although the early policy had been to establish banks facilitating bilateral trade, first with the Soviet Union and then Cuba, the multilateralists quickly won out.

Despairing of any resolution of the Soviet debt dispute, the trustees (representing the Departments of Agriculture, Commerce, State, and Treasury, and the Reconstruction Finance Corporation), who served both banks, voted the Second Bank out of business as of June 30, 1936. Its commitments were absorbed by the original bank.

The bank's common stock was jointly held by the Departments of Commerce and State; its preferred stock was purchased by the Reconstruction Finance Corporation. Stockholders—that is, agents of the federal government—elected the bank's officers, who were—surprise!—other agents of the federal government (from the aforementioned agencies). The bank was headed by a president, who was appointed by the capital-P President.[13]

Exporters and importers could apply for short-term, intermediate, or long-term credit directly to the Ex-Im Bank or via a commercial bank. In the early years of the bank, intermediate (ninety-day) credits were applied primarily "to further the exportation of . . . cotton and tobacco," notes Charles R. Whittlesey.[14] That certainly pacified Southern members of Congress.

Long-term credits were intended to facilitate the export of such durable goods as heavy machinery and railroad and rolling stock equipment, notably locomotives, with special attention given to the Latin American and Chinese markets. The Bank would purchase half to two-thirds of the foreign buyers' obligations.

The Bank, in its statement of policy, assured those concerned about its ambitions that "the Bank expects to supplement rather than compete with existing sources of export and import credit."[15] It had come into being, Export-Import Bank President George N. Peek explained in 1935, because a substantial amount of foreign trade was being unconsummated due to the inability of commercial banks to finance such exchanges. Moreover—and this has been a consistent theme of those advocating that the central government expand into heretofore unexplored regions—other countries put instruments of the central state in charge of overseeing and financing foreign trade, so the United States had best follow suit.

The Cuban loan is an example of how ostensibly high-minded policies—in this case, assisting domestic firms engaged in international trade—are almost always, in practice, payoffs to favored industries. Pressure from silver-state politicians led to the creation of the Second Export-Import Bank of Washington. Writes James S. Olson, "Early in March 1934 Cuba requested help in purchasing and minting silver coin, a demand silver inflationists in the South and Midwest found particularly appealing."[16] The Bank purchased bullion from domestic silver producers, struck Cuban pesos from this silver, and sold the pesos to Cuba. Silver-state politicians were happy.

In its first two years of operation, the Bank authorized loans of $57 million, though only $14 million was disbursed, almost all of it related to the Cuban silver deal. The rest was primarily devoted to financing the export of Kentucky tobacco to the Spanish Government Monopoly.

As chairman of the Reconstruction Finance Corporation, Jesse H. Jones, Houston businessman, owner-publisher of the *Houston Chronicle*, and an early patron of an ambitious Texas politician named Lyndon B. Johnson, oversaw the Export-Import Bank during its early years. (The RFC was a Herbert Hoover creation that fit nicely with the New Deal's interventionist philosophy. Jones was that rarity: a Hoover appointee retained by President Franklin D. Roosevelt, who called the Houstonian "Jesus H. Jones.") In Jones's telling, US Ambassador to the Soviet Union William C. Bullitt persuaded George Peek to take the newly created position of bank president during a lunch with Peek and Jones.

George Peek had an intransigent streak. He was not a New Deal intellectual, and his eventual conflict with the administration was probably inevitable. From the start, he resisted any calls to extend short-term credit to exporters, and his primary focus was on agricultural exports. By 1936 he had defected from the administration and was in Republican presidential candidate Alf Landon's camp.

Peek left a somewhat disillusioned account of his bank presidency, which lasted from February 13, 1934, until December 2, 1935. In *Why Quit Our Own?* (1936), which Peek coauthored with Samuel Crowther, the former Ex-Im president opens by quoting from George Washington's Farewell Address: "Why quit our own to stand upon foreign ground? Why by interweaving our destiny with that of any part of Europe, entangle our peace and prosperity in the toils of European ambition, rivalship, interest, humor, or caprice?"[17]

"I have started with the assumption that we as Americans have as our primary interest the welfare of the American people," writes Peek. This would strike contemporary Ex-Im ears as dangerously xenophobic—doesn't Peek care about Sub-Saharan Africa? Peek was a protectionist, agricultural division. He had been administrator of the New Deal's Agricultural Adjustment Act, though he left over what he later called "socialized farming." Only after assuming his position, he said, did he realize that the AAA was "an instrument to regiment the farmer through acreage control."[18]

The protectionist Peek also accused the Roosevelt administration of the sins of free trade and low tariffs. As to exports, he supported tighter government control thereof for three purposes: "(a) To conserve national assets and resources. (b) To assist American trade, foreign and domestic. (c) To minimize foreign influence or control over American securities markets and American enterprise."[19]

Peek took the position of president of the Export-Import Bank in 1934, he said, because "Every action of the President evidenced a desire to promote a trade policy in which the material interests of the country would be the essential consideration."[20] President Roosevelt also asked him to serve as special adviser to the president on foreign trade.

Peek writes that Ambassador to the Soviet Union Bullitt saw "great possibilities in Russian trade—if only financing could be arranged." Though Peek's interest was in agricultural exports and not furthering trade with the Soviet Union, he yielded to presidential entreaties and accepted the job with a salary of zilch. Of course dispute over settlement of the Soviet debt essentially killed the bank, though the second one was set up, Peek also at the helm, at first to finance the Cuban coinage deal and the Spanish tobacco transaction. "But I had no intention of playing Santa Claus and putting the Government credit behind I.O.U.'s that would have to be renewed and renewed until they died of old age," protests Peek, who adds, "That cramped our activities."[21]

Peek was obviously not a team player. Unlike Nixon science advisor Lee DuBridge, who if you will recall was an SST skeptic who laid aside his doubts once the president made clear that the SST was the plane of the future, George Peek was too refractory, too obstreperous, and he had none of the passion for anonymity that is viewed as the hallmark of a good presidential aide. He was his own man.

Peek stated flatly that the bank would not "subsidize exports at the expense of the taxpayers." He was no libertarian, that's certain. He accepted as a rationale for subsidizing exporters the classic child's excuse that "everyone else is doing it!" The US government, he contended, must aid domestic companies who are competing with foreign interests "who are being actively and heavily backed by their governments."[22]

Yet Peek came to doubt the original rationale for the bank. He wrote:

> The need for government credit in foreign trade, it developed, was not nearly so great as I had been led to suppose. During that time, commercial banks were not lending freely—or at least that was the complaint. I had been told that millions and millions of dollars' worth of goods could not be exported because of the refusal of the banks to finance. I found that generally speaking this was not true and that most legitimate transactions went through the banks without trouble. A not inconsiderable proportion of the applications that came to us were for foreign trade promotions in which the Government was expected to put up all the money, take all the risk and stay away from the profits.[23]

Peek broke with the administration, and decisively, saying, in reference to the AAA, "The farmer ought to know—and I think he does know—that through regimentation he has everything to lose and nothing to gain." This was not music to Rooseveltian ears. "The example of Russia should be enough," he said.[24] Comparing the New Deal to Soviet Communism was a non-starter in the Roosevelt administration. His prescription was for an embargo on foreign farm products, or at least those in direct competition with domestic produce; a high protective tariff and import quotas; and the scrapping of what he regarded as socialistic New Deal policies.

As for the Export-Import Bank, "I could not be a party to making loans which would simply shift the losses to the public."[25] So Peek was gone. The Bank lived on.

Although Ex-Im was granted a two-and-a-half-year life extension in January 1937, "it was generally felt that the Eximbank would be reorganized out of existence."[26] No such luck. In fact, by 1938 the Bank was extending its reach into heretofore unexplored territory. It granted a ten-year, $10 million credit to the International Telephone and Telegraph Company (ITT) to assist in its South American operations. Big business had found a new friend in the swelling federal bureaucracy. It also financed road construction in Haiti performed by a US firm.

The Bank turned to Latin America as a favorite field of operations. Highways were carved out across the Americas, including the Inter-American Highway in Mexico, Costa Rica, Columbia, Paraguay, and Bolivia. The Bank subsidized the export of rolling stock and equipment to wreak roads on Brazil, Chile, and Paraguay. Build, build, build was the Ex-Im's mantra, and well-connected industrialists here and in the targeted countries profited handsomely. Ex-Im sponsored a hydroelectric plant in Uruguay, a luxury hotel and a slaughterhouse (not adjacent to each other) in the Dominican Republic, and a steel mill in Brazil.

"Nowhere did we try to play Santa Claus," protested Jesse H. Jones. Worried that the iron ore deposits in the Masabi Range in Minnesota might not "meet the long drain of a Third World War"—who said Ex-Im wasn't farsighted?—Jones boasted of the bank's investment in the Itabira iron ore deposits of Brazil.[27] (Seventy years later, the city of Itabira is dealing with a welter of pollution problems caused by the extraction of iron ore. Ex-Im wasn't *that* farsighted.)

Warren Lee Pierson, a California attorney who succeeded Peek, spoke rapturously of the Ex-Im's portfolio as containing everything from "the importation of frozen Hungarian pheasants to the construction of mammoth hydroelectric plants in distant lands." No doubt those Hungarian pheasants, once thawed, made for tasty meals, but one wonders just where in the Constitution is located the authority for the federal government to facilitate, via loan, such a deal. (The very question reveals the asker thereof to be a relic.)

The rationale for such loans, according to Jesse H. Jones, was that "commercial bankers are generally allergic" to the granting of medium or long-term credits for construction "in distant climes" and short-term credits for agricultural goods.[28] The Bank was not, however, allergic to controversial governments. In 1939, Ex-Im financed a $16 million loan enabling Francisco Franco's fascist government in Spain to purchase American cotton. Continuing the fascist-tinged theme, that same year found the Bank granting a $6 million loan to aid "30 American cotton shippers in their exports to Italian spinners."[29]

Also controversially, it granted a $25 million loan to a New York-based but Chinese-government-run agency, the Universal Trading Corporation, for the export of "agricultural and industrial products."[30] Repayment was to be not in currency but in tung oil. This last-named transaction was interpreted as a political act, a sign of US support for China against Japan and a symbol of US resolve to maintain trade with the Chinese.

"It is tempting," writes Walter L. Hixson in *The American Experience in World War II: Pearl Harbor in History and Memory* (2003),

> to dismiss the Export-Import Bank's credit as being too small to be of great significance. Several events must be kept in mind, however, when assessing the importance of the Bank's action. While the credit itself was not large enough to be a determining factor in China's struggle with Japan, its importance, both in material and symbolic terms, far transcended its face value. The response of the American government established a precedent which others soon followed. On December 20 [1938], the British government announced the extension of a small export credit for the purchase of trucks and intimated that further credits would be forthcoming. Chinese officials reported that, altogether, they were able to secure $75,000,000 on the basis of the $25,000,000 credit received from the United States.[31]

Despite cursory denials from its officers, the Bank was now being used as a tool of US foreign policy. This was not, of course, how its mission had been sold (though perhaps it was how it was envisioned) at birth, but government agencies accreting new powers is hardly a novel concept. The State Department, in particular, took a warm interest in Ex-Im's potential. There were complaints from antiwar and isolationist members of Congress about the Bank seeming to side with China against Japan, and as a result in 1939 Congress placed a cap of $100 million on outstanding Bank obligations. Representative Edwin Martin Schafer (D-IL) spoke for those who feared the Bank might become a corporate-dominated instrument of US diplomacy when he thundered, "I hope this House will defeat this indefensible, camouflaged, un-American legislative monstrosity."[32]

Schaefer did not get his wish. With the coming of the Second World War, the Bank entered politics in a serious way. The cap on Bank obligations was doubled, to $200 million, as a way of permitting loans to the government of Finland. (Again departing from the Bank's origins, it was now making loans directly to foreign states without the fig leaf of a US commercial interest.)

Fear of Axis penetration of Latin America focused the Bank's intense attention on South America. "No one any longer maintained that the Eximbank was not to be used as a political weapon," wrote Gardner Patterson in 1943. Instead, "it would be a means of keeping [Latin American and other] markets out of Axis hands."[33] The cap on Bank obligations was boosted from $200 million to $700 million. The Ex-Im gaze turned southward, as the dominant policy became, depending on one's point of view, Uncle Sam as Good Neighbor or Intrusive Uncle Sam.

Futile protests were launched by the usual suspects: economy-minded congressmen, those suspicious of foreign entanglements, farm-state representatives unhappy that Ex-Im was effectively subsidizing Latin American agriculture, and those who just did not cotton to the idea of the US government showering taxpayer-fed benefits on large corporations. In other words, the protesters were working within an American political tradition that was hostile to big government and big business—and that ran counter to the prevailing ideology of the New Deal and Rooseveltian interventionism.

So the Export-Import Bank, which less than a decade ago had been founded in order to further trade with the Soviet Union, was now making direct loans to governments, banks, and agencies of state in such nations as Costa Rica, Nicaragua, El Salvador, Mexico, Colombia, Ecuador, and the Dominican Republic for the express—literally—purpose of building roads. Which leads to a fact that Ex-Im publicists leave out of their encomia: Environmental destruction is a common theme running through the Bank's history.

In 1941, a $25 million loan financed half of the construction of a government-owned steel mill in Volta Redonda, Brazil. This was Good Neighborism of a sort, though it had a foreign policy angle, as Krupp Works of Germany had also been part of the conversation before Brazil chose the Americans. Yet it was not without its paternalistic aspect, for the Export-Import Bank had "considerable authority in the selection of the Company's managers, engineers, and contractors."[34] As the Brazilians would learn, when you take handouts from Uncle Sam, the Uncle calls the tune.

The steel mill at Volta Redonda was hailed in 1968 by an American academic as "a hallmark in the development of Brazilian industry" that marked a rejection of Brazil's agricultural past and "an acceptance of industry with its promise of a fuller, more secure national existence."[35] State-owned from its creation in 1941 until its privatization in 1993, the mill, operating under the name of Companhia Siderurgica

Nacional, was long cited as one of the country's most prolific polluters, although accounts suggest that since privatization it has become more ecologically conscious.[36] Nevertheless, it is a fair question—though a question almost never asked—whether or not it is the responsibility, or right, of US taxpayers to subsidize industrial development in Brazil.

Brazil was also the recipient of Export-Import Bank financing for its rubber industry, which achieved strategic significance when Japan's domination in the Pacific cut off a major supply of rubber. (Plantations in Malaysia and Indonesia had supplied 95 percent of the world's rubber.) So Brazil, with its two hundred million rubber trees, filled the vacuum. The results were less than impressive and the cost was considerable, not only in dollars but in lives.

As James A. Brooke reported in the *New York Times*, 25,000 civilian "rubber soldiers" made the arduous journey into the Amazon for the harvest. Half of them never made it out of the jungle. They died in all sorts of spectacularly unpleasant ways: by snakebite, attacks by Amazonian Indians and jaguars, malaria. "From the US point of view, the thing was a colossal failure," said Professor Warren Dean of New York University. "The American investment must have been $30 million, but at the high point, in 1944, only 13,684 tons of rubber were exported to the allies. It was a very, very tiny amount, when you consider that we needed hundreds of thousands of tons."[37]

For Brazilians, the cost was measured in lives, not dollars. Moreover, the would-be "rubber boom" induced by Export-Import Bank financing had no lasting impact: after the war, the rubber industry again flourished in Asia and faded in Brazil, which is today a net importer of rubber.

The same blend of development aid and paternalism, sometimes in the service of US foreign policy, was at work elsewhere in the early 1940s. The Bank granted a pair of $5 million loans to the Haitian-American Agricultural Development Corporation, which was ostensibly intended to promote agricultural development in Haiti but whose primary purpose seems to have been to supply rubber and rope (from sisal) to the US war effort. In addition, part of the price of this loan was securing a seat on the corporation's board for an Export-Import Bank official. The corporation received almost two hundred thousand hectares of land; most was to be dedicated to the planting and harvesting of rubber trees. Like so many subsidized economic projects in the land to the north, farmers—in this case forty thousand families—were thrown off their land to make way for development. The rubber project lost $6.8 million. Those who were permitted to return to their lands after the war and the failure of the rubber experiment often could not even recognize their acres, so changed had they been by the development.[38]

In a similarly imperialist vein, in 1942 the Export-Import Bank financed the Bolivian Development Corporation, a government-owned concern with interests stretching from transportation to petroleum to mining to agriculture. Half of the six directors of this Bolivian government's corporation were appointed by the Export-Import Bank.[39] Why, it's enough to make a Latin American anti-imperialist scream "Yanqui Go Home!" But the Yankee had no intention of going home.

In 1939, Charles R. Whittlesey of Princeton, assessing the bank's first five years in the *American Economic Review*, had concluded that "the actual accomplishments of the Bank have not been impressive."[40] For as Rita M. Rodriguez, a then-director of the Ex-Im Bank, wrote in 1987, "Exports historically have represented a relatively small percentage of the US economy. In 1934, US exports amounted to $2.2 billion, 3.75 percent of GNP. The $11 million in financing authorized by Exim in 1934, or even the $284 million authorized between 1934 and 1939, could hardly be counted on during the Great Depression to reduce unemployment in the export industry, let alone in the economy as a whole!"[41]

As for the other half of the bank's title, Charles R. Whittlesey took issue with the inclusion of the word *import* in the bank's name, since "in a country such as the United States, a transaction that is deserving of credit can be financed through ordinary banking channels." The bank, he said, was an "export credit institution" and would remain so for whatever future it had.[42] He added, however, perhaps in genuflection to the prevailing Washington belief that any program, once born, should never be euthanized, that although the bank's achievements were slight, "it probably should be continued."[43] Not to worry, Professor Whittlesey: the Ex-Im Bank seems to have discovered the secret of eternal life.

It became an independent agency in 1945 and has never looked back.

Ex-Im has survived changes of administration, of governing philosophy, and of the shape of global financial markets. As William H. Becker and William M. McClenahan Jr. write in *The Market, the State, and the Export-Import Bank of the United States, 1934–2000*, FDR ordered into existence the Ex-Im Bank "during the New Deal's earliest zeal for planning and building the power of the state," yet it survives even in our age "where leaders extol the market solutions to economic growth and development in most places in the world."[44] The thing knows how to survive, you've got to grant it that.

Due to the pressures of the Cold War, the Export-Import Bank concentrated on Latin American development in the 1950s and '60s. But it was in the 1970s that Ex-Im came under heavy fire for the first time, really, as critics of corporate welfare focused on the "small number of firms that seemed to benefit most from the Bank's lending."[45] Boeing, Lockheed, General Electric, Westinghouse: did these behemoths really need loan guarantees from Uncle Sam?

Then there arrived in Washington an administration that had given at least lip service to the idea of zeroing out corporate welfare. Might the vaunted free marketeers who rode into the District of Columbia with Ronald Reagan take aim at this reverse Robin Hood?

Not a chance. The ostensible budget cutters of the Reagan administration left Ex-Im standing, despite budget director David Stockman's hostility to the bank. Stockman later called export subsidies "a mercantilist illusion, based on the ideological position that a nation can raise its employment and GDP by giving away its goods for less than what it costs to make them." Such subsidies, insisted Stockman, "subtract from GDP and jobs, not expand them."[46]

A later Republican administration, that of George W. Bush, began by proposing a 25 percent reduction in the authorization for the Export-Import Bank but soon saw the light. A year into his term, Bush was supporting an expansion of Ex-Im's authorization. And so it goes.

* * *

Eighty years after its unprepossessing beginning, the Export-Import Bank—unlike the Reconstruction Finance Corporation, the Works Progress Administration, the Agricultural Adjustment Administration, and all those other three-word New Deal concoctions—survives. Its charter has been amended many times over, but in its essentials— and in its role as bestower of corporate welfare and tool of US foreign policy—it resembles its forerunner of four score years ago.

As in the 1930s, the bank is directed "to supplement, and to not compete with, private capital."[47] Its armaments include loans, loan guarantees, guarantees of working capital, and export credits. The loans, which may be taken out by a foreign purchaser of US goods and services, are fixed-rate and cover as much as "85 percent of the US contract value." The loan guarantees, which also cover up to 85 percent of value, provide that in the event of a default by a foreign buyer of US exports, the Bank will "pay to the lender the outstanding principal and interest on the loan."[48] (These guarantees constitute the bank's largest activity, dollar-wise.) Medium-term loans and guarantees require repayment in between one and seven years; long-term loans stretch beyond that limit. And Ex-Im's insurance program insures US exporters against default by foreign buyers or debtors, whether for commercial or political reasons. (These might include war, government seizure of property, revocation of relevant licenses, etc.)

The Bank's stated mission is to provide government financing, where the private variety is not available, to US exporters of goods and services "with the objective of contributing to the employment of US workers."[49] This objective was tacked on to appease those who might raise the question of just why the American taxpayer should be subsidizing the exports of the corporate giants who are the principal beneficiaries of Ex-Im largesse.

The Bank belongs to those categories known as the *independent federal agency*, which is to say it is not under the control of a Cabinet secretary; and *US government corporation*, which is defined as "a government agency established by Congress to provide market-oriented public services and to produce revenues that meet or approximate expenditures."[50] It is entirely a creature of the federal government. It is chartered by Congress; reauthorized every few years by Congress; receives an annual appropriation from Congress, which caps its permissible loan and credit actions; and is governed by a Board of Directors appointed by the president and confirmed by the Senate. The bank borrows directly from the US Treasury. Only in the lexicon of Washington, DC, could such an institution be tagged with the adjective *independent*.

At the head of the board of directors is the Bank's president, surrounded by the usual complement of subalterns. Congress has oversight function over the Ex-Im Bank, though it does not scrutinize its each and every loan or activity. The Bank is headquartered—of course—in Washington, DC, though it has regional offices in Miami, New York, Chicago, Houston, Orange County (CA), San Francisco, Atlanta, Minneapolis, Seattle, Dallas, and Detroit. Typically, these are opened with great fanfare, as the local members of Congress are prominently displayed before their business constituents and lauded as heroes of trade.

The Bank describes its mission as "to support US jobs by facilitating the export of US goods and services, by providing competitive export financing, and ensuring a level playing field for US goods and services in the global marketplace." It denies that it is in competition with private lenders; instead, it merely "fills gaps in trade financing" by assuming "credit and country risks that the private sector is unwilling or unable to accept." Finally, it helps to "level the playing field for US exporters by matching the financing that other governments provide to their exporters."[51]

This summary of its mission is chockablock with buzzwords and banalities, from the Democratic-tinctured "level playing field," a phrase beloved of unions and protectionists, to "global marketplace," a phrase without which any company's annual report is woefully incomplete, to "competitive," a word that Republicans like and that suggests *competition*, which is exactly what corporate welfare-dispensing entities such as the Export-Import Bank are meant to subvert.

Today, trade is generally "financed through firms themselves rather than banks," but a government bank offers advantages not available in the private sector.[52] As Ralph Nader says, "Corporations generally want loans from the government either because the loans are made at below-market rates, or because the loans include some sort of implicit subsidy (including de facto government insurance)."[53] The favored few profit at the expense of the unsubsidized many.

Ex-Im's establishment supporters are quick to praise what they call "free trade," at least as an abstract theory, but in practice they resort to mercantilism. Their excuse is that everyone else does it: a rationale that is inveracious but that offers a convenient prop on which to hang all manner of government aid, however wasteful, counterproductive, or regressive, just because somewhere, some other nation is pursuing the same destructive policies.

Despite its defenders' claim that Ex-Im exists in some pure realm outside the dirty and compromised precincts of grubby politics, in fact, as two policy analysts from the left-of-center Institute for Policy Studies assert, "The executive branch frequently employs Eximbank financing to reward countries that adopt policies serving US political and economic interests."[54] Yet while the Export-Import Bank has its uses as a tool of US foreign policy, it is, primarily, a means by which the most influential US-connected transnational corporations receive subsidies and deals that would not be available in a free marketplace.

Incredibly, the aviation industry consumes the majority of the Ex-Im Bank's long-term loan guarantees. Or perhaps that's not so incredible, given the transportation industry's long history of dependence on governmental, especially federal, assistance.

Consider the numbers for Boeing *alone*. In FY 2009, according to the Congressional Research Service (CRS), 88 percent of the dollar value of the Export-Import Bank's loans and long-term guarantees "supported the sale of Boeing aircraft to foreign countries."

Eighty-eight percent! No wonder Ex-Im is commonly known as "Boeing's Bank."

In subsequent years Boeing consumed 63 percent (FY 2010) and 56 percent (FY 2011) of Ex-Im's loans and long-term guarantees.[55] All this for the largest aerospace company in the world—the supplier of 75 percent of the world's aircraft fleet.[56] Surveying the absolutely ravenous appetite the company has shown when dining at the Ex-Im table, Timothy P. Carney asks, "How can anyone say with a straight face that Ex-Im does not exist primarily to subsidize one corporation?"[57]

The list of Boeing/Ex-Im projects is long and eye-opening and extends over a considerable period of time, during administrations both Democratic and Republican. In 1998, for example, Ex-Im's deals in China totaled more than $1 billion—and every single case involved Boeing. (China Air has been a Boeing partner, to the displeasure of US-based competitors. Another Boeing partner is the Saudi Arabian national airline, leading economist Robert Higgs to ask, "Can the Saudis not get credit in the ordinary commercial market?"[58])

One of the Export-Import Bank's highlights for FY 2011 was a $117.5 million loan guarantee for the sale of Boeing 737-800 aircraft to flydubai, which was not, naturally, a plucky startup airline backed by gutsy entrepreneurs but rather an airline owned by the government of Dubai within the oil-rich United Arab Emirates.

Fred P. Hochberg, chairman and president of the Export-Import Bank, made it sound as if Ex-Im were in on the ground floor of an exciting new private venture: "This financing is a first for Ex-Im Bank for this successful new carrier in the Middle East, and this export is a great opportunity for Boeing to expand its market reach in the United Arab Emirates. The aircraft financed supported hundreds of jobs at Boeing and its suppliers across the country." Always, always, always, conjure up those jobs-created-in-the-United-States numbers.

For his part, flydubai CEO Ghaith Al Ghaith enthused, "We believed that it was the right time, in flydubai's third year of operation, to diversify the sources of funding for our aircraft . . . as we continue to grow, and we look forward to developing our relationship with them in the future."[59]

There are, seemingly, as many Boeing/Ex-Im deals as there are airplanes in the sky. Bank p.r. puffers boasted in 2013 of a $1.1 billion deal to finance the sale of 230 Boeing 737s—"the largest commercial aircraft order in aviation history"—to Lion Air of Indonesia.[60] The Bank and Boeing claimed that this would support 7,300 American jobs. Support, that is, not create, though even so, it works out to about $150,685 per job.

That via such transactions the Export-Import Bank is subsidizing foreign competition to US airlines has not gone unnoticed in the aviation industry, although the industry as a whole has for so long had such an intimate relationship with the federal government that outright objections to handouts are rare. After all, the company that is harmed today by a subsidy may be receiving a different subsidy tomorrow.

As Timothy P. Carney, tireless journalistic scourge of corporate welfare, notes, in FY 2012, all three of the Export-Import Bank's guarantees of $1 billion-plus went to Boeing through sales to Ethiopian Airlines, LAN Airlines of Chile, and Cathay Pacific Airlines of Hong Kong. The fourth largest guarantee, which topped out just below the billion-dollar mark, went not toward Boeing jets but instead covered "satellites sold by Boeing Space and Intelligence Systems."[61]

Writing in the Washington *Examiner*, Carney details the almost incestuous relationship between Boeing and the federal government. Although Ex-Im has long been Boeing's Bank, the ties have become strangulatingly close in the Obama administration. For starters, Obama named Boeing CEO W. James "Jim" McNerny Jr. to head the President's Export Council, which advises the chief executive on matters of international trade. (Fox, welcome to the henhouse.) As "export czar," McNerny has advised—you'll never believe this—that the Export-Import Bank plays a critical role in fostering the nation's exports. McNerny is the ultimate corporate welfare king, having previously been an executive at General Electric, another Ex-Im client.

But Boeing's penetration of the White House goes far beyond having a well-placed CEO. As Carney relates, Obama raised more than $200,000 from Boeing employees in 2008, which more than doubled the previous largest haul for a candidate, and was more than five times larger than what Republican John McCain raised. In 2012, Obama pulled in $170,000 from Boeing employees (including Boeing's chief lobbyist, Michael Cassel), or about 50 percent more than Republican Mitt Romney raised.

And the beat goes on. The Podesta Group, which Boeing retains as its lobbyist, was founded by John Podesta, who directed the Obama transition team. Lobbyist Linda Daschle is married to Senator Tom

Daschle, an Obama loyalist. Obama chief of staff Bill Daley served on Boeing's Board of Directors. Obama campaign manager David Plouffe was a Boeing consultant. Obama's first secretary of commerce was former Governor Gary Locke of Washington who, like most politicians from the jewel of the Pacific Northwest, served as essentially an errand boy for Boeing. Locke was succeeded at Commerce by John Bryson, who had served on Boeing's Board of Directors.

Why not just turn over the key to the Export-Import Bank to Boeing and be done with it? No wonder Carney scoffs at the common right-wing charge that Obama is a socialist of some sort. Rather, says Carney, he is a "big-business corporatist" who services companies like Boeing in a fashion that would make any honest socialist blush.[62] (Amusingly, in 2008 candidate Obama called the Export-Import Bank "little more than a fund for corporate welfare."[63] But it's amazing what an elevation in station can do to alter one's perspective. The president's new friends showed him that the Bank is one of economic man's best friends!)

And how do the Export-Import Bank's defenders answer the charge that it is Boeing's Bank? They don't, really. They dance around the question, they dissemble, they wander off into thickets of rhetorical irrelevance. The Congressional Research Service provides this choicely lame summary of their defense: "Supporters point out that the Ex-Im Bank's mission is to support US businesses of all sizes and [sic], that the Bank places special emphasis on supporting small business."[64]

Mission statements, as all but the most obtuse business consultant understands, are meaningless. What matters is what the business does. Show us the bottom line. And the bottom line is that a majority of Ex-Im's loans and long-term guarantees go not only to a single sector of the economy, aviation, but to a single firm within that sector: Boeing. This is simply astonishing, and the fact that the Export-Import Bank is reauthorized regularly by Congress with dissent coming only from a handful of free-market Republicans and leftist Democrats is testimony to . . . well, to several things. To the sterling quality of Boeing's lobbyists, for one. To the inattention of the public, for another. And to the shamelessness of the Export-Import Bank's directors, who funnel billions to Boeing while proclaiming, in their not-worth-the-computer-paper-they're-printed-out-on mission statements, that the Bank is committed to fortifying small US businesses and flooding the world with exports from mom-and-pop operations on Main Street, USA. But all the gloss in the world can't hide the numbers. If nothing else, one has to marvel at the chutzpah of Boeing and its Bank.

For its part, Boeing accepts its good fortune as a matter of sublime justice. "We are the largest exporter of manufactured goods in the US," says Cheryl Russell, Boeing's director of federal affairs, "so it is logical that we are the No. 1 user of the Bank."[65] Perhaps so—but *88 percent* in FY 2009?

Even the grossest forms of corporate welfare eventually are accepted as normal, unobjectionable, even healthy. Boeing is not, of course, the only corporate giant to feast on Ex-Im favors. General Electric, Caterpillar, and Houston-based construction behemoth KBR (formerly a subsidiary of Halliburton) annually place in the Top Ten of Ex-Im beneficiaries. The list of companies on which the Export-Import Bank has smiled to the tune of hundreds of millions or even billions of dollars is long and famous: Raytheon, Mobil Oil, IBM, AT&T, Motorola, FedEx, General Motors, United Technologies, Westinghouse, Northrop Grumman, Lucent Technologies, Chevron, Texaco, Bechtel—a regular beggar's banquet. Before its spectacularly messy demise, Enron was an Ex-Im favorite. From 1994 until its expiry at the dawn of the twenty-first century, the ethically challenged energy company was targeted for $675 million in Ex-Im aid. Enron chairman and CEO Kenneth Lay was a tireless champion of the Bank, knowing on which side his bread was buttered.

Enron was not the only disgraced company to profit from Ex-Im philanthropy. In FY 2011, Solyndra, whose case was discussed in the introduction, "received a $10 million loan guarantee . . . which financed a sale of Solyndra products to a customer in Belgium."[66] And this one wasn't even at the request of Vice President Biden.

\* \* \*

If one considers all Bank activities, and not just loans and long-term guarantees, the aviation sector is still far and away the leader in Ex-Im favors granted, accounting for 46.3 percent of "total exposure" in FY 2012.[67] (*Total exposure* is the sum of the principal of all outstanding bank loans, guarantees, and insurance.)

In FY 2012, 50.8 percent ($54.1 billion) of the Bank's portfolio consisted of outstanding guarantees, outstanding loans ($12.3 billion) accounted for 11.6 percent, outstanding insurance ($2.6 billion) constituted another 2.5 percent, and outstanding claims ($1.5 billion) made up 1.4 percent. The remainder of the Bank's FY 2012 portfolio consisted of undisbursed loans ($16.4 billion, or 15.4 percent of the total), undisbursed guarantees ($12.7 billion, or 11.9 percent), and undisbursed insurance ($6.8 billion, or 6.4 percent). In sum, therefore, guarantees accounted for $66.8 billion of the bank's FY 2012 exposure, loans for $28.8 billion, and insurance another $9.5 billion.[68]

A billion here and a billion there, and pretty soon you're talking real money, to paraphrase the late Illinois Senator Everett Dirksen. Nevertheless, for all the Bank's bluster, and for all the billions in loans and guarantees and insurance that it sends hither and yon across the globe, its efforts—even if an unqualified success—would barely affect the volume of US international trade. In 2012, according to the US Department of Commerce, the sum of US goods and services exported came to about $2.2 trillion.[69] This $2.2 trillion dwarfs the Export-Import Bank's $35 billion FY 2012 activity (as opposed to total exposure): indeed, Ex-Im-backed 2012 trade equals less than 2 percent of total exports.[70] The other 98-plus percent of US exports went on their merry way quite without the assistance of the Export-Import Bank. The General Accounting Office admitted the relative inconsequentiality of the Bank when it noted, "Eximbank programs cannot produce a substantial change in the US trade balance."[71]

Since FY 2008, the bank's fee collections from its financial transactions have offset its credit losses. While it is included in the president's budget request, the "net appropriation is expected to be $0."[72] This has emboldened the Bank's backers to claim that it is self-sustaining, which is utter nonsense, of course. For one thing, as Sallie James of the Cato Institute writes, "taxpayers are on the hook if the agency suffers any losses."[73] And the Bank draws on the US treasury for administrative expenses. Moreover, the Bank's activities artificially boost some firms at the expense of others. Ask Boeing's competitors if the Export-Import Bank does no harm to the domestic economy. When Washington picks winners, it creates losers. It redistributes resources according to the coercive mandates of government rather than the free play of the market. And this process is tremendously unfair to those companies that do not scheme and supplicate for subsidies from Washington. They, really, are the unseen victims of the Export-Import Bank.

If the US government were to sever its relationship with the bank, no longer authorizing its loans and expenditures, it would curl up and die. It would not exist on its own. But Boeing and the other corporate giants who receive the tender ministrations of the Export-Import Bank understand that it is good public relations for the bank to assert a specious self-reliance.

Of course the Bank estimates that its effects on the US economy are virtually Midasian. In FY 2011, when its authorization reached $32.7 billion from about 3,700 transactions, the bank claimed, grandiloquently, that its actions supported 290,000 jobs. Interesting phraseology: not *created* but *supported*. The word can mean anything from an intimate involvement to a glancing encounter. A foundation supports a house. A fan supports a professional football team. Their relative contribution to the thing they are supporting varies enormously. But the important thing, from a public relations viewpoint, is that "290,000 jobs" sticks in the mind.

*Jobs* is the mantra repeated by any and all Export-Import Bank spokespeople. Asked by the *New York Times* in 2002 to defend the Bank against charges that it is a flagrant example of corporate welfare, Bank vice president Eduardo Aguirre said, "People who say it's corporate welfare do not understand Ex-Im. Our mission is jobs. Jobs to support exports. Well-paying jobs. What they say is corporate welfare I say is sustaining jobs. We are here to finance exports that would not take place without Ex-Im financing. Tell that to the people who would not have jobs without us."[74]

In FY 2012, Ex-Im's loans, guarantees, and insurance exceeded $35 billion—a record sum—which, the bank's advocates claimed, supported $50 million in export sales and 255,000 jobs.[75] These claims of massive job creation fall somewhere between specious and mendacious. In fact, as trade policy analyst Sallie James writes, "At best, the activities of the bank have no discernible net impact on the number of jobs in the US economy."[76] Yes, subsidizing a foreign government or company's purchase of an American-made product likely produces jobs for the American company. But as with similarly florid claims by economic development agencies, those who trumpet those job-creation numbers ignore alternative uses of the monies loaned. Had the Export-Import Bank not loaned a billion here or a half-billion there to the purchaser of a Boeing plane, that money would not have disappeared into the gloaming. Rather, it would have been put to some other use: perhaps by the US government, or perhaps by the taxpayers and taxpaying businesses to whom the government might have returned those monies in the absence of an Export-Import Bank.

We cannot know. The investments, the purchases, the transactions, and the jobs not created thereby do not show up on any bottom line, but they are real nonetheless. Nor can we know the extent to which the Export-Import Bank, by loaning or guaranteeing loans to hale and healthy companies and even foreign countries, is simply displacing private investment.

Shayerah Ilias, analyst in international trade and finance for the Congressional Research Service, phrases it well. She notes that critics contend that "by providing financing or insurance for exporters that the market seems unwilling, or unable, to provide, Ex-Im Bank's activities draw from the financial resources within the economy that would be available for other uses. Such 'opportunity costs,' while impossible to estimate, could be potentially significant."[77]

These are the invisible casualties of corporate welfare. They are the projects never undertaken, the services never vended, the vessels and factories never built. And they merit not even so much as a footnote in any Export-Import Bank publication. Sallie James quotes Jay Etta Hecker, a Government Accounting Office official who testified before the Senate Subcommittee on International Finance: "Government export finance assistance programs may largely shift production among sectors within the economy rather than raise the overall level of employment in the economy."[78]

In the same vein, CRS analyst Ilias explains that among Bank critics:

> There is doubt that a nation can improve its welfare or level of employment over the long run by subsidizing exports. Economists generally maintain that economic policies within individual countries are the prime factors which determine interest rates, capital flows, and exchange rates, and the overall level of a nation's exports. As a result, they hold that subsidizing export financing merely shifts production among sectors within the economy, but does not add to the overall level of economic activity, and subsidizes foreign consumption at the expense of the domestic economy. From this point of view, promoting exports through subsidized financing or through government-backed insurance and guarantees will not permanently raise the level of employment in the economy, but alters the composition of employment among the various sectors of the economy and, [sic] therefore performs poorly as a jobs creation mechanism.[79]

Shifting jobs from XYZ Aircraft Manufacturer to Boeing may be good for Boeing, but it is emphatically not an unalloyed good.

The percentage of Export-Import Bank financing that flows to small businesses is predictably meager, despite the frequent assurances by bank flacks that the institution has as a central mission the promotion of exports from small American businesses. The Bank claims that in

FY 2012, small business authorizations accounted for 17.1 percent of total authorizations, down from 18.4 percent the previous year.[80]

These figures fall somewhat shy of the pledge in the Bank's charter, which now reads: "The Bank shall make available, from the aggregate loan, guarantee, and insurance authority available to it, an amount to finance exports directly by small business concerns (as defined under section 3 of the Small Business Act) which shall not be less than 20 percent of such authority for each fiscal year."[81]

Now, 17.1 percent is not 20 percent—it's not even 18.4 percent, which was the total in FY 2011—but perhaps we can't fault the Bank for missing this target. After all, Boeing must be served first. (As Sallie James notes, small businesses account for about 30 percent of US exports—so despite Ex-Im's lip service, "small and medium-sized businesses are disproportionately *underserved* by the Ex-Im Bank."[82])

Also in FY 2012, the most recent year for which figures were available, the Bank's "exposure" was highest in Asia, which accounted for $42.3 billion, or 39.7 percent of its activity in dollars. Next on the list came its historic focus area of Latin American and the Caribbean, whose Ex-Im exposure was $22.1 billion, or 20.7 percent of the total. Following those two leaders were Europe ($11.3 billion/10.6 percent), North America ($10.6 billion/9.9 percent), Oceania ($8.3 billion/ 7.8 percent), Africa ($5.8 billion/5.4 percent), and all others ($6.2 billion/ 5.9 percent).

As for exposure by sector, the winner and still champion, in fact the champion as far as the eye can see, the leading recipient of Ex-Im favors in FY 2012—and it's not even close—was, as mentioned earlier, air transportation, which accounted for $49.4 billion, or 46.3 percent of Ex-Im's exposure. This perennial corporate welfare champ was followed by manufacturing ($18.1 billion/17 percent), oil and gas ($13.9 billion/13.1 percent), power projects ($8.6 billion/8.1 percent), and all others ($16.5 billion/15.5 percent). Thus over three-quarters of the Bank's exposure is concentrated in three industries: air transportation, manufacturing, and oil and gas.[83]

The Bank has shifted somewhat from its early focus on national governments—for instance the client states of South America—to private, or quasi-private, foreign entities. Of course the likes of China Air, South Korea's Development Bank, and Pemex, the Mexican state-owned petroleum company, remain clients of the bank. The percentage of Ex-Im exposure to public-sector, or governmental, borrowers only dipped from 40.5 to 30.7 from FY 2008 to FY 2012, as private-sector-borrower exposure increased over that period from 59.5 to 69.3 percent. (Sovereign obligors contribute 8.8 percent toward that 30.7 percent, with the remainder being public non-sovereign entities.)[84]

This is heralded as a step away from statism and toward a dynamic private-sector emphasis, but it does not change the central fact that the Bank is picking winners and losers and subsidizing favored businesses (or states) in a manner wholly inconsistent with the market-drenched rhetoric now in vogue with the planning community. (If only the same respect for the market were visible in their actions and not just their words!)

In March 2010, President Obama announced his National Export Initiative (NEI), a corporatist effort to subsidize those exporters who win the favor of the federal government. The goals of the NEI, which was established by executive order, were ridiculously, unattainably large: a doubling of US exports by 2015 in the service of two million jobs for American workers. As is inevitably the case, this pie in the sky will go uneaten, but don't count on the mass media, which too often function as relayers of White House press releases, to hold the administration to its projection. That's yesterday's news; in the spin cycle, it's always tomorrow's news that matters.

The purpose of the NEI, according to the executive order that snapped it to life, was "to enhance and coordinate Federal efforts to facilitate the creation of jobs in the United States through the promotion of exports, and to ensure the effective use of Federal resources in support of these goals."[85] If only the creation of jobs were that easy.

Ex-Im's role in the National Export Initiative was threefold. In the words of the Bank's draftsmen, it was to:

— Expand awareness of Ex-Im Bank services through focused business development and effective partnerships;
— Improve ease of doing business for customers; and
— Create an environment that fosters high performance and innovation.[86]

Note, again, the use of language that would not be out of place in a Republican congressional caucus meeting or on the pages of one of those *Secrets of Business Leadership* paperbacks that one might buy at an airport kiosk. Words like *awareness, focused, effective, partnerships, ease, fosters, innovation*—these all are right out of Management 101.

And *customers*—why, it's as if the Export-Import Bank has somehow forgotten its founding pledge that it is not a private bank, nor does it compete with private lending institutions.

In its annual report, the Bank even stoops to using such business-speak clichés as the claim that it is an example of "Government at the Speed of Business," a woefully misguided phrase that mistakes coercion and bureaucracy—the hallmarks of government—for voluntary actions undertaken in a marketplace of voluntary actors.[87]

Under its FY 2010 strategic plan, the Bank targeted nine countries for its own special brand of ministration: Mexico, Brazil, Colombia, Turkey, India, Indonesia, Vietnam, Nigeria, and South Africa. The days of the Export-Import Bank's panjandrums disclaiming any foreign policy angle to its activities are long gone. Ex-Im is now frankly in the politics business, though in truth, it has been there since the beginning, when it was used as an instrument of diplomacy in the guise of trade with the Soviet Union.

Authorized loans, guarantees, and insurance for exporters doing business in the newly targeted countries exceeded $1 billion in FY 2012 in only two of them: Mexico ($2.8 billion) and Brazil ($1 billion).[88] In FY 2012, the leading country in terms of outstanding and undisbursed loans was none other than Saudi Arabia ($6.7 billion)[89], that notoriously purse-poor kingdom that is participating in "Ex-Im's largest deal ever: a $5 billion direct loan to subsidize Saudi Arabia's state-owned oil company in building a petrochemical plant" that will be half owned by Dow Chemical. Corporate welfare doesn't get much more plutocratic than that![90]

Second on the loans list was Australia ($3.5 billion), another nation not lacking in wealth. Third was Colombia ($2.7 billion) and fourth was the United Arab Emirates ($2.5 billion), so as you can see, the Export-Import Bank is not yet given over to a Third World portfolio.[91] In fact, it is a mystery why such countries and the Ex-Im recipients therein, whether governmental, quasi-governmental, or private, cannot attract private financing for these projects. But we may be sure that as long as Boeing, GE, and the likes dominate its roster of beneficiaries, exposure in Saudi Arabia will greatly exceed that in Chad, Burkina Faso, and Botswana.

The extent to which public and private merge in some of the Export-Import Bank's client countries is positively dazzling. For example, in 2001 the bank gave a controversial $160 million loan guarantee to the Shin Corporation of Thailand, a telecommunications company that just happened to be owned by Thaksin Shinawatra, Thailand's prime minister. Mr. Shinawatra was also a billionaire. With this loan guarantee his sprawling corporation purchased a communications satellite from Loral Space and Communications, which, as Leslie Wayne of the *New York Times* noted, was "an American manufacturer run by Bernard L. Schwartz, a longtime Democratic Party donor."

A spokesman for an outraged competitor, Franklin G. Polk of the Netherlands-based New Skies Satellites, asked, "How is it that billionaires like Shinawatra and Bernie Schwartz can get the US taxpayers to subsidize their deals?" Polk noted that his company had arranged private financing for the deal, but the terms were not as favorable as the Ex-Im loan guarantee.[92]

The Bank, however, is shameless: subsidizing billionaires is *what it does.*

The Export-Import Bank has also announced its determination to penetrate Africa, assisting US exporters who wish to trade in "high-risk" markets. High-risk markets are precisely the kind that prudent bankers eschew, but when you're playing with taxpayer money, the risks are borne not by investors or clients but by hapless taxpayers who have zero say in the matter. Thus taxpayers are exposed to risks that no private bank would shoulder. (In FY 2012, the Bank allowed $4.6 billion, or 4.3 percent of total exposure, for loan losses and liabilities and defaults on guarantees and insurance.[93])

There is a certain arrogance given off by the Bank in this matter of high-risk loans. It calls to mind former Secretary of State Madeleine Albright's remarkable assertion in 1998 that "we are America! We are the indispensable nation. We stand tall, and we see further into the future."[94] These are the kind of megalomaniacs that one is advised to steer clear of—they are the sort of righteous crusaders who will take your home or expropriate your property or confiscate your savings or even bomb your village, all the while assuring you that *it is for your own good.*

Sallie James limns the mindset: "The bank's attitude reflects a common and misguided assumption in Washington that a few hundred central-agency bureaucrats are more accurately able to price risk and manage economic activities than tens of thousands of private-sector investors and analysts with their own money at stake."[95]

In FY 2012, Ex-Im authorizations for projects in sub-Saharan Africa totaled $1.5 billion.[96] The response that the Bank hopes to elicit when imparting such news is one of praise; the image that it hopes to conjure is of desperately poor people gaining access to critical materials thanks to the loans and loan guarantees of the US government.

But consider the recipients of Ex-Im authorizations in sub-Saharan Africa. There is Boeing—there is *always* Boeing when the Export-Import Bank is concerned—financing through Ex-Im a sale to Ethiopian Airways. There is Boeing again, this time in South Africa. There are Caterpillar and General Electric and Comair . . . the usual suspects receiving the usual subsidies, but in Africa instead of Asia or Europe. From the left, J. C. Shields, writing in *Foreign Policy in Focus*, a publication under the aegis of the Institute for Policy Studies, worries that Ex-Im introduces "inappropriate technologies" into Third World nations with unskilled labor pools. "Exports of mining, petroleum, and infrastructure equipment may help multinational corporations and developed countries access cheaper raw materials," argues Shields, "with few benefits for the residents of developing countries."

Shields also scoffs at the fantasy that the Export-Import Bank is transmitting democracy to the Third World, noting that over a three-year period in the late 1990s, every loan made to Brazil, Indonesia, and Venezuela was used "to purchase equipment for their militaries, including aircraft, trucks, and radio systems."[97] Boeing has used Ex-Im financing to sell aircraft to the Chinese military, who are no one's idea of a liberating force.

The Export-Import Bank, ever sensitive to the prevailing winds of political fashion, has drawn attention to its promotion of US exports that offer "environmentally beneficial goods and services." In FY 2012 these made up less than 2 percent ($614.5 million) of the Bank's total transactions in dollars, but they made for good public relations, especially given the Bank's historic record of financing environmentally dubious projects such as steel mills and rubber plantations. In fact, the Bank boasted of financing a $45 million landfill gas capture in Brazil, site of the infamous rubber soldier experiment of the 1940s, and it proudly noted that "Ex-Im Bank continues to be one of the top financiers of solar projects in India," instancing projects by Mahindra Solar and Kiran Energy.[98]

Yet despite its sedulous application of the gloss of political correctness, the Export-Import Bank is about money and power. As the economist Robert Higgs writes, "The bank is just another contrivance to shift wealth from the politically weak and alienated to the politically strong and connected, while sanctifying the transfer with incantations of economic humbug."[99] That's the kind of bracing rhetoric one never finds in an Export-Import Bank publication.

\* \* \*

The Bank's periodic congressional reauthorizations encounter some turbulence, but it is a manageable turbulence. At its last, in 2012, the Club for Growth, a free-market lobby, spearheaded the opposition. The following year the Club attempted to block the nominations of Bank President Fred Hochberg and two directors as a way to prevent Bank meetings from operating with a quorum.

Chris Chocola, the Club for Growth's president, called Ex-Im "a slush fund for market-distorting subsidies that pick winners and losers in the private sector." He called on Senate Republican leader Mitch McConnell (R-KY) to "demand a plan to wind down the Export-Import Bank and not enable it to continue to hand out massive amounts of corporate welfare benefiting a few select industries."[100]

Both efforts failed, though they did smoke out the corporate-welfare constituency among the capital city's business groups. The National Association of Manufacturers supported the Bank. Its president, Jay Timmons, called it a "vital tool for small manufacturers exporting to new markets."[101]

Thomas J. Donohue, president of the US Chamber of Commerce, a mainstay of the corporate welfare lobby, wailed that a congressional failure to extend the Bank's life "would amount to unilateral disarmament and cost tens of thousands of American jobs."[102] The Chamber's senior director for international policy, Christopher Wenk, said, "Ex-Im obviously plays a vital role for exporters. Not just big companies, but medium- and small-sized companies in particular depend on Ex-Im financing."[103] (This last assertion is just flatly untrue. But then Ex-Im defenders are skilled at the art of exaggeration. They love to claim that more than 80 percent of their transactions are related to small or medium-sized businesses, but of course in terms of dollars that percentage does not even exceed 20.)

The word Boeing, we may be sure, never passed the lips of these Chamber spokesmen. But it did make its way into the arguments of Bank opponents. Delta Air Lines had lodged complaints that Ex-Im financing, by assisting Boeing in selling to Air India, was subsidizing foreign competitors to American firms. Senator Jim DeMint (R-SC) lamented, "We're in a bidding war with China and Europe to see who can subsidize the most loans at a time when all of us are broke. We need to bring this to a close."[104]

Nevertheless, the Ex-Im reauthorization easily passed in the House in May 2012 by a vote of 330–93. Astonishingly, every Democrat voted yea, while Republicans split, with 147 yeas and 93 nays. Anyone laboring under the illusion that the Democrats as a party are in any way, shape, or form hostile to crony capitalism need only examine the Ex-Im vote. A single member of Congress took to the floor to explain his nay vote. Tom McClintock (R-CA) said that the Bank "dragoons American taxpayers into subsidizing loans to foreign companies by making it cheaper for them to buy products from politically favored American companies. . . . Legitimate companies have plenty of access to private capital. They don't need these subsidies."[105]

A week later, the Senate reauthorized the Bank by a vote of 78–20. Nineteen of those twenty dissenting votes came from Republicans; the other was cast by Bernie Sanders, the Vermont socialist who is technically an independent, though he caucuses with the Democrats. Sanders has been a consistent harsh critic of the bank, saying that "Export-Import is generous with taxpayer dollars and we get nothing in return. It's vulgar. At a time when we are having a real crisis in this country and are losing jobs, Ex-Im is sending them overseas. Yet these are the most important corporations in the United States and they get what they want in Washington."[106]

It is a bracing thing to realize that the free-market cause would have done better if only the Democrats had more socialists among them. Predictably, one of the Bank's most ardent admirers was Senator Maria Cantwell, a Democrat from Washington, who presumably has inherited the "Senator from Boeing" seat in that august body.

Senator Sanders has been a longtime critic of the Bank. He has pointed to the numerous instances in which Ex-Im has subsidized foreign competitors of domestic concerns: for example, the Chinese steel mill whose products were sold in the US, and the General Electric appliance-parts factory in Mexico that competed with—and some argue was responsible for the closing of—a plant in Bloomington, Indiana.[107]

The case of the Chinese mill was so outrageous that it even spurred the usually torpid organized labor into action. In 2000, Ex-Im loaned the Benxi Iron and Steel Group $18 billion to purchase US-made equipment. A year later, Benxi was determined to be dumping steel— that is, selling at below-market price—in the US market, and was slapped with a heavy tariff. Given that the US steel industry was in dire straits, the sight of a US government entity supporting Chinese rivals to a struggling American industry roused heated protests, especially from labor and those of its congressional allies who were not in Ex-Im's pocket.

George Becker, former United Steelworkers of America president, thundered, "Why are they pouring money into other countries to build additional steel capacity? This isn't trade. It's dismantling our manufacturing base and robbing our workers of their right to earn a living."[108]

Before giving the Bank a renewed lease on life, the Senate rejected an amendment by Senator Mike Lee (R-UT) that would have killed Ex-Im, giving it a brief time to get its affairs in order. Senator Lee's floor speech in support of his amendment is a concise summary of the Main Street case against the Bank and is worth quoting:

> The American people cannot be the world's financial backstop. The government shouldn't be picking winners and losers. Businesses in Utah and across the country are not receiving government help and are shutting their doors after decades serving their communities. We should not through this government be adding insult to injury by using tax money they contributed to prop up companies overseas.
>
> We need to end the corporate welfare that distorts the market and feeds crony capitalism. The corporations that largely benefit from the Ex-Im Bank should have no trouble marshaling their resources to compete in today's economy. If they are struggling, then they are most likely not deserving of taxpayer help, and if they are turning billions in profit, then they clearly do not need taxpayer-subsidized loans.
>
> Further, government subsidies breed undue favoritism from government bureaucrats who control where the money goes. Unless we want more Solyndras, we should end the practice immediately.
>
> Some have suggested that the Ex-Im bank is good for businesses. Mr. President, what's best for American businesses is getting the federal government out of their way, letting them operate without burdensome government regulations and without a complex tax system. Having the government pick winners and losers does not make industries stronger and makes them more dependent on subsidies, and when government is picking who wins, the loser is always the taxpayer.[109]

Senator Lee's amendment attracted but twelve votes. Not even a baker's dozen of senators would support shuttering this monument to crony capitalism.

Senator Rand Paul (R-KY), another stalwart foe of Ex-Im, explained that opposing the Bank's reauthorization was not tantamount to opposing capitalism. Just the opposite. Senator Paul told the Senate, "I'm a great believer in capitalism, in the jobs that corporations create. I defend profit and the benefit that accrues from leaving that profit large[ly] in the private sector. I'm not one who clamors for punitive taxes, I'm not someone who thinks we need to punish corporations, but at the same time don't construe that to mean that I believe we should be subsidizing profitable corporations."[110]

It is a strange twist by which putative defenders of free enterprise, such as the US Chamber of Commerce, stand up for extensive intervention in the economy, and barely a handful of members of the US Senate are willing to call them on it.

But the Bank is shrewd. It knows how to lobby and it could shame an expert mechanic in the art of wheel greasing. A Treasury official told the *New York Times*, "As a staff member for a congressman, you can call up Ex-Im and say, 'My congressman represents District 13 in the state of whatever.' They will spit out a report saying, 'Here are the businesses by name in your district that receive Ex-Im help.' The bank is politically savvy. It's active in promoting its products in each Congressional district."

In past fights over the Ex-Im budget, corporate heavy-hitters such as United Parcel Service, Bechtel, Oracle, Verizon, United Technologies, Citigroup, and Bank of America have joined the US Chamber of Commerce and the National Association of Manufacturers in lobbying for more, more, more. Thomas A. Schatz, president of Citizens Against Government Waste, told the *New York Times*, "You have an incredibly well-funded lobbying operation led by companies that are not only campaign contributors but also talk about creating jobs. That's a big rallying cry for members of Congress. They think that jobs will help them get re-elected, and once you say that jobs are at risk in their district, they go running for cover."[111]

Another chapter in *Profiles in Courage*.

The Bank rewards its friends. At Ex-Im's spring 2013 annual conference, honcho Fred Hochberg presented Chamber of Commerce president Donohue with the Chairman's Award in gratitude for the Chamber's tenacious defense of the Bank during its 2012 reauthorization battle. Hochberg patronizingly called the Chamber a "rational" force among Republicans, presumably by contrast with wackos, nutballs, and whatever epithets establishmentarians apply to such Ex-Im critics as Senators Rand Paul and Mike Lee.[112]

These annual Ex-Im soirees are grandiloquent exercises in self-congratulation and sedulous flattery of corporate giants. At the spring 2013 meeting Hochberg also presented General Electric with the coveted Sub-Saharan Africa Exporter of the Year Award. This isn't exactly an Oscar, or even a Golden Globe—it's certainly not a Peoples' Choice Award—but the Eximmies, as we might dub them, are every bit as shameless in their celebration of the rich and powerful for being . . . rich and powerful.

President Hochberg presented the Eximmy to GE, declaring: "This transaction is what Ex-Im Bank is all about—improving the lives of people around the world while supporting American jobs in the process."[113] International altruism, jobs, and maybe a few bucks for General Electric: who could object?

Hochberg himself had survived his Senate reconfirmation in 2013 with barely a scratch. He was approved by a vote of 82–17, with the nays coming from such presumably irrational senators as Lee of Utah, who told the Senate that the Bank's "sole purpose is to dispense corporate welfare and political privileges to well-connected special interests. The Export-Import Bank . . . is an example of everything that is wrong with Washington today."[114] Not a single Democrat voted against Hochberg.

Sallie James, trade policy analyst for the Cato Institute, concluded that "Congress should recognize that the alleged justifications for the Ex-Im Bank's existence are hollow and abolish the agency completely."[115] As for the claim that since other nations subsidize exports so ought we, the late William A. Niskanen, onetime Cato chairman and Reagan economic advisor, declared in 2001: "The Soviet Union has collapsed, and there is now an opportunity to end the continuing cold war of export credit subsidies."[116] (And as James points out, the US is hardly in a position to point fingers in this regard. By her calculations, it ranks third among rich countries in export credits used as a percentage of total merchandise exports.)

Unfortunately for taxpayers and those who abhor corporate welfare, the Export-Import Bank's exit is about as likely as Boeing eschewing government subsidies as part of a We Believe in the Free Market campaign. The Export-Import Bank has too many powerful constituents and too low a public profile: those who profit from its subventions are influential, and those who object to its dispensing of favors are too scattered, their voices not quite audible within Washington's corridors of power. As Stephen Moore of the libertarian Cato Institute lamented, "In administration after administration, Export-Import was always on the top of the list to get cut." It survived, however, due to "the full-court lobbying blitz by Fortune 500 companies."

Moore has described Ex-Im as "the poster boy for the anti-corporate welfare movement." There is, he says, "no rationale for the government" to subsidize "the wealthiest corporations" in the world.[117] And yet it does. And every attempt to rein in Ex-Im, let alone abolish it, fails by large margins in the Congress. It's almost enough to make the cynical observer conclude that government gives preponderant consideration to the rich and powerful.

Still, one can hope. J. C. Shields, in *Foreign Policy in Focus*, points to the ideological diversity of Bank opponents, who range from anti-corporate leftists to free enterprisers on the Right.[118] This is, in rough outline, the coalition that has risen in opposition to other giveaways and takeways in the long sordid history of corporate welfare. It has yet to post many signal victories, with the exception of the SST battle of the 1960s and early 1970s, but for reformers, hope springs eternal.

## Notes

1.	Wayne, "A Guardian of Jobs or a 'Reverse Robin Hood'?" *New York Times*.
2.	http://www.taxpayer.net/library/article/u.s.-department-of-agricultures-market-access-program.
3.	http://www.opic.gov/.
4.	Bartlett and Steele, "Corporate Welfare," *Time*.
5.	Nader, *Cutting Corporate Welfare*, p. 103.
6.	Stephen Slivinski, "The Corporate Welfare State: How the Federal Government Subsidizes U.S. Businesses," *Cato Institute Policy Analysis* No. 592, May 14, 2007, p. 17.
7.	Bob Hohler, "Trade Trip Firms Netted $5.5 b in Aid Donated $2.3 m to Democrats," *Boston Globe*, March 30, 1997.
8.	James S. Olson, *Saving Capitalism: The Reconstruction Finance Corporation and the New Deal, 1933–1940* (Princeton, NJ: Princeton University Press, 1988), p. 149.
9.	"Executive Order 6581 Creating The Export-Import Bank of Washington," February 2, 1934, http://www.presidency.ucsb.edu/ws/?pid=14772.
10.	Quoted in Charles R. Whittlesey, "Five Years of the Export-Import Bank," *American Economic Review* (Vol. 29, No. 3, September 1939): 488.
11.	Gardner Patterson, "The Export-Import Bank," *Quarterly Journal of Economics* (Vol. 58, No. 1, November 1943): 66.
12.	Jesse H. Jones and Edward Angly, *Fifty Billion Dollars: My Thirteen Years with the RFC, 1932–1945* (New York: Macmillan, 1951), pp. 215–16.
13.	The First Export-Import Bank capitalized by selling $10 million in preferred stock to the Reconstruction Finance Corporation and $1 million in common stock to the State and Commerce Departments. The Second Export-Import Bank sold $2.5 million in preferred stock to the RFC and $250,000 in common stock to the State and Commerce Departments. William H. Becker and William M. McClenahan Jr., *The Market, the State, and the Export-Import*

*Bank of the United States, 1934–2000* (Cambridge: Cambridge University Press, 2003), pp. 14–15.

14. Whittlesey, "Five Years of the Export-Import Bank," *American Economic Review*: 491.

15. Patterson, "The Export-Import Bank," *Quarterly Journal of Economics*: 67.

16. Olson, *Saving Capitalism: The Reconstruction Finance Corporation and the New Deal, 1933–1940*, p. 151.

17. George N. Peek and Samuel Crowther, *Why Quit Our Own* (New York: Van Nostrand, 1936), epigraph.

18. Ibid., pp. 7, 11, 14.

19. Ibid., p. 37.

20. Ibid., p. 192.

21. Ibid., pp. 193–94.

22. Whittlesey, "Five Years of the Export-Import Bank," *American Economic Review*: 497.

23. Peek and Samuel Crowther, *Why Quit Our Own*, p. 194.

24. Ibid., p. 342.

25. Ibid., p. 196.

26. Patterson, "The Export-Import Bank," *Quarterly Journal of Economics*: 69.

27. Jones and Angly, *Fifty Billion Dollars: My Thirteen Years with the RFC, 1932–1945* , pp. 222–23.

28. Ibid., p. 218.

29. Patterson, "The Export-Import Bank," *Quarterly Journal of Economics*: 72.

30. Ibid.: 70.

31. Walter L. Hixson, *The American Experience in World War II: Pearl Harbor in History and Memory* (New York: Routledge, 2003), p. 90.

32. Patterson, "The Export-Import Bank," *Quarterly Journal of Economics*: 72.

33. Ibid.: 76.

34. Ibid.: 79.

35. Edward J. Rogers, "Brazilian Success Story: The Volta-Redonda Iron and Steel Project," *Journal of Inter-American Studies* (Vol. 10, No. 4, October 1968): 637.

36. Mario Osava, "Brazil's Steel Industry no Longer a Demon," *Tierrameica*, http://www.tierramerica.net/2001/0916/iarticulo.shtml.

37. James A. Brooke, "Manaus Journal: For the Rubber Soldiers of Brazil, Rubber Checks," *New York Times*, May 15, 1991.

38. See "Haiti's Grim History of Being 'Open for Business,'" *Haiti Liberte*, June 5, 2012, http://www.haiti-liberte.com/archives/volume5-46/Haiti%E2%80%99s%20Grim.asp; and Noam Chomsky, *Year 501* (Boston: South End Press, 1993), Chapter 9 online at http://books.zcommunications.org/chomsky/year/year-c09-s01.html.

39. Patterson, "The Export-Import Bank," *Quarterly Journal of Economics*: 81.

40. Whittlesey, "Five Years of the Export-Import Bank," *American Economic Review*: 487.

41. Rita M. Rodriguez, "Exim's Mission and Accomplishments: 1934–84," in *The Export-Import Bank at Fifty: The International Environment and the*

*Institution's Role*, edited by Rita M. Rodriguez (Washington, DC: Lexington Books, 1987), p. 4.

42. Whittlesey, "Five Years of the Export-Import Bank," *American Economic Review*: 500.

43. Ibid.: 487.

44. Becker and McClenahan Jr., *The Market, the State, and the Export-Import Bank of the United States, 1934–2000*, p. 1.

45. Ibid., p. 6.

46. Quoted in Veronique de Rugy, "Bipartisan Corporate Welfare: It's time for the Export-Import Bank to go," *Reason*, October 2013, p. 20.

47. Shayerah Ilias, "Export-Import Bank: Background and Legislative Issues," Congressional Research Service, April 3, 2012, summary.

48. "Management's Discussion and Analysis of Results of Operations and Financial Condition, For the Years Ended September 30, 2012 And September 30, 2011," Export-Import Bank of the United States, p. 6.

49. Ilias, "Export-Import Bank: Background and Legislative Issues," Congressional Research Service, summary.

50. Ibid., p. 1.

51. "Management's Discussion and Analysis of Results of Operations and Financial Condition, For the Years Ended September 30, 2012 And September 30, 2011," Export-Import Bank of the United States, p. 2.

52. Sallie James, "Time to X out the Ex-Im Bank," *Cato Institute Center for Trade Policy Studies*, July 6, 2011, p. 17.

53. Nader, *Cutting Corporate Welfare*, p. 111.

54. Kouros and Barry, "Targeting Eximbank Subsidies," *Foreign Policy in Focus* (Vol. 1, No. 2, October 1996): unpaginated.

55. Ilias, "Export-Import Bank: Background and Legislative Issues," Congressional Research Service, p. 19.

56. "Boeing in Brief," http://www.boeing.com/boeing/companyoffices/aboutus/brief.page.

57. Carney, *The Big Ripoff: How Big Business and Big Government Steal Your Money*, p. 79.

58. Robert Higgs, "Unmitigated Mercantilism," *Independent Review* (Vol. 5, No. 3, Winter 2001).

59. "Ex-Im Bank Authorizes $117.5 Million in First Financing of Boeing Aircraft to flydubai," Export-Import Bank of the United States news release, October 9, 2012, http://www.exim.gov/newsandevents/releases/2012/ex-im-bank-authorizes-117-5-million-in-first-financing-of-boeing-aircraft-to-flydubai.cfm).

60. "Ex-Im Bank Approves $1.1 Billion in Financing for U.S.-Manufactured B737-900ER Aircraft to Indonesia's Lion Air," Export-Import Bank of the United States news release, March 5, 2013, http://www.exim.gov/newsandevents/releases/2013/ExIm-Bank-Approves-11-Billion-in-Financing-for-USManufactured-B737900ER-Aircraft-to-Indonesias-Lion-Air.cfm.

61. Timothy P. Carney, "Boeing and Obama sitting in a tree, K-I-S-S-I-N-G," *Washington Examiner*, December 3, 2012.

62. Ibid.

63. de Rugy, "Bipartisan Corporate Welfare: It's time for the Export-Import Bank to go," *Reason*, p. 20.

64. Ilias, "Export-Import Bank: Background and Legislative Issues," Congressional Research Service, p. 19.

65. Wayne, "A Guardian of Jobs or a 'Reverse Robin Hood'?" *New York Times*.

66. Sallie James, "Expanding Ex-Im's Mandate Is a Big Mistake," *Cato Institute Free Trade Bulletin* No. 48, March 14, 2012.

67. "Management's Discussion and Analysis of Results of Operations and Financial Condition, For the Years Ended September 30, 2012 And September 30, 2011," Export-Import Bank of the United States, p. 3.

68. Ibid., p. 6.

69. "Statement from U.S. Deputy Secretary of Commerce Rebecca Blank on Record International Trade in Goods and Services in 2012," U.S. Department of Commerce, February 8, 2013, http://www.commerce.gov/news/press-releases/2013/02/08/statement-us-deputy-secretary-commerce-rebecca-blank-record-internati.

70. The US trade figure is from calendar year 2012, while the Export-Import number is from fiscal year 2012.

71. Ian Vasquez, "Re-Authorize or Retire the Export-Import Bank?" Testimony before the U.S. House of Representatives Subcommittee on International Monetary Policy and Trade Committee on Financial Services, May 8, 2001.

72. Shayerah Ilias, "Export-Import Bank: Background and Legislative Issues," Congressional Research Service, February 9, 2011, p. 2.

73. James, "Time to X out the Ex-Im Bank," *Cato Institute Center for Trade Policy Studies*, p. 3.

74. Wayne, "A Guardian of Jobs or a 'Reverse Robin Hood'?" *New York Times*.

75. "Management's Discussion and Analysis of Results of Operations and Financial Condition, For the Years Ended September 30, 2012 And September 30, 2011," Export-Import Bank of the United States, p. 2.

76. James, "Time to X out the Ex-Im Bank," *Cato Institute Center for Trade Policy Studies*, p. 4.

77. Ilias, "Export-Import Bank: Background and Legislative Issues," Congressional Research Service (2011), p. 13.

78. James, "Time to X out the Ex-Im Bank," *Cato Institute Center for Trade Policy Studies*, p. 5.

79. Ilias, "Export-Import Bank: Background and Legislative Issues," Congressional Research Service (2011), p. 13.

80. "Management's Discussion and Analysis of Results of Operations and Financial Condition, For the Years Ended September 30, 2012 And September 30, 2011," Export-Import Bank of the United States, p. 14.

81. "The Charter of the Export-Import Bank of the United States," p. 16, http://usaexport.org/research_reports/Updated_2012_EXIM_Charter_August_2012_Final.pdf.

82. James, "Time to X out the Ex-Im Bank," *Cato Institute Center for Trade Policy Studies*, p. 9.

83. "Management's Discussion and Analysis of Results of Operations and Financial Condition, For the Years Ended September 30, 2012 And September 30, 2011," Export-Import Bank of the United States, p. 23.

84. Ibid., p. 24.
85. "Executive Order 13534. National Export Initiative," March 11, 2010, http://www.whitehouse.gov/the-press-office/executive-order-national-export-initiative.
86. "Management's Discussion and Analysis of Results of Operations and Financial Condition, For the Years Ended September 30, 2012 And September 30, 2011," Export-Import Bank of the United States, p. 10.
87. "Export-Import Bank of the United States: 2012 Annual Report," http://www.exim.gov/about/library/reports/annualreports/2012/.
88. "Management's Discussion and Analysis of Results of Operations and Financial Condition, For the Years Ended September 30, 2012 And September 30, 2011," Export-Import Bank of the United States, p. 11.
89. Ibid., p. 22.
90. Timothy P. Carney, "Tea Party fights Obama, K Street on corporate welfare," *Washington Examiner*, April 8, 2013.
91. "Management's Discussion and Analysis of Results of Operations and Financial Condition, For the Years Ended September 30, 2012 And September 30, 2011," Export-Import Bank of the United States, p. 22.
92. Wayne, "A Guardian of Jobs or a 'Reverse Robin Hood'?" *New York Times*.
93. "Management's Discussion and Analysis of Results of Operations and Financial Condition, For the Years Ended September 30, 2012 And September 30, 2011," Export-Import Bank of the United States, p. 27.
94. "The Today Show with Matt Lauer," NBC-TV, February 19, 1998.
95. James, "Time to X out the Ex-Im Bank," *Cato Institute Center for Trade Policy Studies*, p. 7.
96. "Management's Discussion and Analysis of Results of Operations and Financial Condition, For the Years Ended September 30, 2012 And September 30, 2011," Export-Import Bank of the United States, pp. 15–16.
97. J. C. Shields, "Export-Import Bank," *Foreign Policy in Focus* (1999).
98. "Management's Discussion and Analysis of Results of Operations and Financial Condition, For the Years Ended September 30, 2012 And September 30, 2011," Export-Import Bank of the United States, p. 15.
99. Higgs, "Unmitigated Mercantilism," *Independent Review*.
100. Doug Palmer, "U.S. group steps up effort to shut down Export-Import Bank," Reuters, April 16, 2013, http://www.reuters.com/article/2013/04/16/usa-eximbank-idUSL2N0D31RM20130416.
101. Ed O'Keefe, "Export-Import Bank reauthorized by House; Senate expected to act soon," *Washington Post*, May 9, 2012.
102. Ibid.
103. Palmer, "U.S. group steps up effort to shut down Export-Import Bank," Reuters.
104. Jim Abrams, "Export-Import Bank Reauthorization: Senate Votes to Renew Charter," *Washington Post*, May 15, 2012.
105. Sallie James, "Ending the Export-Import Bank," *Downsizing the Federal Government* (Cato Institute), October 2012.
106. Wayne, "A Guardian of Jobs or a 'Reverse Robin Hood'?" *New York Times*.
107. Bernie Sanders, "The Export-Import Bank: Corporate Welfare at Its Worst," *Common Dreams*, May 15, 2002, www.commondreams.org.

108. Wayne, "A Guardian of Jobs or a 'Reverse Robin Hood'?" *New York Times.*

109. "Lee offers Amendment to End Export-Import Bank," press release, May 15, 2012, http://www.lee.senate.gov/public/index.cfm/press-releases?ID=615dc668-99d0-4fc7-bc33-e497a64a125c.

110. "Senator Paul Urges Senate to Reject Re-Authorization of the Export-Import Bank," press release, May 10, 2012, http://www.randpaul2016.com/2012/05/senator-paul-urges-senate-to-reject-re-authorization-of-the-export-import-bank/.

111. Wayne, "A Guardian of Jobs or a 'Reverse Robin Hood'?" *New York Times.*

112. Carney, "Tea Party fights Obama, K Street on corporate welfare," *Washington Examiner.*

113. "General Electric Company Awarded Ex-Im Bank Sub-Saharan Africa Exporter of the Year," Export-Import Bank of the United States press release, April 4, 2013, http://www.exim.gov/newsandevents/releases/2013/General-Electric-Company-Awarded-Ex-Im-Bank-Sub-Saharan-Africa-Exporter-of-the-Year.cfm.

114. Doug Palmer, "Senate approved head of Ex-Im bank for second term," Reuters, July 17, 2013, http://www.reuters.com/article/2013/07/17/us-usa-senate-eximbank-idUSBRE96G0RP20130717.

115. James, "Time to X out the Ex-Im Bank," *Cato Institute Center for Trade Policy Studies*, p. 3.

116. William A. Niskanen, "Should Ex-Im Be Retired?" in *The Export-Import Bank at Fifty: The International Environment and the Institution's Role*, p. 196.

117. Wayne, "A Guardian of Jobs or a 'Reverse Robin Hood'?" *New York Times.*

118. Shields, "Export-Import Bank," *Foreign Policy in Focus.*

# 7

## Conclusion:
# Will It Ever End? Or Is There a Future for an Anti-Corporate Welfare Coalition?

In *Beyond the Broker State: Federal Policies toward Small Business, 1936–1961*, economic historian Jonathan J. Bean describes the difficulty in weaving into the anti-corporate welfare coalition the essential element of small businesspeople, those embodiments of free enterprise who are probably the group most disadvantaged by giveaways to the big guys: "Present-day advocates of small business face the same problem that plagued congressional champions of small business in the past: most small business owners lack any interest in politics and government," writes Bean.

He continues: "Many small business owners are simply too busy to concern themselves with government, even if it promises them benefits. The political scientist Benjamin Mokry concludes that the small business owner is 'by nature independent and antibureaucratic, and may spend little time watching government actions.' Furthermore, many small business owners are hostile to government in general because they feel burdened by taxes and regulations."[1]

Admirable traits, certainly, but not so useful in constructing an anti-corporate welfare movement. What is true of small businesspeople is often true of other ordinary Americans who should be the bulwarks of any such movement: They have better things to do than muck about in politics.

So what can be done?

Solutions range from the comprehensive (legislatively enacted bans on corporate welfare at the federal and the state levels) to the piecemeal. They even include a proposal to further empower the federal government, king of the corporate welfare world, by imposing a federal excise tax on state and local incentives. Arthur J. Rolnick, former senior vice president of the Federal Reserve Bank of Minneapolis and senior fellow at the Humphrey Institute of Public Affairs, says, "You have to make the tax confiscatory, a 100 percent tax, to take away the incentive. Then there's no reason for a company to come knocking at your door. Some have criticized [the federal excise tax proposal], saying, 'We don't want another tax.' And we tell them, 'This is a tax you'll never have to collect.'"[2] The idea, however, is a non-starter. The prospect of the feds leveling, say, a $253.3 million tax on Alabama in retaliation for a future Mercedes Benz-type package is enough to rouse even the most dedicated centralist into a defense of states' rights.

The most direct way to end corporate welfare at the national level would be to enact legislation along the lines proposed by Ralph Nader. Nader has called for a federal law stating that

> every federal agency shall terminate all below-market-rate sales, leasing, or rental arrangements with for-profit corporate beneficiaries, including of real and intangible property; shall cease making any below-market-rate loans or issuing any below-market-rate loan guarantees to corporations; shall terminate all export assistance or marketing promotion for corporations; shall cease providing any below-market-rate insurance; shall terminate all fossil fuel or nuclear power research and development efforts; shall eliminate all liability caps; and shall terminate any direct grant, below-market-value technology transfer, or subsidy of any kind to for-profit corporations.[3]

That would do it. But in Congress, proposals for a corporate welfare ban have never risen to a volume much louder than a soft murmur.

Failing such a ban, Congress might attach sunset provisions to individual pieces of corporate welfare, thus requiring lawmakers to vote at regular intervals in defense of these giveaways. (Alas, this seems as unlikely as a wholesale ban, for if a majority of legislators support subsidies yet understand their general unpopularity, why would they force themselves to cast more pro-subsidy votes than absolutely necessary?)

In 1997, Senators John McCain (R-AZ), Russ Feingold (D-WI), Fred Thompson (R-TN), Joe Lieberman (D-CT), Sam Brownback (R-KS), Ted Kennedy (D-MA), and John Kerry (D-MA) called for a corporate subsidy reform commission, modeled after the military base closing commissions of 1988, 1991, 1993, and 1995. (A later commission deliberated in 2005.) The commission would assemble a list of corporate subsidies that lacked sufficient justification; Congress would then vote yea or nay on the entire package.

The establishment of such a commission would be a frank recognition that members of Congress are cowards. Or if that seems too harsh, that they (with rare exceptions) are unable and unwilling to vote against programs that they believe wasteful if in so voting they endanger their prospects for re-election. A commission, as one of its advocates, Stephen Slivinski of the Cato Institute, puts it, alters the incentives for lawmakers. It also removes lawmakers from a substantial part of the process. In the most common form of the commission proposal, the president and the two houses of Congress would appoint members—persons who are not also members of Congress—to this body. Its purpose: compiling a list of corporate welfare spending (not taxing) programs that ought to be terminated. The commission's recommendations would be transmitted to Congress, which would have sixty days to vote on the commission's report. The vote would be a simple yes or no: no amendments would be permitted. To further insulate congressmen and women from electoral repercussions, "the commission could present to Congress its list of program terminations in a nonelection year."[4]

In theory, as Slivinski explains, the nature of the commission would shield members of Congress from the inevitable pressures brought to bear by those who fear losing their subsidies. A member of Congress could only shrug sympathetically after listening to a lobbyist's sob story; the blame for the commission's recommendations would fall squarely on the shoulders of the commission members. The up-or-down nature of the congressional vote would prevent the usual logrolling and favor-trading and I'll-vote-for-your-program-if-you-vote-for-mine deal making that lubricates the wheels of Congress.

Theory does not always translate neatly into practice, however. In the pages of *Regulation*, Kenneth R. Mayer of the University of Wisconsin-Madison explains the limits of a commission-style approach by a close examination of the Base Realignment and Closure (BRAC) process. The BRAC resulted in the closing of nearly one hundred military bases and many more smaller military facilities, "overcoming decades of congressional resistance to closing bases and saving billions of dollars." Congress, left to its own devices, never would have closed those bases; indeed, our federal solons had actually barred so much as a study of whether or not supernumerary bases should be shuttered.

So the independent commission, created by what Mayer calls "an astonishing delegation of legislative power," was born. It was almost a case of Stop Me Before I Dip into the Pork Barrel again. Members of Congress not only turned over the hard and dirty work of identifying bases for closure to the commission, they also made "it almost impossible to stop the process once the committee had drawn up its list."[5] By prohibiting amendments and requiring an up-or-down vote on the entire list, the BRAC loaded the dice. Members representing bases that were on the commission's hit list could moan and caterwaul and play to the local press, thus gaining points for defending their constituents, but it was all sound and fury signifying nothing, as members of Congress whose districts were untouched by the recommendations far outnumbered those with a stake in the game. The votes, typically, were lopsidedly in favor of the BRAC recommendations.

BRAC produced, as Mayer says, "overwhelmingly positive and long overdue results." Military bases that had long outlived their usefulness were closed down. The downside is that the BRAC was "a largely unaccountable entity that was able to make and enforce decisions in a political vacuum."[6] Its very creation marked a dereliction of duty by Congress. It was, as Mayer writes, "a legacy of the Progressive Era," when anti-populist reformers believed that political decisions should not be made by elected representatives but rather by ostensibly high-minded and dispassionate "experts" who were somehow able to discern the public interest and act on it.[7]

Could a BRAC-type structure effectively take on and slay the most outrageous corporate welfare? Mayer has his doubts, saying, "It is unrealistic to expect delegation to work for multidimensional political issues, such as budget cuts, which require tradeoffs among competing and incompatible programs."[8] Imagine the combined lobbying strength of Boeing, General Electric, Caterpillar, and the entire gallery of Export-Import Bank clients mustered in defense of Ex-Im. Even a purportedly nonpartisan or neutral commission would feel the heat.

If the first step toward the repeal of subsidies is public awareness of subsidies, then another Nader proposal, that every federal agency be required to publish any subsidies distributed under its purview, would be a helpful step. Politicians love to talk about "transparency"; support for exposing just who benefits from corporate welfare would be a genuine effort toward public education.

At the state level, the 1990s plan for multistate no-corporate-welfare compacts might be revived, though its failure and difficulties in enforcement make this a less promising avenue. We've been down it once before—and it led to broken pledges and political weaseling.

More promisingly, state legislators may fasten "clawback" requirements on recipients of corporate welfare. If they don't meet their promises, if the jobs they have guaranteed do not materialize, the welfare takers have to give back a percentage of their alms. New York reformers are currently trying to attach such clawback provisions to IDA agreements.

Also at the state level, and largely in response to the US Supreme Court's controversial upholding of eminent domain in *Kelo v. City of New London* (2005), forty-four states have enacted or strengthened laws protecting private property owners from the depredations, or at least some of them, of eminent domain. A number of these laws are for show and do little, in a practical sense, to keep private property safe from the greedy hands of economic development agencies. But the possibility of a twenty-first-century Poletown has grown dimmer.

\* \* \*

Corporate welfare has no constituency among average taxpaying Americans. The prospect of a coming together, across the artificial divides of Left and Right, of taxpayers, small businesspeople, environmentalists, populists—of everyone from the Tea Party to the Green Party—would strike fear into the corporate hearts of Boeing and General Motors and all those other businesses, from Dick's Sporting Goods to Wal-Mart, that have prospered from public subsidy. Certainly if a referendum were held on individual acts of corporate welfare, the Nays would carry the day in the overwhelming number of cases.

Opinion polls are near unanimous on this. In 2011, a Rasmussen Reports poll found just 29 percent of respondents agreeing that "government should continue to provide loans and loan guarantees to help finance export sales for large corporations"—that is, just 29 percent of voters support the purpose and practice of the Export-Import Bank. Forty-six percent were opposed, and a quarter of respondents were undecided. Rasmussen also found that a huge plurality (70 percent) opposed US subsidies for foreign governments to purchase military weapons from US companies, and a narrow plurality (46–37 percent) would end farm subsidies.[9] Rasmussen also found a large plurality (58–23 percent) opposed to the federal government "provid[ing] loan guarantees to banks, so they will lend money to someone looking to start their own business."[10] So much for the Small Business Administration.

What these numbers show is that across the board, Americans are at least skeptical, and in most cases hostile, to government providing special treatment for some businesses at the expense of other businesses and taxpayers.

But except in such rare cases as the town meeting democracy of New England or in those cities that require public votes on government expenditures for sports stadiums and the like, Americans are deprived of any chance to vote directly on corporate giveaways. Yet the dissatisfaction is real. Corporate welfare violates our most elementary notions of fairness, of justice. Libertarians and free-market conservatives object because it interferes with the workings of the free market. Greens object because it privileges large corporations over smaller concerns. Populists object because it transfers money from ordinary taxpayers to favored and influential interests. Some old-fashioned liberals object because they distrust big business, which is the primary recipient of Export-Import Bank financing.

The last time the lineaments of such a coalition were discernible was in the mid-1990s, when the US House of Representatives was enlivened by dozens of new Republicans who seemed less beholden to corporate interests than were those that had preceded them. Supported by such think tanks and activist organizations as the Competitive Enterprise Institute and the Cato Institute, and with allies among the groups affiliated with Ralph Nader, this left-right movement seemed ready to take on the manifold subsidies to big business, big agriculture, and even parts of the military-industrial complex.[11]

Senators John McCain (R-AZ) and Russ Feingold (D-WI) gave the movement a bipartisan cast. But the effort came a cropper for various reasons: in part because the reformist spirit of the new House Republicans was damped by the capriciousness of Speaker Newt Gingrich (R-GA); in part because the Clinton administration, despite Secretary of Labor Robert Reich's public announcement of November 22, 1994, that "I invite the great think tanks of this city—the Heritage Foundation and the Cato Institute, to pick two at random—to add to the list their own examples of business subsidies that don't make sense," was quite comfortable playing patty-cake with the Fortune 500 and its lobbyists; and in part because it's extremely difficult to end programs that provide enormous concentrated benefits for influential parties while imposing widely dispersed costs on the taxpayers.[12] The parties receiving the benefits have hefty incentives to put forth extraordinary effort to keep receiving them; those taxpayers who shell out for the benefits have no such incentives, since the hit for any particular federal subsidy will seldom amount to a considerable sum on an individual tax bill.

In a postmortem on "How Corporate Welfare Won: Clinton and Congress Retreat from Cutting Business Subsidies," Stephen Moore and Dean Stansel of the Cato Institute noted that of the 35 federal programs they judged "least defensible," Congress had sliced just $2.8 billion of the $19.5 billion budgeted for 1996, a relatively puny amount given the public declarations by Democrats and Republicans that corporate welfare would go under the knife.[13] (This was, recall, a time when there was considerable public unease over the budget, as evinced by the prominence of Ross Perot, whose third-party presidential runs in 1992 and 1996 were largely based on budget hawkishness.)

Despite Secretary of Labor Reich's theatrics, the Clinton administration refused even to support the mildest of cutbacks on corporate welfare. Subsequent administrations have been no better. Despite the pronouncement of his Office of Management and Budget director Mitch Daniels that the federal government should not "subsidize, sometimes deeply subsidize, private interests," the presidency of George W. Bush amounted to a bazaar for corporations which had even the most tenuous connection with defense, intelligence, and surveillance technologies—see my earlier book *Homeland Security Scams* (2006) for an examination of the Homeland Security boondoggle—and Barack Obama has proven every bit as accommodating to favor-seeking corporation giants.[14] From the executive branch, there has been no War on Corporate Welfare.

We might wish that companies, or at least those companies professing fealty to the principles of free enterprise, would voluntarily eschew all forms of corporate welfare. But then we might also wish that every day were sunny, and that chocolate drops flowered in our backyards. Wishing will not make it happen. Even Charles Horn, a longtime Republican Ohio state senator who was among the sharpest critics of government giveaways, said, "We know companies are manipulative, but it's the nature of business to go after every dollar that's legally available. Don't place the blame on the company, place the blame on government. This is government's folly."[15]

It is indeed government's folly. And we pay the bill, year after year.

But if there is no fool like an old fool, nor is there any folly quite so durable as a government folly. Corporate welfare may appall us, it may incense us, it may even amuse us—but until a cross-partisan taxpayer coalition achieves the kind of potency that the anti-SST movement did, corporate welfare isn't going anywhere other than into the treasuries of the Boeings of this country.

# Notes

1.  Jonathan J. Bean, *Beyond the Broker State: Federal Policies toward Small Business, 1936–1961* (Chapel Hill: University of North Carolina Press, 1996), p. 177. Like the Export-Import Bank, the Small Business Administration provides loans and loan guarantees to private businesses, though on a scale smaller than that of Boeing. What the SBA lacks in profile, however, it almost makes up for in profligacy: in the 1980s, delinquency rates for SBA loans exceeded 20 percent. Although Reagan's budget director David Stockman called the SBA a "billion dollar waste, a rat hole," the canny titling of this agency has probably saved it from abolition. Jonathan J. Bean, *Big Government and Affirmative Action: The Scandalous History of the Small Business Administration* (Lexington, KY: University Press of Kentucky, 2001), p. 119. Exceedingly few "small businesses" benefit from SBA loans, but the very existence of the SBA serves, in the mind of its defenders, as a rebuke to those who charge that corporate welfare is only for the big boys. In fact, the SBA's primary constituency today is the banking industry, which is happy to loan money to risky businesses when those loans are backed by the federal government.
2.  Bartlett and Steele, "Corporate Welfare," *Time*.
3.  Nader, *Cutting Corporate Welfare*, pp. 116–17.
4.  Slivinski, "The Corporate Welfare State: How the Federal Government Subsidizes U.S. Businesses," *Cato Institute Policy Analysis* No. 592, p. 11.
5.  Kenneth R. Mayer, "The Limits of Delegation: The Rise and Fall of BRAC," *Regulation* (Vol. 22, No. 3, 1999): 32.
6.  Ibid.: 33.
7.  Ibid.: 34.
8.  Ibid.: 37.
9.  "Voters See 'Corporate Welfare' Programs as a Good Place to Cut Government Spending," September 6, 2011, www.thinkbynumbers.org.
10. "58% Want to End Small Business Administration Loan Guarantees," August 17, 2011, *The Financial*, www.finchannel.com.
11. See Janice Shields and James M. Sheehan, "Left and right come together on ending corporate welfare," *Washington Times*, June 13, 1995.
12. Stephen Moore and Dean Stansel, "Ending Corporate Welfare as We Know It," *Cato Institute Policy Analysis* No. 225, May 12, 1995, p.1.
13. Moore and Stansel, "How Corporate Welfare Won: Clinton and Congress Retreat from Cutting Business Subsidies," *Cato Policy Analysis* No. 254, p. 1.
14. Stephen Slivinski, "The Corporate Welfare Budget: Bigger Than Ever," *Cato Institute Policy Analysis* No. 415, October 10, 2001, p. 2.
15. Bartlett and Steele, "Corporate Welfare," *Time*.

# Index